ALSO BY HELEN LEFKOWITZ HOROWITZ

*Alma Mater*

*Culture and the City*

# CAMPUS LIFE

# Campus Life

## UNDERGRADUATE CULTURES FROM THE END OF THE EIGHTEENTH CENTURY TO THE PRESENT

### Helen Lefkowitz Horowitz

THE UNIVERSITY OF CHICAGO PRESS

*Chicago and London*

The University of Chicago Press, Chicago 60637
The University of Chicago Press, Ltd., London

©1987 by Helen Lefkowitz Horowitz
All rights reserved. Published 1987
University of Chicago Press edition 1988
Printed in the United States of America

97 96 95 94 93 92 91 90 89 88   5 4 3 2 1


*Published by arrangement with Alfred A. Knopf, Inc.*


Library of Congress Cataloging in Publication Data

Horowitz, Helen Lefkowitz.
  Campus Life.

  Reprint. Originally published: New York : Knopf,
c1987.
  Bibliography: p.
  Includes index.
  1. College students—United States—History—19th
century.   2. College Students—United States—History—
20th century.   3. College students—United States—
Attitudes.   4. Universities and colleges—United
States—History—19th century.   5. Universities and
colleges—United States—History—20th Century.
I. Title.
LA229.H569   1988         378'.198'0973          87-30226
ISBN 0-226-35373-7 (pbk.)

To

*Benjamin Horowitz*

*and*

*Sarah Esther Horowitz*

# Contents

# Preface

This is a book about college students and their lives on campus. It attempts to describe the variety of ways that undergraduates have defined themselves, viewed their professors and fellow collegians, formed associations, and created systems of meaning and codes of behavior. Although my story begins at the end of the eighteenth century, my real concern is the present. The primary question that I am asking is: How did we get where we are now? Because I have a historian's cast of mind, the answer to the question lies in the evolution of the past into the present.

This is not the first effort to explore the ways of college students. Since the late nineteenth century the American reading public has had an intense curiosity about college life, fed by magazine articles and books on college customs. In the 1920s the deeds of flaming college youth, seemingly squandering their opportunities, alternately frightened and titillated an older generation and led to a minor genre of college fiction. The political and cultural radicalism of some American college students in the 1960s grabbed headlines and occasioned a vast literature. More quietly, psychologists and sociologists have been researching and writing about undergraduates since the early twentieth century, focusing especially on student values.

A few works have attempted an overview of the college experience. Why write another? Most simply, because I am not satisfied. What has been written generally stays within the literature of a discipline, such as social psychology or history, and therefore fails to connect to studies and accounts outside its boundaries. And none of the broader works confronts the divisions between students that have separated American collegians since at least the late eighteenth century.

This book offers a new synthesis and a new perspective. Critical to my understanding of undergraduates and their lives on campus are three elements. The first is that college students in the past, as in the present, are not all alike. In 1910 the sons of Boston Brahmins and of Russian Jewish immigrants came to Harvard for fundamentally different reasons, as do the young athletes and first-generation Asian Americans entering Stanford today. These differences shape both the experience and the behavior of students in college. To be specific, out of my research I have located three distinct ways of being an undergraduate with their male and female variants: college men and women, outsiders, and rebels. The term *college life* has conventionally been used to denote the undergraduate subculture presumably shared by all students. My study clarifies that college life, in fact, is and has been the world of only a minority of students. I have therefore reserved the terms *college life* and *college men* and *college women* to a particular undergraduate subculture and to those students who partake in it.

The second element is that the past has shaped the present. Not just in the usual sense that all children have parents or all events have causes, but in the sharper, more direct sense that some students in the past created undergraduate subcultures that have been passed down to successive generations and that continue to shape how students work and play in college.

The third is that as America has changed, so too have the institutions of higher education been changing in the last century. Because of their goals and associations, some students have been in a better position than others to comprehend the meaning of those changes. Some undergraduates have never noticed any changes at all.

This perspective derives from my biography. I went to Wellesley in 1959 and found myself initially attracted by college life. Over the course of four years, I was pulled in another direction by a growing interest in the life of the mind and the questions rebellious contemporaries were raising about personal goals, discrimination, and foreign policy. In graduate school at Harvard and early teaching at MIT, I observed the 1960s, and I was troubled both by the policies which evoked protest and by the protests themselves. As a historian in the 1970s and 1980s at Union College, Carleton, the University of Michigan, and Scripps and at the National Humanities Center in North Carolina, I have watched and talked to generations of students in many different settings as they have tried to make their way in the college minefield. All this time, but especially during the past five years, I have been both studying undergraduates and teaching them about their collective history. I have examined the books and articles that attempt to describe them and their situation directly, and I have probed the indirections of fiction and autobiography.

Then about three years ago I got angry, angry enough to begin this book. Students were refusing to grow up, I thought, holding themselves in because they had to get A's not only on tests but on deans' reports and recommendations. What had gone wrong in college? I set out to interview students, read their college newspapers, and find out. Because I am a historian I had to go back in a systematic way to beginnings. I found that these beginnings were not in the 1960s, as I had anticipated, but in the late eighteenth century. And I found that anger had been the characteristic mode of college professors for just that long a time.

In the course of writing this book I have been challenged by skeptics, especially those committed to close disciplinary research, that I have no subject. I have been told that the differences between past and present are too vast and the disparities today among institutions of higher education too great to allow me to explore undergraduate experience in the last two hundred years.

I must concede that critics have a point. Differences between present and past are immense. In the 1980s over 7 million young people attend college or university full-time. This constitutes roughly half of American youth between the ages of eighteen and twenty-one, in contrast to an estimated 2 percent in the early 1800s who went to college. The college population of 1800 was white and male and largely of British descent; today slightly more women than men attend college, and the ethnic mix on campus mirrors, with the significant distortion of the underrepresentation of blacks and Hispanics, that of the population. College has always served disproportionately the privileged, but the field of privilege has widened to include greater reaches of the middle and working classes.

Moreover, intrinsically connected to the broadening and deepening of the student body is the basic change in the relation of the college to the society. In a largely agrarian and mercantile society, college served as one of many competing routes to adulthood. In our industrial, bureaucratic one, it has become the pre-eminent channel for those who aspire to gain or keep middle-class status. Once admission to college could be reached in a number of ways. Throughout the twentieth century college has normally required high school graduation. In an earlier period informal apprenticeships or freestanding schools trained young Americans for the professions, and neither built necessarily on the B.A. degree. Today college graduation has become the necessary prerequisite to professional school. As American society has become transformed in the last two centuries, so has the purpose and function of its institutions of higher education.

Two hundred years ago the college taught a prescribed curriculum to all who entered. Now students choose among a vast array of programs, the less technical of which offer a wide range of electives. Then each class recited together each day. Today's students—depending upon their particular majors and preferences—attend lectures, participate in discussion classes, take labs and studios, work on independent studies, and enter internships. The notion of a prescribed body of knowledge that all educated men must know has moved to the background, while to the foreground has come a commitment to inquiry, to teaching male and female students how to ask questions and to undertake the appropriate research to find answers. Initially the route to the acquisition of the culture of a gentleman or to ministerial training, the undergraduate course has become the standard rite of passage for youth, adapting to meet their highly divergent needs.

In addition to the problems posed by the vast changes over the last two centuries, there are those generated by the wide range of institutions that call themselves colleges and universities. At one end of today's spectrum are the small, highly selective private four-year residential liberal arts institutions. At the other are two-year public commuter community colleges. And ranging between is the vast complex of public and private colleges and universities, with student populations of fewer than 100 to those of more than 40,000. Although scale has increased, diversity has been characteristic of American institutions of higher education since the early nineteenth century, as many different types of schools have called themselves colleges and universities.

Given heterogeneity and change, why have I persisted in trying to establish patterns in undergraduate life and in linking together past and present? I have done so because I am convinced that student subcultures, created in particular historic moments, persist over time and that they still, at some level, inform the present. More particularly, male college life, created in the wake of revolts that rocked colleges throughout the new nation, has proved to be remarkably adaptive to new situations and settings and to changes in educational purpose and scale.

Moreover, because my research has shown that undergraduates have not shared a monolithic student subculture but rather have been divided among competing ones—of college men and women, outsiders, and rebels—any individual institution is unique in its particular mix. Some of the phenomena I describe depend upon the clash of different groups coexisting on campus and therefore require a residential college with a traditional college life; but other aspects are independent. Therefore, although my narrative and analysis capture most clearly the undergraduate world of the residential four-year liberal arts college, nonetheless readers familiar with commuter campuses and more technically oriented schools may find something of interest. In this account, outsiders are as important as college men.

Many who are or have been college students may find themselves located not in one undergraduate subculture but in several. How can this be? Two explanations are essential to understanding what follows. First of all, in examining college men and women and rebels, I am looking at subcultures, not individuals. That is, I am exploring the complex of values, attitudes, and behavior held by undergraduate groups and transmitted to those entering them. Individual students vary in the degree to which they assume a collegiate subculture. Outsiders remain immune from them all. To simplify language, I adopt common parlance to write of *college culture,* rather than employ the more technical word *subculture,* but I remain aware that students in American colleges exist within the broader national culture. Secondly, in delineating these subcultures and in describing the outsider, I am simplifying and organizing characteristics to create ideal types. An ideal type has no objective existence but is a mental construction that strives to represent reality. While an ideal type may approach truth, it invariably is far too clean and uncomplicated for the messy world of actual historical phenomena.

Reliance on autobiographies and memoirs compounds this distortion. Autobiographies are hardly raw data. They are contrived writings that attempt to create order out of their subjects' lives. As autobiographers reflect on their pasts, they seek to clarify and give meaning to their experiences. In writing about college, they seek patterns and governing principles, many of which spring from knowledge coming long after the events they describe. Moreover, some autobiographies are not accurate or honest. Although autobiographies are tainted sources, they remain indispensable to the student of undergraduate lives, for they are in many cases the only record that exists of what it has meant to be a student in the last 150 years. Some distortions can be useful, for they delineate mature reflection upon college cultures by subjects who are always interesting and occasionally wise.

Finally, in attempting to capture undergraduate experience, I have chosen to use a wide-gauge net. I have been looking at commonalities across a wide range of institutions in different periods, rather than at the particularities of institutional settings in different moments. Because of this I pick up only large fish and thereby miss many subtleties and shadings. A better analogy comes from aerial photography. Although photographs taken at close range make all sorts of hills and valleys perceptible, from those at a distance only the broadest features of the landscape can be discerned. Knowing this does not invalidate the distant image; it merely points out its limitations. Others are at work on the close-up image. I have chosen to examine at a distance so that I might describe the basic contours of the world of college students.

My hope is that this book may clarify the varieties of undergraduate life. To alumni it may illumine a meaningful part of their past and connect it to the bewildering present. To entering students and their parents it can serve as a road map, pointing out choices. To the many actors in today's college dramas, it may provide some guidance as they try to devise new roles and plots in the months ahead.

I believe that an understanding of the past frees us from its unconscious hold. As students in college today reshape their cultures perhaps they will be able to create forms appropriate to their own experiences and not to that of their great-grandparents.

# Acknowledgments

During the writing of this book I was fortunate to live in three academic communities in three sections of the country: Claremont, California; Ann Arbor, Michigan; and Chapel Hill, North Carolina. I benefited greatly by the contact this gave me with diverse students and faculty.

I began and ended my inquiry in Claremont, and my questions were initiated in conversations with students and colleagues in the Claremont Colleges over a decade that began in 1972. Whatever differences I may have with them, I am grateful to my students, advisees, and undergraduate friends for exploring issues with me. Long before I began thinking about writing this book, I discussed and argued every issue that it raises with Daniel Horowitz, colleague, husband, and friend. As the research and writing progressed, we differed about many substantive issues. Dan's unfailing willingness to engage in the subject and to confront my prose cheered me on in early months. His disagreements opened my eyes to key questions and contradictions. His own preoccupations and responsibilities gave me needed perspective.

The Claremont Colleges provided important support in a variety of ways. Daryl Smith first led me to sources in the literature of student values. James Gould extended to me his clipping file on undergraduate activism. Jack Schuster of the Claremont Graduate School assisted me at a later stage as I focused on the links between higher education and American society. As always, the Honnold Library staff, especially the Interlibrary Loan office, aided my work. Marilyn Bazzett brought to the final stages her characteristic helpfulness and good spirits. Scripps College faculty research funds helped me pay for the photographs and the index.

## Acknowledgments

A year as a Visiting Associate Professor of History at the University of Michigan was invaluable. I am grateful to David Hollinger for his instigation. Conversations with David and Joan Hollinger and Diane and Peter Hughes enlivened the year and stimulated the prose. Don Brown proved to be an extraordinary resource. His knowledge and personal library opened up to me the extensive social science literature on college students. I had useful conversations about students with Marion Evaskeski and Greg Fawcett, who extended the resources of the Office of Student Services to me. Marvin R. Peterson was most gracious in suggesting names and contacts. I enjoyed discussions with Jean Campbell about students, then and now. Through her I had the good fortune to meet Daniel Katz and discuss his survey of Syracuse University students. The extensive collections of the University of Michigan Library facilitated research.

The Rockefeller Foundation generously supported a year of research and writing. The National Humanities Center, Research Triangle Park, North Carolina, appointed me a Fellow for the 1984–85 academic year. I am deeply grateful to both institutions.

The National Humanities Center provided office space, library access, supportive services, and the pleasure of fellowship with scholars from many different fields. I am especially indebted to the library staff for their massive help throughout the year. I applaud Charles Blitzer, Kent Mullikin, and the entire staff of the Center for their spirit and good cheer. It has been hard to get the tar unstuck from my heels.

Colleagues at the National Humanities Center, the University of North Carolina, and Duke provided stimulating discussion and camaraderie. I recall with relish conversations with Philip Berk, William Bouwsma, Michael Confino, Emilia Viotti da Costa, Morris Eaves, Peter Filene, Elizabeth Fox-Genovese, Eugene Genovese, Jefferson Hunter, Pamela Hunter, Leon Kass, Joy Kasson, John Kasson, Karen Kupperman, Phoebe Lloyd, Lucinda Mac-Kethan, Stuart Marks, Tom Regan, Armstead Robinson, Charles Royster, Diane Sasson, Jack Sasson, Ann Scott, Bonnie Smith, S. Cushing Strout, Jr., Jean Strout, Larry Tempkin, and Jack Wilson. No-holds-barred criticism of my seminar presentation by Fellows at the National Humanities Center was uncommonly useful.

College and university archives assisted me with photographs. I particularly enjoyed research when able staff joined in the search for images. I especially thank Edwin Southern of the Duke University Archives and Kevin B. Leonard of the Northwestern University Archives. I am indebted to the many institutions who waived or reduced their fees for permission to publish: University Archives, Princeton University; University Archives,

Harvard University Library; the State Historical Society of Wisconsin; the Western Reserve Historical Society; and Special Collections Division, University of Washington Libraries. I am even more indebted to those institutions who have no such fees: Friends Historical Library of Swarthmore College; Bentley Historical Library, University of Michigan; Duke University Archives; Special Collections, University of Chicago Library; North Carolina Collection, UNC Library at Chapel Hill; Department of Manuscripts and University Archives, Cornell University Libraries; Bryn Mawr College Archives; Radcliffe College Archives; Barnard College Archives; Lyndon Baines Johnson Library; American Jewish Archives; Stanford University Archives; Northwestern University Archives; Eugene C. Barker Texas History Center, University of Texas at Austin; Williams College Library; Union College Archives; University Archives, University of Minnesota; Amherst College Archives; Library of Congress; Reed College; Wellesley College Archives; Bancroft Library, University of California, Berkeley. I would like to thank Harold Forsythe for the use of his photograph from the Hampton Institute.

The AERA gave me the opportunity to air my findings as the Invited Speaker for Division F. I profited by the lively interchange among historians of higher education that followed my talk. The *History of Education Quarterly* published a version of the talk, which contains much of Chapter 10, in its Spring 1986 issue. I am grateful to the editor for permission to reprint. In addition, as I have presented pieces of my work to audiences as diverse as undergraduate Phi Beta Kappa initiatees at Duke to scholars in the humanities at the Fourth Humanities Conference at Berkeley, I have learned from critics and commentators. Harold S. Wechsler and Michael H. Ebner led me to important sources.

Several scholars honored me by reading and commenting on the first draft: Arthur Cohen, Joseph Kett, Peter Filene, Diane Ravitch, and Peter Wood. Although I was not able to amend all the flaws they perceived, I tried to come up to the high standards that they set in their own work and as critics of mine.

Research assistance comes from the most unlikely sources. I called on my willing and able father-in-law, William Horowitz, far too often. Other family members inadvertently helped, although they should be exonerated from any responsibility for the opinions herein expressed. I was particularly fortunate in having as windows on the undergraduate world in the 1970s and 1980s Henry Lefkowitz, Jeffrey Katz, Linda Katz Kaminsky, and Andrew Katz.

I promised to protect the privacy of the students I interviewed, a few of whom I have quoted in these pages. They should know, however, that I am thankful for their willingness to talk with me frankly about their present experiences and future aspirations. I learned a great deal from them, and what I learned altered my perspectives.

Jane Nuckols Garrett has assumed the duties of sounding board, counselor, and friend, along with those of editor. I am delighted to report that the new responsibilities have not diminished her editorial acuity or the power of her tactful persuasion. Without her the book might have been shorter and more quickly written, but it would have been far less interesting.

Ben and Sarah Horowitz constantly reminded me that immediate needs demanded attention, especially during the Ann Arbor teachers' strike and North Carolina ice storms. They also kept me alert to the importance of future generations of undergraduates. My dedication to them goes far beyond this book.

# CAMPUS LIFE

# Introduction: The Worlds That

# Undergraduates Make

In the spring of 1983, a black freshman at the University of Michigan summed up his first year in college: "I'm having no fun." The students around him were so bent on work that they walked to class without looking up and then rushed back to study: "nobody is willing to stop and talk to each other." All he heard around him was GPA—grade point average: "three letters that I am tired of hearing." He mimicked what he disliked: "Why should I mess up my GPA? Why should I do this to my GPA?" He had come to college because he saw it as a chance "to get away, to find yourself." But college had turned into "study, study, study." With everyone thinking about grades, he felt cheated: "You don't have time to expand."

A white friend down the hall agreed. He had not found what he had looked for in coming to college, "that other side of college life besides academics." He did not hold his professors or deans responsible for the competitive, tense atmosphere. Rather he blamed his fellow students, who —"too ready to grow up"—wanted to jump from high school to career. What he heard around him was "I have to get a 3.5 to get to med school." As a result "the stuff in between is kind of lost," what he had come to college for: the "freedom to find out what to do."[1]

As these freshmen realized, this is a difficult time to be a college student. The pressures are great; the life, often grim. Although undergraduates enjoy partying on weekends that can begin on Wednesday night, they confine their friendships to the narrow social groups from which they spring. For some, extracurricular activities form part of their work or recreation, but the college no longer inspires any sense of community or service. Few college students ask existential questions about the meaning of life. As they

3

compete for the grades that will get them into professional schools, they allow themselves little room to grow and become. College moves them along to a job or a career, but for most it no longer serves to liberate their souls.

What is the cause? Are undergraduates really only children of whom we should expect little? No; earlier collegians, equally youthful, were not content to be dependent sons and daughters. They demanded to be considered adults. Are contemporary students less villains than victims, caught by economic forces beyond their control? Perhaps; but other generations of students confronted in college the harsh challenges of an unfriendly future and yet allowed themselves the pleasures and the pains of an intense college world. What makes the 1980s different?

The answer lies in the collective experience of undergraduates inherited from the nineteenth century and transformed in the 1960s and 1970s. In entering college, freshmen step into a complex environment containing alternative student cultures, each with its own standards and values. These particular undergraduate worlds give form to students' lives and meaning to their experience. Collegiate canons shape how students perceive both their formal education of courses, classes, and books and their informal education of social relationships, organizations, and rituals. Although college authorities have attempted to mold undergraduate worlds, they have succeeded only in setting the outer parameters of permissible behavior. College faculty has seen itself as determining students' lives through the courses that it teaches and through the power of personal influence. But professorial words and gestures have been filtered through the evolving cultures of students' own devising.

Eighteen-year-olds who leave home to enter college feel as if they are embarking on a great adventure in which all the choices are theirs. In part this is true, for the college world contains a number of possibilities which give the appearance of choice. But college students enter a social order that, like the communities they are leaving, has emerged from an earlier time. The undergraduate cultures that today's students inherit have traditions that shape the way those within them see their situation and act.

The multiple contexts in which these traditions operate have undergone radical transformation. As the United States became an industrial nation and world power, higher education shifted from a marginal to a central force in the polity. The number and proportion of young people going to college greatly increased. Their socioeconomic composition shifted. And the relation between higher education and their futures changed.

In 1800 roughly 2 percent of young men went to college. They were a motley crew, ranging in age from the early teens to the thirties. The youngest were the sons of Southern landed and Northern mercantile wealth eager for the polish of the gentleman. Also young were the offspring of the small urban professional elite, in college to attain skills comparable to their fathers'. The oldest came from modest farms with the clear intention to become ministers. At first counting in 1840, 16,233 students were reported in 173 institutions.[2]

The nineteenth century saw important changes in higher education. As the population rose, the numbers of enrolled students increased: by 1880 there were 85,378 students in 591 colleges and universities. New types of schools came into being, offering courses that challenged the traditional curriculum. Through the Morrill Act of 1862, the national government attempted to foster agricultural and mechanical training and the spread of public institutions. Philanthropists endowed separate colleges for women and blacks, and some institutions integrated them. But despite these changes, until the 1880s the proportion of young Americans in college remained relatively stable.[3]

Agrarian and mercantile America was largely uninterested in formal credentials and gave youths the chance to learn occupations in a wide variety of ways. College had limited usefulness. For well-placed young men, it proffered the good times they had come to expect, contacts with others of their own kind, and the foundation for the culture of gentlemen. For the small numbers of the urban elite with professional fathers, college promised to extend status into the next generation. For the striving, it opened a way into the professions, yielding entry into the middle class and at least a modest income. By the late nineteenth century, such industrious students were shifting from the ministry to education, journalism, engineering, scientific agriculture, pharmacy, and medicine. They now included women, who, like their brothers, came to college for general culture or to train for the professions, especially for schoolteaching. For young men looking forward to careers in business as entrepreneurs or as managers, however, there was little incentive to go to college. Far better to begin working early and gain useful experience. Even some doctors or lawyers might bypass college (or even secondary school) and study with a practitioner or go to an independent professional school without benefit of the liberal arts.

By the end of the nineteenth century the rate of college-going began its steady rise. In 1880 less than 2 percent of those between eighteen and twenty-one attended college; by 1890, 3 percent did so. In the first half of the twentieth century, the numbers roughly doubled every ten or twenty years. By 1900, 4 percent of those between eighteen and twenty-one attended college; by 1920, 8 percent; by 1940, 16 percent; by 1950, 30 percent; by 1970, 48 percent.[4]

What explains this increase? Changes within the educational system provided the necessary support. Higher education built on the elementary and secondary school system that vastly expanded in the nineteenth and twentieth centuries, preparing larger numbers and proportions of children over increasing numbers of years. Except among those training to become schoolteachers, however, this did not in itself generate new college enrollments. In the course of the twentieth century, the ratio of students in colleges and universities to those in primary and secondary schools shifted from 1 in 80 to 1 in 10.[5] This suggests that more important than the number of students prepared to go to college was the proportion of those prepared students who chose to enter college. The twentieth century saw the founding of new institutions of higher education to attract students. So had the nineteenth century. The difference in the twentieth century was that students came to the colleges, old and new.

The true source of the pull of higher education on American youth was the transformation of American society. In the nineteenth century the United States became an industrial nation. Beginning with textile mills and railroads before the Civil War, the application of machinery to the process of production vastly increased the output and the scale of manufacturing. After the war the development of heavy industry and growing production greatly intensified the process. Natural increase and immigration swelled the population. Agriculture, which once occupied the bulk of the population, required fewer hands.[6] Changes in sources of power from water to coal brought factories to cities. As manufacturing was added to mercantile enterprises, cities grew and spread across the continent and attracted dwellers from American farms and from Europe and Asia. The wave of consolidation gathered firms into large combinations. Beginning with the railroads and the federal government, bureaucratic organization spread to these combines. American business and manufacturing corporations began to hire new kinds of employees: a vast army of white-collar workers, such as bookkeepers and clerks, and a smaller number of professionals, such as corporate lawyers, accountants, engineers, and architects. Growing urban populations and greater wealth meant the increasing need of goods and services of all kinds and the more frequent resort to experts—doctors, dentists, architects, and lawyers. In the four decades after 1870 the number of professionals increased over four times to total 1,150,000 by 1910. In the same period, those in finance, real estate, and trade more than trebled, amounting by 1910 to 2,760,000.[7]

In the post–Civil War years higher education was altering in form and content. Out of the many experiments of the nineteenth century came the university with its new approach to knowledge and conception of the curriculum. Empiricism reshaped the liberal arts. In addition, with the decline of apprenticeship, frankly vocational subjects, such as engineering and accounting, became college-level courses. Innovative teachers introduced empirical methods and reshaped graduate and professional education to incorporate scientific and technological knowledge. Newly created or strengthened professional associations devised standards for entry that required graduation from accredited schools and licensing examinations. Professional schools, once independent, associated with universities and increasingly required a B.A. degree for entrance.

As work and education in America changed, so did the prospects for youth and the place of college in their lives. While the bulk of white-collar positions required only high school, those that promised movement upward through management gradually began to prefer college men. American business had always favored those with capital and connections. College became the place to extend these benefits, broaden acquaintances, and learn how to lead. As more and more middle-class youth came to college, some of them aspired to these advantages. They saw college as instrumental for acquiring not only business and accounting skills but also contacts and style. By the 1920s going to college became normal for youth from the broad reaches of the middle class. They came from American farms and cities because they perceived college as their principal access to jobs with futures —careers.

While many in the middle class had their eyes on business, some looked to the professions, old and new. In this they were joined by some sons of wealth and by the small number of working-class youth in college. Family backing, connections (now enhanced by college), imagination, grit, and luck might account for financial success in many businesses, but, especially in larger corporations, engineering provided one of the surer routes to management.[8] The substantial salaries of the new vocations and professions demanded competence proven through disciplined training. The elite looked to professions, such as corporate law, that promised the highest prestige and income. The few of the aspiring poor who entered college continued to prepare themselves for occupations that promised upward mobility.[9]

For those hoping to enter the professions, new standards began to apply. An engineering degree or admission into law school may have required only passing grades, but to some employers academic achievement began to matter. Industry looked to high marks in the hiring of engineers. To make law review became a source of prestige respected by prominent law firms.

By the early twentieth century, a coherent, though heterogeneous, educational system had emerged in which the institutions of higher education sat at the top. Children moved up the grade ladder of elementary and secondary schools. Upon graduation, those with backing and motivation entered college. In 1910 there were approximately 150,000 undergraduates in American colleges and universities. Roughly one-third took the classical course, as it was then defined, to prepare themselves in a general way for business or for professional school. Two-thirds took courses geared to vocations, such as engineering or accounting.[10] After receiving a B.A. or its equivalent, those intent on a profession, such as law or medicine, that required an advanced degree then attended a graduate school within a university.

College students increasingly went to schools under public control. At the turn of the century, there were almost 3 students in public colleges and universities for every 2 in private; by 1965 there were almost 2 in public institutions for every 1 in private.[11] The two-year community college arose to open access to higher education to new segments of the population, claiming enrollments of over one-half million by 1950.[12]

Certain colleges and universities became competitive by the mid-twentieth century. Their graduates fared far better in occupation, leadership, and income. In all institutions, but especially those with open admissions, grades became the means to sort students. Poor grades forced some to leave, flunking out. Of those who remained, some stayed in place, merely graduating. Others made high grades and advanced to graduate and professional schools. In 1960 over 75 percent of Yale students anticipated postgraduate training, in contrast to 20 percent in 1920 going on to graduate work.[13]

Despite the emergence of a stratified educational system channeling its most achieving students into the professions, a dual relation between the American occupational structure and higher education has persisted. Although in the twentieth century more positions of high income and prestige have required high grades in college and professional school, sectors have remained where academic achievement has counted for little, and family background, confirmed only by college admission, all. Until the 1960s the children of alumni still had preference in Ivy League colleges and universities. Right connections led to the right clubs and the right firms. Quotas in private institutions limited the number of Jews; outside the Negro colleges or the public institutions of the North, racism effectively barred all but a few blacks. Jews might make law review, but discrimination within major corporate law firms limited their entry into jobs and partnerships and relegated them to less prestigious and less lucrative forms of legal practice.[14] Although discrimination has eroded in the last decades, the white Gentile enclave has been partially able to protect itself from the claims of academic achievement. Moreover, entrepreneurship continues to bring rewards to a few. Although large firms have dominated the economy, a sector has remained open to small business. Here, where good fortune, determination, and an idea or product count, no high-level educational credentials have been necessary, although they might help.

But as the twentieth century has progressed, an increasing proportion of positions of high income and prestige have required both the B.A. and professional training. Because of the manner in which the U.S. Census sorted the labor force there are no accurate totals for professionals as a group. However, specifics are illuminating. In 1900 there were 131,000 in health callings, which included healers and chiropractors as well as physicians and surgeons. By 1920 there were 157,000 physicians and surgeons alone, a number that rose to 195,000 by 1950. During the half century, lawyers and judges rose from 108,000 to 184,000; accountants and auditors, from 23,000 to 390,000; scientists, from 12,000 to 302,000.[15]

Beginning with World War II, the demands of industry and government created new positions in engineering and experimental science: almost 150,000 new jobs in engineering appeared during the decade of the 1940s. For those with educational credentials, industrial and government bureaucracies had jobs with the possibility of rapid advancement. Professional schools and firms softened their quotas. Colleges and universities largely ceased to discriminate in their professorships. Between 1950 and 1970 the proportion of the employed holding professional positions grew from 6.9 percent of the work force to 12.1 percent. The number of government officials, salaried businessmen, and non-profit managers—many of them trained as professionals—rose markedly. In contrast, both the relative position and the absolute number of independent businessmen declined.[16]

During these years higher education underwent enormous expansion at all levels—community colleges, four-year institutions, and universities. The great growth was in the public sector, and it received the lion's share of students. By the late 1970s the ratio of public to private enrollments was over 3 to 1. Increasing numbers went, at least for their first two years, to community colleges, which drew roughly 40 percent of undergraduates. At the same time, a small number of prestigious private colleges and universities faced a rising flood of applicants competing for scarce places in the "hot" colleges. Graduate education mushroomed to include over 1.3 million taking graduate and professional courses.[17]

Shifts in employment patterns and educational opportunities in the past and present matter because young people have their eyes on the future. Their initial decisions of whether or not to enter college and of which college to attend are shaped by their economic and social position and career expectations. So, too, are their choices once in college. On campus they are confronted with conflicting worlds. To a large extent existing student societies do the choosing, sorting students out by wealth, status, and gender. But to some degree assent is necessary, requiring students to decide which group to join and whether or not to try another.

In addition to economic and social position and hopes about the future, undergraduates have brought basic human differences to the creation of their college worlds. They have varied not only in that they have been rich and poor, male and female, Jewish and Gentile, black and white. They have also differed in their need for others, their casts of mind, their approach to knowledge, and their desire for action. When all undergraduates studied the same curriculum, formal higher education did not take their variety into account. As the higher learning grew and changed, greater flexibility in courses of study accommodated many more kinds of students. Though wide-ranging in its offerings, college has nonetheless presupposed that its young population was willing to spend long hours alone in study. This may have satisfied the inquisitive or contemplative who enjoyed being by themselves. Gregarious doers, however, may have felt compelled to seek company and action outside of class.[18]

Humans differ profoundly, but in any society and era certain types tend to dominate. On a familiar level we think of the distinctive traits of Americans and those of other nations, and look to foreign observers such as Alexis de Toqueville to inform us about ourselves. We also implicitly accept the notion of a Representative Man, one who from Ralph Waldo Emerson's time until ours has captured the spirit of the age. David Riesman perceived a basic shift in the American type from the individualistic, inner-directed men of the nineteenth century to the peer-oriented, other-directed ones of the mid-twentieth century. In the 1960s Kenneth Keniston and Robert Jay Lifton posited that the needs of post-industrial society were creating a new protean man. In the 1970s Christopher Lasch characterized the American—emerging in what many were calling the age of "Me-ism" —as narcissistic.

In the twentieth century it has been a fashionable intellectual pursuit to link these changing types of Americans to evolving child-rearing practices. This reached absurd levels in the 1960s as critics rushed to blame student unrest on the advice of Dr. Benjamin Spock. Although the linkage is subject to abuse, it is too useful to relinquish. It helps us understand how students have sorted themselves out in college.

Young people have come to college from widely divergent backgrounds with very different life histories. In some households they have been implicitly encouraged since birth to be gregarious and expressive; in others, introspective and obedient; in others, independent and questioning. Parental expectations and rewards and punishments have shaped young minds and bodies. Undergraduates bring to their higher education a great deal of baggage from their short pasts.[19]

Wealth and status have set the outer dimensions of possibility; the psyche, the inner dimensions of choice. Because family position is frequently related to child-rearing practices, the external and the internal have often fit, and undergraduates have found the form of college experience that has satisfied them. But college students have been confronted with only a limited repertoire of possibilities. Given the many varieties of human beings who enter college, some students have not had a recognized path open to them. This has created the conditions that have made for personal unhappiness, individual resistance, or collective change.

By the late eighteenth century American youth in college divided into two basic paths. Undergraduates might become college men or remain outsiders. As women entered coeducational and all-female institutions of higher education in the nineteenth century, distinctive female variants emerged. In the early twentieth century, a third route opened, collegiate rebellion, available to both men and women. These three contending male undergraduate cultures and their female counterparts arose from particular historical contexts and were linked to socioeconomic position and personal style.

*College life* was born in the violent revolts of the late eighteenth and early nineteenth centuries. All over the new nation colleges experienced a wave of collective student uprisings, led by the wealthier and worldlier undergraduates. College discipline conflicted with the genteel upbringing of the elite sons of Southern gentry and Northern merchants. Pleasure-seeking young men who valued style and openly pursued ambition rioted against college presidents and faculty determined to put them in their place. In every case, the outbreaks were forcibly suppressed; but the conflict went underground. Collegians withdrew from open confrontation to turn to covert forms of expression. They forged a peer consciousness sharply at odds with that of the faculty and of serious students and gave it institutional expression in the fraternity and club system.

College life was altogether agreeable to affluent male adolescents of the nineteenth and early twentieth centuries. In the competitive world of peers, *college men* could fight for position on the playing field and in the newsroom and learn the manly arts of capitalism. As they did so, they indulged their love of rowdiness and good times in ritualized violence and sanctioned drinking. Classes and books existed as the price one had to pay for college life, but no right-thinking college man worried about marks beyond the minimum needed to stay in the game. Faculty and students faced each other across the trenches. If cheating was needed to win the battle, no shame inhered in the act. No real college man ever expected to learn in the classroom, not at least the kind of knowledge that bore any relation to his future life in the world. No, college life taught the real lessons; and from it came the true rewards.

The culture of the college man took its mythic shape in the late nineteenth century. In 1896 Henry Seidel Canby dragged a suitcase of books from the train to the Yale campus. As he crossed the New Haven Green he felt himself joining the thousands of collegians who had left their families and the past to step "overnight . . . through the opening door into tradition, a usable, sympathetic tradition of youth. It was our privilege to be born again, painlessly, and without introspection." What he saw in the Yale he approached was not "the dingy halls ornamented with pseudo Gothic or Byzantine," nor the high-minded world of scholarship cultivated by the faculty. Rather before him loomed the prospect of college life, "a little space of time . . . where the young made a world to suit themselves."[20]

As traditional college life created an adolescent peer culture, it linked students on any particular campus in a network of shared assumptions and joined them to their fellows in other institutions. Youthful high spirits, insubordination, and sexuality helped to shape its forms. But equally significant was that part of adolescent mentality that looked to the future and saw college as a staging ground for adult life. College students had their eyes on the society that they were about to enter. To an important degree, the college world that they made was their reading of the present so that they might claim it for their future. To those heading for the combat of American capitalism, the trials of the extracurriculum appeared to offer valuable lessons.

Yet traditional college men were not just adolescents. They were adolescents in a particular context: they were a subject people. They entered a society in which they did not make or enforce the rules. The world that some of them created—college life—was their effort to protect themselves from the harsh and seemingly arbitrary authority of their faculty.

College authorities generally insisted that students regard college as a period of self-abnegation in which they denied present needs in the hope of future reward. Fearful of disruption, college masters forbade students the freedoms and pleasures generally accorded the youth of their era and subjected rule-breakers to censure and punishment. College men saw the four years as a staging ground for their adult lives; they insisted, however, that it not be merely a time of preparation. For them life was now. Thus their eager pursuit of the pleasures of the table and the flesh and their high tolerance for the excesses that accompanied indulgence. They refused to judge each other as they were judged and offered mutual aid to those threatened with being caught and sympathy to the convicted.

College men placed a high value on mutuality, on the bonds that united them with each other against their faculty. They insisted that they did not share the social prejudices of their era and boasted of their "democracy." While their words suggest a degree of egalitarianism, their social structure was intensely hierarchical. What collegiate democracy meant was that college men did not fully accept the status system of the broader society but created their own where athletic prowess, social grace, and a sense of fair play weighed significantly.

Male college life proved both stable and adaptable. It remained constant in its belief in the war between students and faculty, its devaluation of academic work, its willingness to cheat, and its disdain for those outside its circle. It continued to attract the wealthier students and to emphasize polish and style. However, it changed in significant ways. In the early twentieth century, as presidents and deans empowered college men as the official student leaders, the canons of college life shifted from antagonism to support of the administration. When sex came on campus, the codes of the college man made dating as important as male life among peers. Going out with the right girl became a way to confirm prestige on campus. Hedonism, always one of college life's distinct features, incorporated the new elements of each era. Men had always smoked and drank and enjoyed their kinds of music. Now they did so in the company of women, and the music shifted to jazz. As later in the century new temptations, pleasures, and threats were added, they, too, joined into the play of the college men.

One unchanging element of college life has been its code of fair conduct. To protect themselves from the demands of faculty, college men of the nineteenth and twentieth centuries have attempted to define a reasonable amount of academic work. They have perceived the especially diligent student as the "grind" and the student seeking faculty friendship as the "fisherman" or "brownnose."

Such terms of derogation have been necessary because college life has always had to contend with a significant number of students who have wanted no part of it—the *outsiders*. To the early colleges came some men for whom higher education was intended, those studying for the ministry. By the early nineteenth century their numbers increased, as poor men, often in their twenties, came off the farm, fired by the ambition to become ministers. Either by inclination or out of fear, the future ministers avoided the hedonism and violence of their rowdy classmates. Studious, polite, and respectful of authority, these hardworking students sought the approval of their teachers, not of their peers. Of an evangelical temperament, they brought their highly developed conscience with them to college. Throughout the four years they remained within the culture of their parents, a culture shared with their faculty. Some were ministers' sons and patterned their lives after those of their fathers. Others were poor and ambitious: college offered to them the chance to rise in the world. During college vacations they frequently taught school. Such men were rewarded with tutorships upon graduation and pulpits a few years later. The ministerial claim weakened in the nineteenth century, but not the pattern these students had established.

When the fraternities formed, these students stood outside. At some schools they banded together in an anti-secret society; but mainly they remained independent. College was for them not a time for fun, but a period of preparation for a profession. They focused on academic, not extracurricular, success; sought the approval of their teachers; and hoped, by dint of hard work, that achievement in the future would compensate for the trials of the present.

Beginning in the mid-nineteenth century other outsiders took the pastors' places: ambitious youth from all over rural America; the first college women; immigrants, especially Jews; blacks; veterans after World War II; commuters; and, beginning in the 1960s, women continuing their education. Such students have looked askance at their more playful classmates to wonder how they could waste their time with foolishness. Some outsiders entered with a clear vocation which, whether it was Greek grammar or engineering, absorbed all their energy. Others became infatuated with the content of what they were studying. But whether vocationally or academically motivated, the outsiders avoided looking at other students and directed their gaze at the faculty.

Nineteenth-century college professors had a clear notion of the good student. They tried to form him through penalties and rewards. Faculty offered students high grades, membership in honor societies, and awards for excellence. Those who called themselves college men created an alternative system that distributed status by their own standards, not those of professors, and denigrated the good student; the outsiders, however, who hoped to rise above their station, worked for high marks and professorial recommendations.

The transformation of American society created new demands on American education and new opportunities for youth. The numbers and proportions of young people in college began their dramatic rise. The emergence of the university and changes in the colleges altered many of the conditions of undergraduate life. To this new situation, college men and outsiders reacted differently. College life shielded those under its canons from many of the changes, and they continued to emphasize the extracurriculum as the way to business success. Outsiders saw and used the emerging system to their own advantage. Heading for vocations and professions, old and new, they focused on the curriculum and sought to do well. They accepted the hard discipline of study and its stimulating challenges. They saw the classroom as the arena of combat, and sparred with each other and their professors. They connected to their teachers, perceiving them as mentors and allies, not as antagonists. Many achieved, moving into jobs in the expanding professional and managerial sectors of the economy. A few entered the exciting terrain of the life of the mind.

Gaining an education from the curriculum was not to be limited to outsiders. Beginning in 1910 a few rebellious collegians directly challenged traditional college life and called it false and exclusive. Arriving at Harvard a decade later than Canby, Walter Lippmann unpacked his trunk of well-tailored clothes in preparation for his ascent to the top of Harvard's undergraduate society. He quickly learned that no major athletic team took Jews, nor did the *Crimson,* nor did any of the final clubs that confirmed college social prestige. Lippmann turned elsewhere. The world that he created with friends such as John Reed broke with college codes. It denounced Harvard's exclusions and claimed both the politics of the broader society and the intellectual commitments of the faculty.

Individuals had long dissented from college life, finding personal strategies to confront its conformity, but Harvard in 1910 saw the birth of college *rebellion.* This third path collectively opposed college life. College *rebels* took their language from early modernism, whose creative currents they identified with the ideal university. Initial partisans came from nurturant families of the middle class whose deviance—often the mere fact of being Jewish—barred them from college life. As excited by ideas as any outsider, college rebels could be as cavalier about grades or as hedonistic as a college man, for they did not see their four college years as instrumental to future success. College rebels demanded the content, not the form, and identified keenly with artists and writers breaking conventions and with the few iconoclastic professors moving into the academy. College rebels fought the social distinctions that sorted out college students and reveled in difference, not uniformity. Not content with individual resolutions, they began to battle with college men for positions in student government and on undergraduate newspapers.

With its heady mixture of iconoclasm, radicalism, intellectuality, bohemianism, and opposition to traditional college life, collegiate rebellion traveled quickly. By 1920, when Margaret Mead transferred to Barnard, the Columbia-Barnard rebels composed a lively group.

Because college iconoclasm has always stood as a counter to the collegiate way, it has never appeared as a college culture in its own right. Each succeeding college generation believes it alone has discovered the truth. But since 1910 collegiate rebellion has existed as an alternative available to entering freshmen. Once the pattern was cut, iconoclastic youth needed no special spur to become rebels, only a conception of themselves as nonconformists. They were supported in their struggles on campus by rebellious graduates out in the world, who publicized their efforts, goaded them in periodicals and books, and helped them form a national organization.

Beginning in the 1920s, when innovation in the arts split from radical politics, college rebels divided into two streams. Some students of an independent cast of mind withdrew from political discourse to struggle for inner psychic freedom. Others continued their openly political fights to link questions on campus to broader national issues. In the 1930s political rebels moved into the ascendancy. At the University of Minnesota, Eric Sevareid and his friends took control of college publications and student government. They sympathized with truckers on strike; and they successfully fought to abolish compulsory ROTC. They also discovered the world of ideas in the classroom.

The confidence in their own cause that stimulated college rebels in the 1930s disappeared as the United States entered World War II. In its wake nonconforming undergraduates searched for inner transcendence, a quest that often took them off campus. The Columbia outcasts and poets, such as Allen Ginsberg and Jack Kerouac, who found each other in the 1940s, turned to the streets of New York and the highways of America. Later known as the Beats, with their underground poetry and novels they shaped the consciousness of experimental undergraduates in the 1950s, who began to gather to read their work, listen to folk music, and take their clues about the mind-expanding powers of drugs. In the same period most observers claimed political rebellion to be dead. But Willie Morris found it on the pages of major college dailies and revived it in full at the University of Texas.

The first women to go to college were as serious and aspiring as any male outsider. Many had only the diffuse wish to continue study, but some looked to schoolteaching as their future profession. They had a choice between the women's colleges and the coeducational institutions. Those who ventured to the all-female schools such as Vassar College had a chance to define themselves on their own terms. The more outgoing created a robust college life. Although these women students were independent and hedonistic in their way, their college life did not incorporate male hostility to the faculty or disinterest in study. As the colleges attracted the daughters of affluence, they brought society on campus with its divisions and exclusions. Those of humbler backgrounds or with serious commitment to study found themselves partially outside this world. To this degree the women's colleges imitated their masculine counterparts. But female collegians lived within a community of women. As they competed in athletics or ran for offices in campus organizations, they learned new skills which took them beyond the canons of feminine behavior. No future positions awaited them upon graduation. Unlike college men geared up for capitalism, some of the all-round girls of the women's colleges became unconventional women who turned to public life and causes.

At coeducational institutions the pioneer women students, such as Alice Freeman at Michigan, saw themselves cast in the role of outsiders. It fit their serious purposes and those of generations of women from modest backgrounds preparing themselves for paid work. As more affluent and conventional women entered college at the end of the nineteenth century, they found a way to get partly inside: they created the sorority world that allied them with male power on campus. Conservative and cautious, sororities insisted on social distinctions and feminine behavior. In the twentieth century, as college men partially traded male solidarity for female companionship, the organized women became the sought-after dates of college men. A few gained a moment of glory when their beauty or popularity singled them out for social honors. Less affluent women or those with intellectual ambitions remained outsiders. The more freewheeling joined male rebels and entered the political fray.

As young men and women have entered college, they have surveyed the campus scene and asked the question: Where do I fit? Implicitly they have wondered if they were college men or women, outsiders, or rebels. But throughout the twentieth century educational reformers have questioned the cultural system of undergraduates, the structure of college life. Influenced by their own college memories and prejudices, educators have worked to reshape undergraduate experience. For some the problem was that outsiders, not college men, were gaining academic glory. How could undergraduate leaders, so spirited and attractive, be made to study? How could their energies be harnessed to the academic ends of the curriculum? Others, less elitist, opposed the divisions themselves that denied respect to scholars and denigrated their activity. The focus of concern of educators shaped their answers to the instrumental questions that followed. Should clubs and fraternities be abolished, controlled, or ignored? How might fruitful relationships with faculty and administrators be established? How might college men come to value academic excellence and give prestige to scholars? Should outsiders be brought inside or limited by quotas?

Educators experimented with a wide range of reforms, some constructive, some vicious: new colleges without fraternities or intercollegiate athletics; undergraduate residential houses staffed by tutors; Jewish quotas; systems for recognizing and empowering student leaders; honors programs. In some places, efforts at change worked, and larger numbers of students took to their books.

Pushing them were not only presidents and deans, but a new perception of economic forces. Students, even college men, came to college as a way to improve their chances as adults. College was for them the staging ground for future success. They had once believed that college life alone prepared them for American life. Gradually, the worldly success and prestige of former outsiders and rebels called into question the assumption that the extracurriculum had future value. By midcentury it was becoming clearer, even to undergraduates, that disciplined training leading to the professions —the curriculum—had the surest potential economic benefits.

In the 1960s cultural currents strong enough to feel like a revolution in consciousness opened college youth to new ways of thinking and behaving and caused some of them to question the nature and the goals of higher education. Triggered by the civil rights movement, political college rebels became more radical and more numerous, collectively creating the New Left, what they called the Movement. It provided them with increasingly radical explanations for their discontent, a common identity, and linked plans of action.

In the late 1960s as New Left radicals changed their strategy, they turned to protests designed to teach idealistic students about the collusion of the university with the system. They brought conflict—sometimes violent conflict—to campus. Although radicals remained in a small minority, they found a newly responsive audience among their fellow students. In the democracy of rock music and denim, the boundaries that had formerly divided college men and women from outsiders and rebels softened. The escalation of the Vietnam War and the extension of the draft personally threatened many male undergraduates and caused them to question not only governmental authority but all authority. As radicals tangled with administrators and police, they drew on undergraduates' loyalty to each other and their sense of common cause against adult power. Although the increasing radicalism of the New Left isolated it politically, campus actions drew into their wake undergraduates terrified by the draft and outraged by the violence and tear gas turned against protesters. Student strikes of the late 1960s altered the consciousness of those who participated and of those who observed.

Until May 1970 only a minority of students ever involved themselves in the campus protests of the 1960s. Why this period felt unique, even compared to the 1930s—when a larger proportion of undergraduates had engaged in radical campus politics and strikes—was that the dissenting minority of the 1960s was different. As observation showed and reports confirmed, protest drew in those who, a decade earlier, would have been college men and women—the campus leaders. Some joined radical groups and led campus actions; others provided the reformist outrage that turned these actions into strikes. The athletes—no longer the pre-eminent college men, but a special breed of student whose career aspirations centered on sports—split off in opposition. The vast army of outsiders, once the principal support for college radicals, divided. Academically committed students, influenced in part by liberal social science and humanities faculty, tended to become rebels or their supporters; the vocationally minded, especially in science and engineering, frequently imitated their more conservative faculty mentors and eschewed politics or took cautious positions.

The cumulative events of the 1960s ended the hegemony of college life. At the end of the decade it remained as one option, but hardly the most important. Divisions persisted on campus, but they signified personal preferences unconnected with prestige.

The killings at Kent State University and Jackson State College in May 1970 evoked an outpouring of protest unmatched in earlier periods. When undergraduates returned to campus in the fall, however, an era had ended. The termination of the draft and the winding down of the war, repression, the death of innocents, self-destructive forces within youthful radicalism, a turn in the economy, and ennui worked their way. Protest stopped. Observers who had anticipated an ever-growing radical movement among college youth were caught off guard. In the place of building takeovers and rallies, calm descended. Students suddenly took to their books and began a period in their history that has persisted now for over a decade and a half. All the energies that had once gone into campus high jinks or political demonstrations focused on the curriculum. In the permissive social environment of the 1970s hedonism continued unabated. Colleges had largely withdrawn their oversight of manners and morals, leaving undergraduates relatively free to experiment. Drugs and sex continued to be part of the campus scene, and alcohol returned. But the demand that life and learning join was no longer heard; and students separated their private pleasures from academic work.

As they returned to study, college students of the 1970s dropped earlier concerns for relevance and societal well-being and concentrated on enhancing their competitive advantage for professional schools. A narrow feminism that advocated women's advancement within the existing society encouraged female students to pursue formerly male-dominated professions, thereby adding to competitive pressures. The majority of all students looked to the professions as their route to financial well-being and security. The claims of meritocracy, apparent to some since the beginning of the century, now appeared invincible, drowning out the actual possibilities in the economic order for chance, connections, and entrepreneurship. Undergraduates responded with a vengeance to the message that they make high grades for medical or law school. They wondered if there was anything for them in fraternity life or political action groups. The corrosive effect of this question decimated the ranks of collegians and rebels. In the 1970s the culture of the outsiders triumphed over the ethos of college men and women and rebels. But what had once been the province of aspiring youth, optimistic about their futures, became that of prosperous collegians fearful of downward social mobility. Beginning in the 1970s the New Outsiders transformed the campus.

The classroom retrieved its centrality as increasing numbers of students vied for high grades. A feeling of entitlement soured the air as undergraduates fought over the scarce goods of library books and laboratory space. The sense of community eroded, and ethnic, racial, and gender relationships became clouded by the hostility of the established defending their prerogatives. Faced by the anarchy of the war of each against all, many students retreated socially into the lives they had known before college.

By the mid-1980s changes in the economy and a growing sense of routine have moderated slightly the harsh world of the New Outsider, but its essential dimensions remain intact. Boundaries between student groups remain permeable, and thus the ethos of the New Outsider shapes those who currently choose to be college men and women or rebels. The fear of economic and social erosion, of not being able to reproduce the comfortable world of one's parents, continues to dominate undergraduate consciousness. In this atmosphere education is largely being reduced to the quest for grades through the application of all the strategies of grinding that college men once imagined outsiders pursued. Despite their seriousness, today's New Outsiders do not connect to the life of the mind: ideas are far too risky in the game of grade-seeking that they play. Holding themselves in as carefully as did high school students in the past, these undergraduates fail to follow individual interests that might lead them to find true vocations or to develop autonomy from parental standards. They work for a grade, for the cumulative grade point average that will get them into law school. If college today is "no fun," it is not just because professors are piling on work, but because students see that work in a different way.

Those who choose to become college men and women share much of the culture of the New Outsider as well as assume the traditions of organized life. The Greek-letter fraternity system is attracting more takers, offering as it does the pleasures of an established group and of a clear place in the campus firmament. Because service to the college remains devalued, its primary attractions are personal and social. Hedonism is no longer the preserve of college men, but fraternities continue to support communal cheating, violence, and rape. Elitism and conformity do not set sorority women apart from independents, but nonetheless can be located in their more vicious forms in the houses. While those outside the system do not recognize Greek superiority, those inside work to convince each other of the rightness of their choice. At a time when the consciousness of the New Outsider pervades the campus, fraternities and sororities have added the rhetoric of academic excellence and future connections.

Collegiate rebellion has returned in its more politicized forms to campus, but, by this writing, few students see the point of demonstrations. More pervasive among college students is an emerging consciousness that questions rather than attacks. The objects of 1980s college rebels are not college men and women, who—however caught in their own positive self-estimation—remain marginal to others. Contemporary rebels confront the New Outsider. They attempt to distance themselves from the careerism and grade-grubbing of their classmates. Many rebels outwardly conform, adopting no special costume or hairstyle. The struggle they wage is within their own minds to frame an independent course, to mediate the pressures of parents, professors, and peers. Their stance is cautious and wary. Their quiet achievements, however, are solid and real.

The calm of the 1970s has continued into the mid-1980s. Because no rapid swings of student mood blur our vision, we can now see for the first time certain constants in undergraduate culture as well as new elements that have reshaped old forms. The clarity of the present makes this the moment for understanding.

## College Men: The War between Students and Faculty

College life was born in revolt. Not just the insubordination inherent in youth, but a wave of violent, collective uprisings in the late eighteenth and early nineteenth centuries against the combined authority of college professors and presidents. In every case forcibly suppressed, the conflict went underground. Losing the preliminary battles, college men won the war. Collegians withdrew from open confrontation to turn to covert forms of expression. In the interstices of the nineteenth-century college, college men forged a peer consciousness sharply at odds with that of the faculty. They created college life.

I do not mean to suggest that the collective life of students was a creation of the new Republic. Undergraduate culture has a long and rich history. In fact, it long preceded the first English settlements in North America. The recorded history of associations of university students began in the twelfth century, at the very origins of the university itself. When students and teachers first gathered in urban centers in Italy, students organized to protect themselves. The word *university* means "totality of a group" and was first applied to these student organizations. Faculties in Bologna and Paris formed guilds in response, protecting their right to give examinations and to grant degrees. Endowments of colleges or halls of residence to house penurious students gave faculties, most importantly those of Oxford and Cambridge, some ability to control the unruly bands of young men who gathered for instruction. But everywhere students threatened established society by their rowdy ways.[1]

Records of youthful hedonism and collegiate customs in North America go back to Harvard's beginnings. Its poverty, simplicity, piety, and small scale may have initially inhibited adolescent enthusiasm, but Harvard in the heart of Puritan New England caught its students playing cards, drinking, and stealing the turkeys of their Cambridge neighbors. As early as 1667 the Overseers complained that upperclassmen were sending freshmen out on private errands, that the English practice of "fagging" had reached Massachusetts. High spirits continued to plague college authorities. By the eighteenth century the faculty recorded a new kind of misdemeanor: students put live snakes in their tutor's room and drank his wine. Such pranks suggested disrespect as well as distance.[2]

Eighteenth-century American collegians enjoyed a vigorous, creative fellowship in the literary societies of their own devising. Beginning in 1750 at William and Mary and at Yale, these student societies supplemented the formal course of study. Open to all, the societies organized debates, criticized written compositions, established libraries, and gave to students meeting places and public events. Students also formed clubs of a social nature, starting in the 1770s at William and Mary. Harvard's Porcellian began about 1791 as friends gathered to dine on roast pig.[3]

Although student culture has existed as long as the university, that particular American form we call college life—still with us today—was forged in the faculty-student warfare of the post-revolutionary years.

The revolts were extensive. Students rioted at the long-established colonial colleges and at the newer denominational ones. Some disturbances lasted only a few hours. Others placed the colleges in a state of siege for weeks. The North Carolina legislature suspended its university's endowment after the violent riot of 1799.[4] None of the New England colleges was immune from revolt in the years between 1820 and 1860. A few colleges went into permanent decline, losing students, faculty, and patronage.

The continuing conflicts at Princeton give some sense of the temper of both sides. In 1800 students disturbed morning prayers by scraping, insulting the speaker by rubbing their boots against the rough floor. President Samuel Stanhope Smith called in three seniors and, when they admitted their wicked deed, dismissed them from the college. When their fellow students learned of this harsh penalty, they set off a riot. They shot pistols, crashed brickbats against walls and doors, and rolled barrels filled with stones along the hallways of Nassau Hall, the principal college building. One of the expelled seniors did not leave the area and returned to the college two weeks later. He beat up the tutor whom he suspected of reporting on him. This set off a second riot that Smith quelled only by threatening to close the college.[5]

Seven years later the suspension of three students again angered their classmates. This time undergraduate leaders acted responsibly and drew up a letter of remonstrance that questioned the justice of the dismissals and requested that the three be allowed to return. President Smith found this conscious, collective act more threatening than spontaneous violence: Princeton students had illegally combined against proper authorities. At evening prayers, he, his faculty, and a trustee presented their case against the letter and began to call the roll. Each student at the calling of his name had to disavow the letter and remove his signature from it. Refusal meant suspension. A student leader led the way out of the room, followed by 125 Princetonians. Riot followed. Angry students seized Nassau Hall, smashed windows, and armed themselves with banisters against villagers who had assembled at the request of the president. The revolt ended when Smith closed the college for an early recess.[6]

What is particularly interesting about the 1807 riot is the division it demonstrated between students. At least six of those expelled or dismissed were Virginians, including Abel P. Upshur, later to become Secretary of State of the United States.[7] Between 30 and 40 students did not walk out with the 125. Of the 125 suspended students, 55 ultimately submitted and re-entered Princeton. A later conflict confirmed this divide. In 1817 students rioted once again. This time they yelled "Fire!" from the top of Nassau Hall, after they had nailed up the entrances and also the doors to the rooms of tutors and religious students.[8]

Even we who lived through the 1960s find the violence directed against persons in the early 1800s hard to comprehend. At the University of North Carolina students horsewhipped the president, stoned two professors, and threatened the other members of the faculty with personal injury.[9] Yale students in the 1820s bombed a residence hall. In a later Yale conflict, a student killed a tutor who tried to break up a melee.[10]

What was at issue? A few generations ago, the answer was simple. Underlying undergraduate unrest was an antiquated curriculum of *quadrivium* and *trivium*—arithmetic, geometry, astronomy, music, logic, grammar, and rhetoric—inherited from the medieval university, sorely out of touch with the new currents of thought. New scholarship on the early American college, summarized by Frederick Rudolph, has demonstrated that this was not so.[11] However meager their resources, the colonial colleges inherited from England not only the tradition of scholastic learning but also Renaissance ideals of humanism and the educated gentleman. Moreover, the colonial colleges responded to the intellectual revolution of Isaac Newton.

Quietly, by a series of measured steps, college presidents, professors, and tutors transformed the content of higher education in America. The "New

Learning" of mathematics and natural science reshaped the course of study and introduced the radical notion that the mind could discover the unknown. Its English texts for the study of science broke the hold of Latin as the language of instruction. The study of language itself shifted to include literature, history, and rhetoric. Moral philosophy emerged as the capstone of the curriculum, taught by the president to the senior class. Moral philosophy sought to develop a guide to human behavior based not on divine law, but on the exploration—through observation and reason—of the social order as revealed to man. Student debates and graduation oratory reflected the shift from syllogistic disputation in Latin based on deductive reasoning to English forensic debate that required empirical thinking. In Rudolph's words, "the curriculum had shifted from explaining the ways of God to exploring the ways of man."[12]

If undergraduates were not reacting to the boredom of an outmoded curriculum, what then provoked the outbursts? Like participants in the early student riots in the 1960s, students at each college had a particular grievance. At Union College they wanted a professor dismissed. At Dickinson College they demanded the right to take all classes simultaneously, making graduation possible with a single year of study. Princeton undergraduates, restive under monastic rule, insisted that the college not suspend their fellows for minor breaches of public order. When their demands were ignored, students rioted.[13]

Despite these varied demands, at bottom collegians fought over power. College students of the early Republic inherited a system in which they were completely dependent upon their faculty not only for their system of education but also for their living arrangements. The prescribed student role was to pay, pray, study, and accept. If they found their instructor vindictive or their food rotten, they had no legitimate recourse other than withdrawal. That may have suited young scholars of 1740, but it no longer fit those of 1805. What had happened?

Undoubtedly the Revolution had worked its way. During the years of conflict, college men had been remarkably untouched by revolutionary fervor. A generation later, however, the patriots' sons entering college were less willing to exhibit those marks of deference faculty had traditionally expected. Nineteenth-century collegians simply had been trained to less hierarchical manners. A frequent, illuminating demand was the right to call each other Mister or Sir.

In addition, these young men came to college for reasons less clear than those of earlier scholars. Far fewer were headed for the ministry. College was for them the literary society where they gathered in comfortable quarters to write on and debate issues of philosophy and politics. At Princeton, influential members of these societies led the revolts. At all the colleges wealthier students broke the rules and turned out for the fight. They could afford to. They did not depend upon college for a position in the world.

Moreover, their inner selves conflicted sharply with the college order. Philip Greven has argued that three basic temperaments divided Americans during the era of the Revolution and the new nation.[14] The "genteel" temperament—especially strong among elite Southern families, but also present among the wealthy Northern merchants—arose in children reared indulgently in large households of extended family and servants. Parents gave fond attention to highly individualized, beloved children. They used physical punishment, but let it be administered largely by surrogates. Genteel parents thereby created pleasure-loving, extroverted sons who valued outward appearance and good manners, accepted the play of ambition and the open pursuit of power, and did not suffer pangs of conscience.

In contrast, the "evangelical" temperament encouraged introspection and guilt feelings. The intense piety of evangelicalism ordained that a nuclear family keep close watch over its young, who came into the world tainted by original sin. Through physical restraint and psychological warfare, parents sought opportunities to break the will of children. They created introverted sons submissive to parental authority and anxious about their psychic states.

By gradually bending the will, "moderate" parents sought to train their children to grow in grace. Such households dropped prohibitions against pleasure, even dancing and gaming, to let the rule of moderation and reason prevail. Moderate families fostered youth who were tolerant of others and who accepted diversity. Their child rearing aimed at the ideal of self-control in the young, so that they might live without apparent monitors.

Greven did not focus on the behavior of college students, but the relation between his typology of temperaments—genteel, evangelical, and moderate—and the revolts is clear. Genteel sons who went off to college took their extroverted ways with them along with their servants. They brought to college a love of pleasure, an attention to manners, a restless ambition, and an easy conscience.

Early-nineteenth-century colleges, however, were institutions created and sustained by those of a different spirit. Presidents and professors trained as ministers in eighteenth-century colleges could comprehend neither the changes of their era nor many of their students. To shift from absolute monarch to consultative ruler threatened the known order. As men of evangelical temperament, they assumed they could break the will of the young and errant. Instead of compromise they insisted on their traditional prerogatives. Although the heads of all colleges shared similar assumptions, the conflicts these evoked were particularly acute in the Southern institutions where planters' sons confronted rules invented in New England and largely maintained by New England-trained clergy. "Young Georgians at Athens, young North Carolinians at Chapel Hill, young South Carolinians at Columbia, young Mississippians at Oxford—all objected to such a system," suggestive to them of the subordination of slavery.[15]

The refusal of college faculty to hear and act on complaints or reconsider disciplinary judgments often provoked the original outburst. Gregarious, moderate young men presumed that they were reasonable adults. If they met with respect, they were apt to accept the world that they found; if denied respect, they might join in opposing what they regarded as unjust authority. The orthodoxy and intransigence of college heads convinced students of a moderate temperament that the authority over them was unreasonable, and they joined their more spirited brothers in rioting in protest.

As colleges moved to suppress disturbances, they found support outside in a public that feared civil disorder. College heads seemingly triumphed after every riot. At the end of each conflict the seditious apologized and sought mercy, withdrew, or were suspended. Colleges were determined to put students in their place.

Technically they did. Presidents supported by faculty reasserted their right to determine who taught what, and how. They wrote the rules. They admitted students and could expel them. But the apparent victory hid the reality. Suppressed though it was, the mutinous spirit survived. It ceased to confront authority directly but turned to covert forms that grew in strength during the nineteenth century.

The student culture that emerged from the revolts differed profoundly from its eighteenth-century predecessor. The literary society that held a dominant place from its mid-eighteenth-century founding until the 1820s offered a means for self-improvement, the "junto" of the leisured college man. Did the required course of study ignore the basic education desired by collegians aspiring to become men of culture? Then build outside its bounds a fellowship to address contemporary philosophy and politics. Did recitation allow no real cultivation of manners and style? Then use the society to improve writing and public speaking. Did the college not provide the necessary books to study the great questions of the day? Then organize a library within the society.

What is striking about the eighteenth-century society is its seriousness of purpose. Its members made, as James McLachlan has put it, the Choice of

Hercules, choosing virtue over pleasure, the virtue of the man of letters. The literary society offered an excellent education for public life. Though its course of study remained outside the formal curriculum, the two were complementary, not antagonistic. Professors neither organized nor led these associations, but they were welcome on their premises to use the library or to attend the debates. Generally each campus had two rival societies, each of which engaged with its competitor in a lively contest for newcomers' loyalty. The two included in their ranks all undergraduates who sought membership.[16]

The revolts ended such a judicious, amicable system. Combatants emerged from the conflicts with a sense of deep injury and anger. Many students saw themselves at war with their faculty and with fellow students. They turned away from the literary society to create in the college fraternity an institutional expression of both their grievances and their divisions.

In 1825 Union College was growing into the largest college in the nation. It too had been wracked with disturbances, though none as violent as those of Princeton. Its student body reflected the range of its region, drawing the sons of upstate New York aristocrats along with young men from the country and the new frontier towns. A few prominent students confirmed their friendship by adopting the name Kappa Alpha, choosing the watch key as an emblem, and surrounding the society in vaguely Masonic ritual. Within two years other students founded two other fraternities at Union, and in 1831 students at Hamilton College formed a branch of the Union fraternity Sigma Phi.[17] By 1840 fraternities had spread to most New England colleges and would take solid root in the Midwest before 1850. By the Civil War, Williams College had six branches of national fraternities on its campus, comprising at least 50 percent of its student body. The rapidity of the fraternity's adoption and its early strength suggest that Union students hit on the right form for the age.[18]

The fraternity appealed because it captured and preserved the spirit of the revolts. Unlike the eighteenth-century literary society, the fraternity consisted of a small, select band pledged to secrecy. Although rhetoric paid tribute to serious, high-minded purpose, the real concern of each fraternity was to create within the larger college a small group of compatible fellows for friendship, mutual protection, and good times.

On most campuses the conflicts had disclosed a sharp division among students. Only a small minority of young men attended college in the early Republic, perhaps 2 percent. Two groups deemed college as appropriate: the wealthy who chose it to "finish" their young and the poor who hoped to become ministers. Very few in the middle class brought their aspirations to college until later in the nineteenth century, when higher education emerged as the principal route to the professions. In this bifurcated world, the wealthier students tended to fight authority, the poorer complied. The future ministers came to college for the formal training it offered. Raised in evangelical households, introspective sons expected to work hard, be governed by their professors, and strive intensely for self-improvement.

Brothers of Sigma Phi on the porch of their house, Williams College, 1866. *Williamsiana Collection.*

Affluent, secular classmates looked askance at these good students. They labeled a studious classmate a "dig," a "fag," a "grub," or a "blue." English university students divided themselves into "reading men," the diligent students, and "rowing men," those specializing in sports and play, but American collegians had no equivalent antonyms. The language of college life lacked any positive term for hardworking classmates or for study. The line collegians drew between those who took their studies seriously and those who tried to ingratiate themselves with their professors was a thin one.

A "blue" studied hard; a "blue-light" spied on other students for the faculty.[19]

The division between students went back at least to the early eighteenth century and underlay the disrespect that many undergraduates had for their tutors. Wealthy Boston families sent their high-spirited sons to Harvard. As they gambled and drank, they offended both their more restrained classmates and college authorities. By midcentury at both Harvard and Yale, the blades confronted tutors whose origins and demeanor repelled them. The tutors tended to have minister fathers; as college students, the future tutors' pious and obedient manner had pleased their presidents enough to secure an appointment.[20]

The demography of early-nineteenth-century New England swelled the numbers of such serious students in Northern schools. Younger sons sought an alternative to the family farm that could support only an elder brother. With little time for socializing and no money, the pauper scholars did not join in the hell-bent amusements of their peers. Reared in evangelical homes, in college they encountered professors whose expectations fit their own internal standards. As fraternities formed, some of them stayed aloof; others formed counter-groups committed to teetotalism or to non-secrecy. Economic and psychic disparities among students dissolved the basis for collegiate community. The fraternity system underscored these differences and gave them form.

In the South, although conflicts between faculty and students remained explosive, the more homogeneous body of affluent undergraduates had less need for exclusive organizations. Thus, in places such as Franklin College, renamed the University of Georgia, literary societies remained vital until after the Civil War, and communal celebrations such as commencements attracted wide attention. Only in 1866—on a campus that included for the first time state-supported veterans and future teachers and ministers on scholarship—did the first Greek-letter fraternity at the University of Georgia take hold, with effects as disruptive of the old societies and celebrations as elsewhere.[21]

Differences existed among colleges, not only of region, but in scale, class origins of students, and intention of faculty. Behavior acceptable at one institution caused expulsion from another. In 1847 Greenville Tutor Jenks came to Amherst from New York University, bringing with him membership in Psi Upsilon. Though he was "wild as a hawk," the Gamma chapter at Amherst took him in. William Hammond, an academically ambitious brother, determined that Jenks would do "well enough with a little *training*" and dedicated himself to the task of reform. Jenks in return gave Hammond "glowing descriptions of 'life' and 'the fellows'" at NYU. Hammond's influence came to nought, and after nine months the Amherst faculty wrote to Jenks' stepfather to remove him. Protected by a vigilant faculty, Amherst in the 1840s attracted few "blades" and expelled those few it mistakenly admitted. Its fraternity men were less genteel than moderate in their temperament. William Hammond was the son of a Newport, Rhode Island, lawyer and minor public official, who himself chose the law. If he is at all representative, to an unusual degree his world valued scholarship, intellectual discourse, and cordial relations with their faculty—along with their good times.[22]

Such deviations were the exception, rather than the rule. In general, college life, buttressed by the fraternity, sustained the mentality of the students who had joined the revolts. Its representatives, who have left us the major accounts of college experience from the mid-nineteenth century until World War I, presumed to speak for all students. They did not. They spoke for that wealthier, secular sector of male undergraduates who joined or wanted to join a fraternity or club. The strength of this segment varied on each campus. Where it dominated, as at Williams and other New England country colleges, fraternities accounted for a majority of students. Where weak, as at the University of Nebraska, the organized undergraduates formed only a small proportion of the college population.

Our best source for the mind of the undergraduate under the sway of collegiate canons is Lyman Bagg, a Yale student of the late 1860s. Despite the presence at Yale of a significant number of undergraduates who remained outside college life, our informer seldom qualified his statements. In its directness and simplicity, his language is difficult to resist. Moreover, his presumption that he speaks for all men in college is itself critical to his cast of mind. In drawing on his report I will retain his language, with the warning that in this context *students* and *undergraduates* really mean only those who assumed the mantle of college men.

Bagg reported that undergraduates retained a collective memory of the outrages of the revolts. Faculty victory over students in the antebellum years convinced students that any "fight against the faculty would be a hopeless one." What collegians meant was any direct, open fight, for students believed in "the irrepressible conflict between themselves and the faculty."[23]

In such an atmosphere students cheated with impunity. Because students perceived faculty power, however "arbitrary and unreasonable," as absolute, an undergraduate defended himself by "sharp practice and every mode of deception which his wits can conjure up." Flunking out posed the greatest danger to students. Their professors sought to rid the college of weaker scholars, an intolerable attack on the student community. Students had the duty to protect themselves individually and by mutual aid. Against the common enemy, all measures of defense were acceptable. Undergraduate lore was filled with the more ingenious stratagems for "shining," or cheating. Fingernails, cuffs, and boots served as obvious slates for formulae and outlines. The daring hid texts in holes dug in the floor or on the other side of windows, and devised ingenious mechanical devices to keep rolls of notes up their sleeves. Whole classes cheated on examinations. The use of ponies (translations of texts) was almost universal. At Yale in the 1860s, perhaps less than half of the compositions were actually written by the supposed author for the occasion.[24]

Students approved of all cheating necessary to stay in college. Unlike those of later, more competitive eras, good students risked their places for weak ones. Because grades (or "stand" at Yale) had little value, students with high grades substituted their exams for those of failing friends. A student who refused to help another to cheat was "thought little better than a monomaniac on the subject of honor." Mutual aid was one thing; competition another. Students fully accepted cheating to stay in college, but to "skin for a stand" (to cheat to better one's record) was considered "mean and contemptible."[25]

Students themselves valued intelligence, but they insisted that it be measured by their own standards. Scholastic rank, the faculty measure of a student's success in recitation and exams, carried no prestige. "Stand, in the abstract, is a thing which is laughed at by the great body of the students, including the good scholars as well as the poor ones." Students normally did not know each other's scholastic rank very clearly. For a student to regard it as important, "to 'talk stand,'" assessing the relative position of colleagues, or "to seriously compare their 'chances,'" signaled a weak character. Classmates who won honors met with "good-natured ridicule at the hands of their friends." Thus the prizes the college offered did not necessarily carry prestige. Men might receive them by "accident" or as "successful cheats." The prizes for mathematics and postgraduate scholarships, awards most clearly connected to grades, possessed little value. Prizes for literary composition, debate, and oratory, on the other hand, came as great honors, especially savored if meted out to a student with low marks.[26]

Success by faculty standards bore no relation to success in the world. Andrew D. White, later the founding president of Cornell, recalled one of his first recitations as a Yale student of 1850. He contrasted Delano Goddard's performance in Greek with that of a highly praised classmate, whose translation struck White as "without one particle of literary merit" and whose tongue on conjugating a verb reminded him of a "clapper of a mill."

When the scholar sat down, White's neighbor confided, " 'that man will be our valedictorian.' This disgusted me. . . . It turned out as my friend said. That glib reciter did become the valedictorian of the class, but stepped from the commencement stage into nothingness, and was never heard of more. Goddard became the editor of one of the most important metropolitan newspapers of the United States, and, before his early death, distinguished himself as a writer on political and historical topics."[27] So much for professorial judgment.

"In Memoriam de Mattie Matix" or "Cremation of Mathematics," in which the Amherst College class of 1886 celebrated the end of an infamous course (Clyde Fitch on couch). *Amherst College Archives.*

According to the codes of college life, students had no interest in getting to know the faculty in or outside of class. A man's real distinction as a scientist or scholar remained unrecognized and unappreciated by students. White took courses from Benjamin Silliman and James Dwight Dana, but failed to be affected by either. He later reflected that he could not forgive himself "for having yielded to the general indifference of the class toward all this instruction. It was listlessly heard, and grievously neglected."[28]

At a more personal level, an undergraduate might be cut if he insulted a professor to his face, but students approved of cheating and lying to him and of cursing him in private. The official doctrine of the colleges encouraged faculty to exercise paternal regard for their charges, but students resented any idea that there should be "any familiarity between the two 'hostile elements,' either in the recitation room or outside it."[29]

Nineteenth-century undergraduates condemned with a long list of negatives those students who tried to gain teachers' approval. They labeled such behavior with the terms "bootlick," "coax," "fish," or "baum." Such slang confirmed the divide between teachers and students. Many decades earlier, John Popkin, a professor at Harvard, had written to his younger brother with suggestions about how to conduct himself. Popkin knew that if his brother followed his advice, the young man would be exposed to the "opprobrious epithet, *fishing.*" To the professorial brother, the term had done great harm, suggesting that

> every one who acts as a reasonable being in the various relations and duties of a scholar is using the basest means to ingratiate himself with the government, and seeking by mean compliances to purchase their honors and favors. . . . If a scholar appeared to perform his exercises to his best ability, if there were not a marked contempt and indifference in his manner, I would hear the whisper run round the class, *fishing.* If one appeared firm enough to perform an unpopular duty, or showed common civility to his instructors, who certainly wished him well, he was *fishing.* If he refused to join in some general disorder, he was insulted with *fishing.* If he did not appear to despise the esteem and approbation of his instructors, and to disclaim all the rewards of diligence and virtue, he was suspected of *fishing.* [30]

A professor perceived a word so used as undermining his position. For a student eager to partake of the dominant culture of college life, however, such a word served to protect the social and emotional distance necessary to maintain student bonds. It drew the line between students who sought the esteem of their peers and those disloyal ones who believed that faculty set the standards for behavior and offered the rewards of success.

Any "code of honor" in the nineteenth century existed only between college men. They regarded it as unthinkable that one of their fellows might tell a member of the faculty that another broke college rules. College men did not inform against each other. They preferred expulsion from the college to the ostracism of classmates that would follow from bearing tales. Faced with cheating, damage to property, or even injury, college authorities found it impossible to gather evidence against wrongdoers. Such students simply did not talk.[31]

A few institutions, such as Princeton and the University of Virginia, established honor systems that made cheating more difficult, but even at these places the basic dynamic remained intact. At the University of Virginia the term was not *fishing* but *sticking your neck out.* As Virginius Dabney described its usage in the early twentieth century: "It was sticking your neck out if you spoke up in class and answered a professor's question to the group as a whole. It was likewise regarded as bad form to do reading for the course above and beyond the assignment and to let that be known." Although a professor's son, Dabney was a member of Delta Kappa Epsilon. In college he partook of the mentality, not of the professor, but of the college man. He recalled his righteous anger at a student who said in class that he had done extra reading. When Dabney received a higher mark he "rejoiced idiotically for no other reason than that I felt he got what he deserved for having gone so far beyond proper bounds."[32]

To put it directly, college men and faculty remained at war. Students who assumed the culture of college life avoided any contact with the enemy beyond that required. Knowing they would lose in open conflict, such students turned to deception, using any means to circumvent rules and fool their faculty, including lying and cheating. College men protected each other's honor, no matter what the offense, even at the risk of expulsion. No shame adhered in low grades, a six-week suspension, or even severance from the college. As the faculty's measure of quality, grades counted for nothing; the real measure of success was the judgment of peers.

Although the fraternity did not initiate cheating or derision of the scholarly or the sense of common bonds, it did link them in a coherent culture which it passed on to successive generations of college men. The fraternity perpetuated the mentality of the revolts. It was created in the wake of uprisings which had sharpened the intensity of faculty-student conflict and had pointed out divisions among undergraduates. Secret societies of select students initiated each incoming group of pledges into a way of thinking and behaving that kept the spirit of Princeton in 1807 alive.

The fraternity had great appeal. For those undergraduates with the wealth, inclination, and leisure to join, the new Greek-letter organizations gave an arena of privacy away from college eyes. In colleges founded by Protestant denominations that demanded abstinence and self-denial, members could break the official codes among trusted brothers. Fraternities provided the economic and social basis for feasts, strong drink, loose talk about women, cardplaying, and gambling. Moreover, they provided a useful base for the politically ambitious to seek college offices and honors. A group of friends pledged to fellowship and secrecy gave a definite advantage to one of their number seeking votes.[33]

The first effect of the fraternity was to disrupt the literary society. The open, inclusive eighteenth-century associations became forums for compet-

Fraternity pins became jeweled symbols of the elect. *Courtesy Northwestern University Archives.*

ing fraternities seeking to elevate their own members to prestige. At Williams, for example, a fraternity coalition appeared as early as 1843. Fraternity electioneering repeatedly weakened the societies until the 1840s and 1850s, when most of them disappeared.[34] The fraternities then moved their campaigns to the rest of the campus, where they helped create aggressive, competitive organizations more in keeping with fraternity style.

The second effect of the fraternity was the erosion of class feeling. It had been strong in the eighteenth century. The young men who came together each autumn to form a class constituted a social group that remained together for four years. Numbers were generally small, normally under a hundred. Faculty instructed the class as a body. Such conditions had bred group loyalty. A lexicon of college slang compiled by a student in 1851 contained seventeen entries beginning with the word *class*. *Class marshal, class supper,* and *class tree* marked the importance of the word and the strength of the bonds that college class once created. *Class* carried with it connotations of shared experience and comradeship, conveyed by the example of correct usage under *classmate:* "the day is wound up with a scene of careless laughter and merriment, among a dozen of joke-loving *classmates.* "[35] But by 1851 such sentiment was anachronistic, drawing on the college literature of a past era.

Divisions among students sharpened by the fraternity turned class occasions into conflicts. Fraternity brothers not only made distinctions between Greeks and Barbarians; they fought against members of rival societies. As fraternities pushed their own members for awards and prizes, they disrupted class days. Williams College had to cancel the class day of 1870 because the disputes between two rival fraternity coalitions could not be resolved amicably.[36]

One element seems inexplicable: small, select bands of students pledged to secrecy formed under the noses of college authorities. Why did presidents and professors—who had suspended students for lighting firecrackers and ringing college bells—not check the fraternity at its outset? Some of them tried. In 1832 President Eliphalet Nott offered this threat from the Union College chapel to the students under his charge: "The first young man who joins a secret society shall not remain in College one hour!" But within a year he relented and lifted the ban.[37] Mark Hopkins tried to abolish fraternities at Williams, but his board of trustees overruled him.[38] In the hope of a united action, Edward Hitchcock of Amherst wrote to the presidents of a number of Northern colleges to seek their aid in collectively suppressing fraternities. Although he learned that his colleagues disapproved of these secret societies, most of them felt powerless to end them. They feared driving them further underground.[39]

Public opinion strongly favored these new associations. The early fraternities bore much resemblance to Masonic lodges (and retain elements of this in their ritual and symbolism). Colleges found that fathers, who had generally sympathized with efforts to check their sons' unruly behavior, supported the sons as they created and joined associations. Fraternities seemed eminently American. In 1849 University of Michigan professors—alarmed at what they saw as "a monster power, which lays its hand upon every College Faculty in our country" and threatens to bring "debauchery, drunkenness, pugilism, and duelling . . . disorder and ravagism" to Michigan—expelled fraternity founders and early members. The townspeople of Ann Arbor called for their reinstatement and the expulsion of the faculty. The loss of students and the ill will that resulted forced the faculty to compromise.[40] Fraternities in antebellum America seemed an expression of the right of free association.

Moreover, they were simply inevitable. One college did succeed in suppressing fraternities—Princeton in 1855. But students created local associations that served the same functions of exclusion and fellowship. No one has ever accused Princeton's eating clubs of bringing equal opportunity to campus.

Once they took hold, fraternities, whether national Greek-letter or local clubs, entrenched themselves in colleges with a strength and intensity that has baffled observers for over a century. One element of their power is that, unlike earlier student associations, they served as the base out from which the undergraduate moved, not the final stopping place. The fraternity gave the college man his group of trusted fellows, his college home. Membership, however desired, did not define his success. This remained to be won. The fraternity, if powerful on campus, gave him strong support. But the collegian still had to go out and try to win.

College men of the mid-nineteenth century began to look for more ways to compete and win. They ignored or devalued success by faculty standards, but they increasingly rewarded leadership won in the competitive trials of undergraduate life. Arenas for achievement multiplied during these years. Such students perceived college as a field for combat. This led collegians to create a panoply of teams, newspapers, journals, and societies.

Sports came to claim collegians' deepest involvement, with football, baseball, and rowing taking center stage. Informal competitions began before the Civil War, but the real organization of athletics came in the 1870s, when students at many colleges started teams and set rules. Interclass rivalries gave way to intercollegiate competitions, calling forth intense fighting spirit and loyalty to the college among students. The rows of athletes gathered for team pictures offer carefully posed self-presentations of virility and newly acquired adulthood. As they steeled themselves for the flash of the camera or for the battles of the playing fields, college men drew on the traditions of Anglo-American schoolboy fiction that, since the 1857 publication of *Tom Brown's School Days,* had linked virtue with athletic prowess.

Under the legendary coach Alonzo Stagg, the University of Chicago brought football into its official life. *Special Collections, Regenstein Library, University of Chicago.*

College athletes as campus heroes: Yale baseball team, 1900. *Manuscripts and Archives, Yale University Library.*

They also took onto themselves the postures and attributes of homegrown groups of elite men who had formed teams in the antebellum years. Although irregular students found themselves on the playing fields to increase team chances, the ordinary college athlete, in the years between the Civil War and the turn of the century, was an amateur rather than a professional, recruited from the ranks of ordinary students and destined for a career in business, not sports. But his special skills put in the service of alma mater made him a campus hero.[41]

Those with other talents and interests could try out for college newspapers, literary magazines, drama clubs, music groups, and debating societies, all of which provided alternative fields for competitive play. Each college man had something he could do. The codes of college life exempted no student from some form of extracurricular activity. To hold oneself off from the group life of the college to preserve time for study or private interests was simple selfishness.

The years after the Civil War saw the full development of college life. College men came into their own. Out of the varied possibilities of the early nineteenth century, collegians shaped a student culture of tremendous power. Whatever the faculty thought it was doing in providing the liberal arts, college men learned little from the curriculum and much from the world of their own creation.

What did a young man learn from college life? Frederick Rudolph has cogently argued that, through the literary society and the fraternity, students of the 1830s turned their provincial, religiously orthodox colleges into urban places teaching them the ways of the world.[42] Williams College's real education in the years before the Civil War was in gentlemanly behavior. Continuing his logic, one can see that the postwar years brought changes that reflected a new purpose. The trials of college life turned the boy into a man prepared for success in the competitive world of American business.

Implicitly, collegiate codes taught undergraduates that only men were important, and thereby strengthened the masculine hegemony of the late nineteenth century. Many of the most prestigious private colleges had been founded in the era when higher education was reserved for men. Yet two of the great developments in the post–Civil War period were the opening of women's colleges and the significant expansion of coeducational institutions. The women's colleges offered special possibilities for women, isolated from men. At coeducational institutions, such as Cornell and the University of Michigan, college men put women into the established groove of the pauper scholar and ostracized them accordingly. Many of the women were serious and hardworking and saw the college as a way of becoming schoolteachers or doctors. But some of them desired the pleasures of college life. Coeducational schools forced their male students to sit beside females in class, but they allowed the men to dominate the all-important life outside the classroom. Insisting that the extracurriculum be for men only, the organized male students moved to exclude women completely from their organizations.[43] A popular group of Cornell short stories depicted a manly college life little different from that of Yale. Coeds, mentioned in passing only twice, played no part in the struggles and passions of the fraternity men.[44] Thus for many men in coeducational institutions, as in all-male ones, college life offered full immersion into the group life of male peers. If American boys needed a period of separate trial and initiation before entering adult society, this was it. Removed from their homes, the community of boys entered their own social system to emerge at the end ready for adulthood.

This male world was violent. College men battled each other in interclass rivalries and outsiders in town-gown conflicts. They fought local toughs for turf, both on campus and off. City police and firemen represented, not legal authority, but townsmen in uniform, as eager to get even as to calm civil disturbance. Students confronted each other in "rushes," violent free-for-alls that pitted sophomores and freshmen against each other. To enter college the freshman endured the physical and psychological pain of initiation. The sophomore, his primary enemy, made him feel distinctly unwelcome, fighting him in the streets, denying him the right to carry the principal undergraduate weapons of defense, the club or cane, excluding him from the turf of the college, the fence or the wall. Sophomores stole the personal items of freshmen, forced them to endure humiliation, and subjected individuals who refused to be good sports to brutal hazing. Having endured the violence of his first months, the freshman felt he became more manly because of the ordeal, a manliness confirmed by the rowdiness of his later college years.[45]

Freshmen learned early in the college course that they could openly enjoy pleasures frowned on by parents and hometown gossips. Male college culture was assertively hedonistic. When he arrived at Yale in 1896, Henry Seidel Canby's "first sensation in this new world was of a wholly delightful irresponsibility. . . . We kicked up our heels in that pleasant college town like colts in a pasture."[46] Nineteenth-century colleges may have had regulations against drinking, cardplaying, and profanity, but these rules were honored only in the breach. Except for strongly denominational schools, colleges increasingly left students to their private lives. A complex scheme of marking tracked students' attendance and promptness at college functions,

The male world of college men paid a strange tribute to the opposite sex in undergraduate theatricals: Stanford men in *Rambling Rameses*, 1912. *Stanford University Archives.*

The violence of college life knew no region: freshman-sophomore rush, Berkeley, turn of the century. *University Archives, The Bancroft Library.*

Freshman–sophomore snow fights had dramatic results: three Princeton freshmen of the class of 1895: Darwin R. James, Jr.; John P. Poe, nephew of the poet; and Arthur L. Wheeler. *University Archives, Princeton University.*

but this supervising hand did not extend outside of classroom and chapel.[47] Many students moved out of college buildings and into fraternity houses or private rooming houses, but even the students who lived in college halls had considerable freedom from supervision. On their own, they set their own standards. Yale students, according to Lyman Bagg's 1871 report, approved of "moderate drinking," and did "not disapprove of one's 'getting comfortably tight,' occasionally." They played cards, smoked, swore, and engaged in loose talk about women.[48]

But escape from the mores of home or boarding school meant entry into a new community. "Therefore the freshman changed his tie, his hat, his slang, as a manifesto of his escape from rule, but also of his new allegiance. He was no longer a boy from Rochester, he was a Princeton undergraduate, admitted to the rights and privileges of college life . . . sensitive to every push and pull of his new environment."[49] The flip side of escape was conformity, the intense conformity to college custom and fashion of the college man. College yearbooks give an annual record of this attention to style, as each year students chose to be photographed in the uniform of the day. Virginius Dabney recalled the power of student dress codes at the University of Virginia in the early twentieth century. "For at least one whole year the only good form at Virginia was to wear a white shirt and a solid black four-in-hand tie. This stylistic edict reportedly came down from Yale. At all events, one saw herds of students wearing nothing but white shirts and black ties, the over-all effect being that of a morticians' convention."[50]

The undergraduate under the spell of college life believed that what you knew did not matter very much. Whom you knew, however, mattered a great deal, and in college he believed he made contact with the best. What constituted quality and how was it judged? Students insisted that they alone evaluate another's worth. Not only did they not accept faculty standards; they denied that they were influenced by a man's social origins. Lyman Bagg insisted that "prejudices as to birth, or State, or politics are quite unknown to the college. It is a useless recommendation to say of a man that he comes of a good family . . . he will be judged by himself alone."[51] It is in this independence that the much-vaunted "collegiate democracy" lay. It was not that all were equal in college. Rather that students made natural, not artificial, distinctions that they based on success gained in college competition, not on family social standing.

Statements about the democratic nature of college life flew in the face of the divisions actually separating students. Early-nineteenth-century undergraduates were divided between the serious ministerial candidates and

What the well-dressed Virginia man wore in the 1890s. *University of Virginia Library.*

Theodore Roosevelt, graduation portrait, 1881.
*Harvard University Archives.*

their more prosperous secular classmates, a division confirmed and heightened by fraternities, clubs, and secret societies. On each campus, the existing members of an organized clique asked versions of the 1836 question used by a Williams fraternity as its final test in selecting members: "Would you want your sister to marry him?"[52] Family position, money, and style certainly weighed in the answer. (Tests of religion and ethnicity awaited the more open student body of the twentieth century.) Although groups might point to an exceptional member from a modest background taken on the basis of character or talent, clubs did divide up the college into a hierarchy of prestige that conformed rather closely to the social stratification of the outside world.

Even so enthusiastic a Harvard undergraduate as Theodore Roosevelt carefully scrutinized the backgrounds of his college friends. In the fall of 1876, his freshman year, he confided to his sister that he wished "most sincerely" that he knew "something about the antecedents" of his friends, and that "on this very account I have avoided being very intimate with the New York fellows." He rather quickly formed an eating group with his Boston acquaintances, all of them highborn. His wealth, family connections, and high spirits opened the doors of Boston society, and he was accepted into the set of well-bred Bostonians at Harvard. They had him out to their homes on Sundays; invited him to their dancing parties, sleigh rides, and picnics; and ultimately accepted him as the husband of one of their liveliest debutantes.[53]

Roosevelt's Harvard career requires me to pause. Already at Harvard he was breaking certain codes of his social class. Although he never strayed beyond the world of proper society, he behaved differently in it. When Harvard canons required undergraduates to be blasé, he was enthusiastic, running between recitations, rather than imitating the "Harvard swing," a nonchalant shamble. Male college peers may have drunk, smoked, and womanized, but Roosevelt kept himself to the rigid standards of purity that he associated with his father, a commitment made the stronger by the tragedy of his father's death during his sophomore year. He taught Sunday school throughout his four college years. Group norms may have encouraged inattention to classes and study, but Roosevelt studied hard, took pride in his marks, and interrogated his professors in the classroom. He caught his own mixture of seriousness and conformity when, at the beginning of his senior year, he announced proudly to his family that he ranked nineteenth in a class of 230; "only one gentleman stands ahead of me."[54] A classmate later remembered "looking hard at him," wondering to himself whether Roosevelt was "the real thing, or only the bundle of eccentricities he appears."[55] Yet he was elected to several clubs, including the Porcellian, that he was "delighted to be in . . . there is a billiard table, magnificent library, punch-room &c and my best friends are in it."[56]

Only a young man with Roosevelt's native gifts, vitality, wealth, and social pedigree could enjoy the luxury as an undergraduate of being a true original; but at one level nineteenth-century Harvard was more open than many other places. Harvard students never lost their respect for brilliance.

Undergraduates at nineteenth-century Harvard had an unusual respect for the intellect: O.K. Club at Harvard, Bernhard Berenson seated second from the left of hassock. *Harvard University Archives.*

Throughout the nineteenth century they conferred honors on those of unusual gifts. Although he had the proper pedigree, Henry Adams remained outside "what were known as popular men," but his fellows chose him the 1858 class orator. In 1884 Bernhard Berenson, an impoverished Jewish immigrant, arrived as a freshman, but he joined O.K. Club, whose members included George Santayana, wrote for the *Harvard Monthly,* and ultimately became its editor-in-chief. Though Robert Morss Lovett had gone to the non-prestigious Boston English High School, after he became president of

Phi Beta Kappa and editor-in-chief of the *Monthly,* his classmates elected him 1892 class poet, and the Hasty Pudding took him in. Adams, Berenson, and Lovett experienced and remembered the divisions separating undergraduates at Harvard. (Berenson, particularly, continued in later life to nurse his wounds at the slights he had received from other students. Nothing, he later wrote, was "so clicky and exclusive as the schoolboy or the schoolboy-minded Anglo-Saxon of all ages.") But in Harvard's particular nineteenth-century collegiate world, talent opened doors that would have remained shut elsewhere.[57]

Just as Yale's chronicler of college life denied that college men paid attention to family status, so, too, did he insist that politics were inconsequential. His juxtaposition suggests that undergraduates did not see politics as an ongoing debate about philosophy and policy that ought to engage all citizens, but as a family habit that if brought into the college could divide students against each other. The Civil War had turned classmates into the soldiers of warring armies. In its aftermath, students sought harmony rather than division. Moreover, as college life expanded and became more elaborate, those under its canons grew more insular and inward-looking. By the late nineteenth century collegiate canons identified political concern with the world external to the college, a world that held no real interest for the undergraduate.[58]

In his first week at Yale, Canby went to the New Haven Green to hear William Jennings Bryan. The Great Commoner hurled the accusation: "Ninety-nine out of a hundred of the students in this university are sons of the idle rich." Undergraduates began to shout repeatedly, "Nine, nine, ninety-nine," drowning out his speech. Democratic newspapers reported the uproar as a conservative political gesture directed against Populism; but it was not. The freshmen in the crowd belonged to the class of 1899, and they picked up on Bryan's inadvertent invocation of their class name. Canby recalled that he had yelled like the others because he "had entered a state within a state, and joined a faction of that state, the student body, aware really only of themselves, their own life, their own ideals."[59]

As flippant as this college world appeared to the outside, it was in fact a harsh taskmaster. It insisted that every student "do something." Study was for the self alone, but reporting for the college paper or singing in the glee club was "doing something for the college." At their meetings fraternities tracked each member's achievement, worrying about scholarship only to protect their exposed flank against the faculty. Canby recalled that "the toil was supposed to be fun, but the rewards were serious. No one that I remember did anything that was regarded as doing, for its own sake. No, the goal was prestige." The collegian believed that his strenuous life "demonstrated loyalty to . . . the college, that thus the selfish man transcended his egoistic self-seekings, and 'did' something for Harvard, or Amherst, or Yale."[60]

As he moved up the hierarchy of classes as a college leader or an admiring onlooker, the undergraduate under the sway of college life believed that he

Some served who only yelled: Chris Bradley leading Stanford men in cheering the football team, 1897. *Stanford University Archives.*

was experiencing a rehearsal of the real world. College was not a moratorium; it was a trial run. Its outcomes gave an accurate prediction of future success. As he gained the respect of his peers, the collegian experienced a certain confidence. He sloughed off his provincialisms and learned an ease of manner and a style designed to ensure his acceptance in society. If he had become a "big man," a leader on the playing fields or in the newspaper room, this augured well for his future. In the competitive struggle for place, he had learned how to get ahead, a lesson that would serve him in the conflicts to come. He believed that the heroes of the college, especially those of the gridiron, were destined for greatness.[61] Distinguished alumni, particularly those recognized in college, confirmed this feeling. Natural leaders surfaced and gained the respect of the class. College life buttressed belief in the Survival of the Fittest.

College men also believed that success in college brought real rewards. The contacts one made lasted for life. In the corridors of wealth and power, the "big man" would have friends, a place, an edge. "From henceforth he would be not Jones of Columbus, but Jones of 'Bones' or some other tight-ringed fraternity. Thanks to his ability to catch a ball, or to organize, or to be friendly, or to drink like a gentleman, or even to capitalize on his charm, he was tapped as of the elect at age 20 or 21."[62] In the archetypal Yale story, a poor, brawny, and likable Westerner makes friends with the prep school son of a successful businessman. After a difficult trial in which the fundamentally decent fellow from the West proves himself, personally and on the gridiron, he is welcomed into the chosen circle. And after he graduates, he enters his wealthy friend's family business.[63] Jay Gatsby could hardly have dreamed it better.

Despite the promise it offered to such Westerners and small-town boys, college life essentially confirmed and intensified the growing elitism of late-nineteenth-century American life. College men gained contact with young men of other regions, but they did not become tolerant of those from other ethnic groups, for, although there were a few Jews, Catholics, and Negroes in college, they remained essentially invisible in the nineteenth century. Nor did a collegian under the sway of college life generally cross the boundaries of social class. Poor white Protestant students continued to go to college in the late nineteenth century, but the dominant undergraduate culture taught the more affluent to ignore their modest classmates who chose the path of serious study.

Such was the power of college life that it shaped the experience of undergraduates in far-flung settings. In 1885 a privileged young man from Sacramento entered the University of California at Berkeley. Thus did Lincoln Steffens, the future reporter and muckraker, set out on "an adventure into a new world, and a very strange and complete world too." Stories had prepared him and his fellows for college life. Even though his predominantly male classmates of roughly one hundred came from California, not western Massachusetts, to a new institution set in the brush across the bay from San Francisco, they shared the "typical undergraduate customs, rights, and privileged vices" of students of the older colleges. "The stories and the life are pretty much the same for any college."[64]

Unlike other college-bound youth, young Steffens wanted to *know*. He had taken an extra year of study before entering college (after flunking his entrance examinations), a challenging year that had posed to him the great questions about the nature of God and the universe and the just society that were troubling intellectuals in the late nineteenth century. But Steffens quickly learned that college was no place for such matters. "There were no moot questions in Berkeley. There was work to do, knowledge and training to get, but not to answer questions. I found myself engaged, as my classmates were, in choosing courses." Hemmed in by requirements and prerequisites, Steffens found himself merely working mechanically for a degree in courses that bore no relation to intellectual growth. At Berkeley, "knowledge was absolute, not relative, and it was stored in compartments, categorical and independent. The relation of knowledge to life, even to student life, was ignored, and as for questions, the professors asked them, not the students; and the students, not the teachers, answered them—in examinations."[65]

So Steffens went the route of the college man. He had gotten a taste of this life when he first arrived on campus to find upper-class students rallying to defend their ways against the university's president, who had attempted to regulate their "private lives and . . . public morals." Steffens joined them as they dramatically pointed out the limits of student tolerance. They put a ladder through the front window of the president's house and "to the chant of obscene songs, swung it back and forth, up and down, round and round, till everything breakable within sounded broken." With his courses chosen, Steffens turned with the other freshmen "to the socially important question: which fraternity to join." The upperclassmen put aside their superior airs for a time "to 'rush' those of us whose antecedents were known and creditable. It was all snobbish, secret, and exclusive." Once initiation was out of the way, Steffens turned to the "next great university question . . . athletics."[66]

Steffens' independence of mind and failure to make a team limited his life as a college man. His one great skill was as the military drillmaster of the freshmen and ultimately of the whole undergraduate corps, "the most unpopular and meaningless of undergraduate activities," earning himself the nickname "D.S.," for "damned stinker."[67] He also learned to gamble and to cheat at cards, a profitable extracurricular activity. Most extraordinarily, in his last two years, Steffens turned away from requirements and college life to prod his teachers into introducing him to an education. For this he had to ignore the codes of the college man and ask his professor after class for references. Thus did his intellectual—as opposed to his college—life begin.

Such college life as Steffens described sprang from collegians' efforts, free from any institutional direction or support. Faculty and presidents not only opposed student organizations; they felt bewildered by the mentality behind them. In 1863, when Edward Hitchcock recalled how he had dealt with students as president of Amherst College, he confessed that he had adopted a principle that he came at times to believe—that college students were "deranged." College exposed them to "the influence of views, feelings, and prejudices, so different from those of men in common life" that they were best treated as "men under strong hallucination, if not partial insanity." How else explain how men, who later became quite respectable, could "abuse one another, oppose the Faculty, justify convivial excesses, and sympathize strongly with those disciplined for gross immoralities, so as even to organize rebellion against lawful authority."[68]

But gradually a change took place. Students under the influence of college culture failed to perceive the new spirit and continued to assume that they were at war with their faculty, but by the late nineteenth century, many of their professors were calling a truce. A faculty member, by definition, was once a student. Some of them had taken the path in college of the future minister, and had thus been both serious and temperate; but not all had entered academia by this route. Some had been college men, even "big men," leading the team on the athletic field and enjoying fraternity life. As they became professors, they brought their memories into their new positions, and saw themselves, not as their students' adversaries, but as their supporters.

Such a man was Edward Hitchcock, Jr., the son of Amherst's president. A member of the class of 1849, he had joined Alpha Delta Phi fraternity and remained loyal to it the rest of his life. Trained as a doctor, he joined the Amherst faculty in 1861 to become its first professor of hygiene and physical education, a position he held until 1911. During these years "Old Doc," as generations of students affectionately called him, campaigned unceasingly for greater attention to the health of college students, for their regular physical training, and for gymnasia and playing fields. He understood the "animal spirits" of college men. What he tried to do was to give them outlets better than masturbation and the town saloon. Thus he insisted on daily gymnastics and encouraged athletic games, college songs, and even a billiard table in the gym. Hitchcock had no will to oppose college life, which he had enjoyed. He did, however, want to channel it into safe, morally upright lines.[69]

Few faculty were as committed to reshaping and supporting the extracurriculum as "Old Doc" Hitchcock, although each campus seems to have had his counterpart. Once scorned at Princeton as "low and unbecoming gentlemen and students,"[70] athletics came into the curriculum, and colleges hired coaches as part of the regular faculty. College authorities found sports to be useful, for they channeled student violence into organized, controllable games and provided a focus for alumni loyalty. Colleges hired coaches, created physical education programs, and built gyms. A good number of professors, some of them alumni of the colleges where they taught, maintained their fraternity ties and joined with students in supporting college teams. In the competitive social atmosphere of the late nineteenth century, college football became an immense spectacle and winning teams the objects of devotion.[71]

College life memorialized in brick and mortar: Pratt Gymnasium, Amherst College, 1882. *Amherst College Archives.*

A new factor entered as successful alumni, grateful to their alma mater for its contribution to their careers, began to give large sums to support the extracurriculum. Alumni did not return, as Hitchcock suggested, to simple sanity. They retained special memories of college. This could strengthen the anti-faculty strain in undergraduate culture, as, for example, in 1877 when the Yale alumni supported the performance in New York at the Union League Theater of a student minstrel show that the faculty had canceled.[72] Memories could foster college hedonism, as presidents learned when they observed alumni who returned to their fraternity houses on football weekends. But alumni became valuable, especially in their giving.

Alumni found athletics a worthy enterprise to support. In 1882 Charles W. Pratt, who three years earlier had been the gymnastics captain of the class of 1879, gave Amherst a large well-equipped gymnasium that included a student lounge, bowling alleys, a billiard room, and a room for memorabilia. He and his Amherst-educated brothers continued to support college athletics richly throughout their lives. In colleges across the country, alumni imitated the Pratts' generosity. George Walker Weld gave to Harvard its handsome boathouse; Henry Lee Higginson, Soldier's Field; and Augustus Hemenway, the gymnasium.[73] Alumni members of fraternities and clubs built handsome houses. In 1897 it was estimated that fraternity property in colleges across the nation was worth over two and a half million dollars.[74] College newspapers and literary magazines got well-equipped rooms or, in some cases, buildings; musical and dramatic groups began performing in new theaters and auditoria. College life—which had begun in the interstices of the early-nineteenth-century college—emerged by the end of the century as the handsomely endowed center of the campus.

The official language of the college shifted. College life assumed its place as a valued element of a man's education. No professor or president could endorse collegiate violence and hedonism, given the threats they posed to town and gown, but he could welcome fraternities, sports, and the whole spectrum of associations that trained students through the extracurriculum. Strengthened by endowments, valued by many faculty and presidents, and dominant among students, on American campuses at the end of the century college life seemed poised for a magnificent future.

# 3

## Outsiders: The Loyal Opposition

There was, of course, another side of the story. College life had never included all students. The very prestige of the fraternities consisted in leaving out the majority, or as Amherst president Edward Hitchcock put it, making them "the mud-sills on which the secret societies rested."[1] The fraternity had arisen out of the conflicts with faculty and the divisions among students exposed during the revolts. Not all undergraduates had turned out to riot. Some of them had given the names of those who had "scraped" in chapel.

Who were the thirty to forty Princetonians who in 1807 refused to walk out with their fellows in protest, who remained docile while classmates rioted in Nassau Hall? Who were the tattletales?

They were the pious ones. As more secular blades spoiled for a fight with their professors, religious classmates worried about the future in both this life and the life to come. They came to college to become ministers. For them the formal curriculum had real bearing on their future work, for the liberal arts with their strong emphasis on the ancient languages provided them with professional training. They studied hard, for they had to win the approval and backing of their professors in order to get a pulpit. This required them to remain circumspect in their personal behavior and to seem at least to obey all rules. Their own upbringing made such conformity natural. They shared with their professors not only religious belief but also a highly developed conscience and an intense anxiety about the state of their souls.

College presidents promoted successful students to positions as tutors. This provided a probationary period for further observation. The faculty then recommended those who passed the tests of intelligence, character, and piety to congregations as proper ministerial candidates, or possibly to other colleges as professors and ultimately presidents.

The numbers of these serious students swelled in the early nineteenth century in New England.[2] Western settlement created new opportunities for ministers and teachers. Farmers' sons, especially the younger ones who had no hope of inheriting the family farm, saw the chance for a better life. Revivals intensified religious feeling and the commitment to spread evangelical Christianity across the continent and to the far ends of the globe. Missionary societies set aside scholarships to send poor, aspiring youths to college to prepare for the ministry. The colleges themselves kept tuition low and living costs down.

In New England villages local ministers recruited promising lads, coached them in Latin, and recommended them to the nearest college. The lack of money created a serious obstacle for many of these village scholars. Again the town minister intervened to help them find personal patrons or get them scholarships from the American Education Society or its regional branches. A good many of these poor youths delayed college to earn tuition money as schoolteachers, making them older than the conventional student. During their years in college, they extended their winter recess to keep school. At a time when more affluent students took rooms in town, the poor inherited the dormitories on campus. Such young men had to be circumspect. They had to justify their ministers' faith in them, to retain their positions as teachers, and to have good reports for the patrons or societies helping to finance their education. Years of sacrifice for the chance of social mobility were not to be thrown away by careless actions in college.

In a world that increasingly valued style, the village scholars cast a short shadow. Nathaniel Hawthorne, an 1825 graduate of Bowdoin, where over half of the students had received some sort of aid, knew the type well. In 1838 he observed the graduation exercises of Williams College. The assemblage included a considerable number from the surrounding country towns: "Country graduates,—rough, brown-featured, schoolmaster-looking, half-bumpkin, half-scholarly figures, in black ill-cut broadcloth,—their manners quite spoilt by what little of the gentleman there was in them."[3] To admirers of Brom Bones, they were the Ichabod Cranes.

One such country scholar was Julian Sturtevant, whose family had pioneered in the Western Reserve, establishing a small family farm in Tallmadge, Ohio. Tallmadge had no pastor, but the one in the neighboring town encouraged Julian and his brother to prepare for the ministry. The Sturtevant family was very poor. Tallmadge Academy took the two boys without tuition. Both parents encouraged their sons, for they wanted them to have "a superior education." Advisers reassured the family "that funds were contributed to aid deserving young men in preparing for the ministry," and, in fact, the American Education Society supported three of Julian's four college years. Another local lad, the son of the principal of the academy, decided upon Yale. The three Ohio youths set off on one broken-down horse for New Haven. Julian characterized the long journey as a pilgrimage to a sacred place. As he recalled in later life, his enthusiasm proved justified, for "Yale, or some other college very much like it, was an indispensable condition of my entering any career."[4]

As might be expected, Sturtevant studied hard. Despite his somewhat spotty preparation, especially in arithmetic, he vied for honors. College achievement encouraged him. Unlike boyhood competitions in which his "inferiority in all contests with those of my own age" had discouraged him, at Yale he found he "had entered a new world" in which he was not "a weakling." He resolved that he would not "be outdone by anyone."[5] In both his junior and senior years, he ranked among the first fifteen who made college honors.

Early in his college course Sturtevant went to his tutor before recitation for help with his arithmetic. The tutor "bowed me out of his room, telling me that it was not customary in Yale to help a student in his lessons until after the recitation." The professors held themselves at an even greater distance. They assumed their students had no interest in their studies and insulted them accordingly. James L. Kingsley announced to his class after they had read Tacitus Agricola, "Young gentlemen, you have been reading one of the noblest productions of the human mind without knowing it." Despite his respect for his drillmasters and his admiration for his professors, Sturtevant found it bewildering to be cast adrift without adult guidance. "Professors and tutors held themselves aloof from the students and met them only in an official capacity. For the most part a student could hope for sympathy and help in his moral and religious struggles only from his fellow students."[6]

Sturtevant found this especially difficult because of the conflicts among students. The years in which he attended Yale, 1822 to 1826, were ones of "singular disorder," even "anarchy." Violence rocked the college. One November night during a northeast storm, college vandals broke all the windows of his fellow student and friend Horace Bushnell. As disorderliness mounted, Sturtevant felt himself surrounded by evildoers in power: "the wicked bore rule." "The perpetrators of all this mischief governed the college with a terrorism seldom surpassed."[7] When rowdy students blew up the chapel, shattering the glass in all the windows, Sturtevant and three close friends decided to act.

Yale undergraduates called anyone reporting to the faculty on fellow students a "Blue Skin." "No one who was not in Yale College at the time, can have any conception of the peculiar sting which the term carried. We decided to disarm that scorpion." The four formed the "Blue Skin Club" to report all violations of college rules. They gathered allies, pledging about a hundred to secrecy. When the scheme became known, three members of the opposition came to discipline the deserters. As one of the "ruffians" raised his cane, he was checked by friends gathered to protect fellow "Blue Skins" and forced down the stairs. Sturtevant's group reported the incident, and the faculty dismissed the intruders. Collegians sympathetic to the culprits called a meeting to protest the "tyrannical government" of the college, but the "Blue Skins" prevailed. The violence ended, but for many weeks the club members kept a nightly watch to protect themselves.[8]

Sturtevant understood the conflict between forces in the college in both regional and class terms. He saw the ruffians as Southern aristocrats who disdained the "Mudsills," the poor Northern students who had to earn money for college by waiting on tables or by ringing the bell for morning prayers. It chagrined these men and their Northern allies that the poor rustics took college honors. In their fight against the government of the college "they condemned the poorer students as its servile tools." To this future abolitionist the Yale conflicts of 1824 were "premonitions of the Great Rebellion," an early illustration of the corruption of both the South and the moneyed North.[9]

How many Julian Sturtevants were there? In his memoirs Sturtevant claimed that there had been over a hundred in his band in 1824 and that ultimately a majority of the college supported the "Blue Skin Club"; but he may have exaggerated. No one measure allows a simple answer. In general, the new struggling denominational colleges attracted from rural or small-town families "mature, purposeful, . . . career-minded" sons who went about their work without troubling college authorities with high living or riot.[10] While younger students attended the 83 Catholic colleges founded between 1789 and the Civil War, many of which combined preparatory and collegiate training, religious and ethnic ties between faculty and students and the mission to train future clergy intensified student seriousness.[11] Oberlin Collegiate Institute, founded as an outpost of evangelical Christianity in the West, allowed only the devout and earnest within its gates. Strict moral oversight and manual labor to lower costs discouraged all but the most dedicated. By 1866 its college had graduated 465 (out of the more than

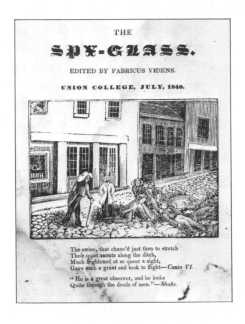

*The Spy-Glass*, July 1840, title page. *Schaffer Library, Union College, Schenectady, New York.*

James A. Garfield, right, with William Boynton, ca. 1852. *The Western Reserve Historical Society.*

11,000 who had matriculated in all its branches).[12] The American Education Society supported only those able to prove themselves destitute. In the years around 1840, these numbered roughly 15 percent of all New England college students. Slightly less than 40 percent of Amherst students before 1845 demonstrated to the college that they were poor enough to receive charity funds. Perhaps the best overall indicator of the proportion of serious, pious youth among the Eastern college population is that between 1800 and 1860 one-fourth of all New England students graduated after age twenty-five.[13] Although all colleges had some, these mature students congregated at the country colleges close to home, such as Williams and Amherst.

When the fraternities formed, these were the students left outside. Most of them ignored the strenuous organizing going on about them and remained secluded with their books. On some campuses, however, the serious students fought back. In 1834 at Williams thirty "moral . . . and religious members of College" formed the Social Fraternity, pledged to anti-secrecy. By 1838 it enrolled two-thirds of the college.[14] At Union College the promoters of the anti-secret fraternity met in President Nott's home. In 1840 they published *The Spy-Glass,* an exposé of the immorality and drunkenness of the Greek societies. The title page shows a member of the anti-secret fraternity gazing through a spyglass from an upper-story window at a group of "drunken fraternity men staggering through the streets."[15]

As this anti-secrecy movement gathered chapters, it gradually took on the coloration of its enemy, evolving into the national fraternity Delta Upsilon. One can see this transition in the diary of a prominent member, the future President James A. Garfield. A religious young man, he had vowed on entering Williams that he would "stand at least among the first in that class. The bare thought of being far behind makes my flesh crawl on my bones." Garfield kept his vow, but to his dismay found himself "by degrees and almost imperceptibly to be drawn into the currents of College partizanship [sic]." He wondered if in becoming a "College Statesman" he had lost sight of his "inner self and inner life."[16]

Neutrals replaced members of anti-secret organizations as the opposition to fraternities. By 1850 at Williams the fraternities claimed the greatest number of students, followed by the independents, and then by the anti-fraternity society. Some sense of the strength of religious opposition to the fraternity can be seen by the number of Williams graduates between 1833 and 1872 who became pastors. Roughly 42 percent of the alumni of those years had belonged to fraternities; but the Greek societies claimed only 131 ordained ministers, in contrast to the 413 who had been neutrals or members of the anti-secret society.[17] Even more dramatically, in Amherst's class of

1851 all but two of the fourteen members of the anti-secret society became ministers or college professors, but Delta Kappa Epsilon produced no ministers and only one professor.[18]

The anti-secret movement hardly threatened the fraternity brothers. It only clarified the power of the Greek system. The fraternity was by its very nature exclusive, cutting from consideration those not in the magic circle. In 1861 a member of Kappa Alpha at Williams made the distinction between the fraternities and the anti-secrets explicit. Unlike the fraternity, the anti-fraternity group on campus failed to exercise any real discrimination: its members were "chosen not because they possess in any marked degree those qualities which will render them desirable companions." The only thing the anti-secrets had in common was that they were "supposed to 'practice strict morality.'" They did not form a select group, but constituted "a motley set of good, bad and indifferent young men . . . thrown together, having no interest in or congeniality with each other."[19]

In fact, however, at Williams and elsewhere, those who did not join a fraternity often had a good deal in common. They did not partake in a distinctive collegiate culture, but they did share certain characteristics. Despite their numbers and predominance at certain colleges, because they stood outside the select circle of college men, I have chosen to call them *outsiders*.

What outsiders held in common was the perception of college as preparation. Whatever pleasures the four years might hold were incidental to the primary pursuit—an education to lead to advancing in the world. Outsiders sought to succeed in the classroom, not in the extracurriculum. They typically admired the president and faculty and sought professorial approval. They looked to their teachers, not to their peers, to learn how to behave. They hoped that by hard work and imitation they might gain academic mentors to ease their way in a calling. Though striving to move above their station, in spirit they often remained close to home. Unlike college men who entered the insular world of college life, outsiders generally retained the values and manners of their cultures of origin.

By the mid-nineteenth century, new groups of serious students were joining the ministers. Unlike affluent college men who confidently looked to futures in business, those of more modest means who chose college—the outsiders—often focused on professions that offered to aspiring young men with little capital the chance for upward mobility: law, medicine, dentistry, engineering, education, and journalism.[20]

Some of the ambitious ventured to college with little more than the suits on their backs. In 1884 Abraham Flexner, later the founder of the Institute for Advanced Study at Princeton and perhaps the leading critic of American higher education, left his German-born mother in Louisville for the new Johns Hopkins University in Baltimore. Ill prepared, but ambitious and hardworking, Flexner overcame his deficiencies in Latin and Greek to earn his B.A. in two years. He revered his professors: "I thought them all superior beings, as indeed they were. I followed their advice without question, feeling myself fortunate in my close contact with outstanding men."[21]

In his later critiques of American colleges and universities Flexner assumed that his undergraduate experience was both normal and desirable, and

Higher education carried special meaning to those who had once been slaves: graduating class, Hampton Institute, 1877; William Alexander Forsythe, Sr., second row, fourth from right. *Courtesy Harold Forsythe.*

he set out to remake higher education in the image of his Johns Hopkins years. What he was drawing on in his reforms was an extreme version of the outsider's existence. As an undergraduate, Flexner had had no interest in or conception of college life. In part, the intention that Johns Hopkins be a research university, not an ordinary college, shaped Flexner's perceptions. Johns Hopkins had no dormitories, no such thing as divisions by freshmen or sophomore class, and no interest in the life of its students outside the classroom. Despite this, however, other Hopkins students created a pale version of college life, complete with fraternities. That Flexner remained unaware of this was a measure of his Jewishness, his poverty, and his psyche. In his two years he became friends only with Dr. and Mrs. Kaiser, with whom he boarded, and with the family of his classmate Julius Friedenwald, who often had him to the Sabbath meal on Friday night. As he put it, "I did nothing in these two years in Baltimore but work, for the time was short. I had no money to spend, and I became homesick the moment I became idle." Although in Baltimore, psychologically Flexner remained at home. Throughout the two years Flexner wrote a daily postcard to his mother.[22]

While Flexner had to travel from Louisville to Baltimore, ambitious poor youth who lived near institutions of higher education could commute each day. In the early twentieth century William Langer, later the renowned historian of modern Europe, traveled from Dorchester Heights to Harvard Yard. Unlike Johns Hopkins, Harvard had a rich tradition of extracurricular life, organized and informal. Langer never entered that world. He learned a great deal, but later recalled that he could "hardly say that I enjoyed college life. I could not enjoy or hate it, because I simply did not have it." He ate his "homemade lunch in solitude between classes and spent at least two hours a day in commuting between my home and Cambridge."[23]

When his older brother Rudolph astounded Harvard's dean by passing his entrance examinations without having completed high school, Langer's widowed mother moved the household to Cambridge. Although immersed in his courses, William Langer remained within the culture of his mother's home. In the evenings he sat with his two brothers and mother "around the dining room table, a boy on each of three sides and the fourth appropriated by my mother," to talk over the content as well as the frustrations of college work.[24] When he moved outside home circles, Langer remained within the German community of Boston. The young woman that he squired came from a German family, as did Harold Kurth, his one close college friend. Langer's experience typifies that of generations of commuters, before and after, who go to college intellectually, but psychologically and culturally remain at home.

As higher education moved West with the land-grant colleges, the number of eager young men and women increased. They came to college off the farms, filled with seriousness and impatient with what appeared to them to be the childish silliness of many college students. They were not so much pious as ambitious and sometimes poor. They came to the university for the chance that it offered for mobility into the emerging professions. They

College men had no monopoly on humor: announcement of Prof. Charles Hill's lecture, April 24, 1896, Denny Hall, University of Washington. *Historical Photography Collection, Pacific Northwest Collection, University of Washington.*

wanted to become lawyers, doctors, teachers, and occasionally ministers. Some of them did join fraternities and introduced extracurricular life to the campus. But in the nineteenth century many more state university students eschewed this organized world. At the University of Oregon, students founded the first fraternity only in 1900, almost twenty-five years after the institution opened its doors.[25]

Alvin Johnson, later the head of the New School for Social Research in New York, recalled his student years at the University of Nebraska of the 1890s. The undergraduate college was small, graduating only about 150 students. Johnson was older than the average student, and, in his struggle to advance as quickly as possible, he took graduate courses as a college sophomore. With serious interests and no real anchor in a class, Johnson stayed aloof from campus politics. A Populist and a man who questioned received wisdom, Johnson also felt alien from the conservatism of the university and from its intense religious life. "A tattered flap of the Southern Bible Belt had covered much of Nebraska and was very much in evidence in the university. A very considerable proportion of the students I knew refused to register for any course under an instructor addicted to that horrible anti-religious doctrine Darwinism."[26]

While the Greek system at Nebraska was well established, "the majority of the students were anti-fraternity." Johnson found the fraternities imposing artificial social standards at a time when he wanted to enjoy the widest possible friendship. He consciously sought to know a German immigrant struggling to learn English, a talented Negro, and a number of Jewish classmates. As a "Barb," his primary recreation was the literary society, which met weekly. "Each Friday evening the boy members of the Palladian society were expected to escort the girl members to the meeting. I . . . was always rather sorry for the girl whose evening was sacrificed to me. I had no small talk and felt hesitant about indulging in large talk—Plato's real place as the prince of the Sophists, Kleon as not at all the monster figured in upper-class Greek accounts but merely an ancient William Jennings Bryan, or the tragedy of the proposed Populist merger with the alien Democratic party." The University of Nebraska proved to be, however, a good place for an unconventional young man. Johnson not only got an education but to his surprise and pleasure found a wife. Just when he had despaired of ever falling in love, into the classical library of which he was custodian came a graceful junior whose talents as a writer Johnson had already admired.[27] At the University of Nebraska in the 1890s those outside the fraternity system found themselves at little disadvantage in games of courtship.

The reporter Edwin Slosson summarized well the fluid quality of nineteenth-century undergraduate life at the state universities. As he studied the great universities at the beginning of the twentieth century, he found himself amazed by the hold of tradition among undergraduates at Yale. When he had been a student at the University of Kansas, only one custom prevailed: each class disregarded "the customs which the preceding class had attempted to establish. And if a visitor from the University of Nebraska had ventured to hint that the University of Kansas had traditions, there would have ensued a physical infraction of intercollegiate amity."[28]

As late as 1910, women students brave enough to enter Cornell classrooms banded together in front. *Department of Manuscripts and University Archives, Cornell University Libraries.*

The first college women came with high ambitions and determined independence. They had defied feminine conventions to take their minds and aspirations seriously. They ventured to college to become teachers or doctors or scholars. A few, such as Florence Kelley or M. Carey Thomas, were the daughters of affluence; but far more had struggled alongside their parents to accumulate enough to buy college training. Where they entered an all-female world in the women's colleges, they began quite early to develop a college life with many parallels to that of their brothers. Where they penetrated into formerly male preserves, such as the University of Michigan and Cornell, they were as unwelcome as any uninvited guest. College men organized in fraternities rejected them as outsiders. At Michigan, women could not join the regular staffs of the *Daily* or the yearbook. Michigauma, the primary honorary society, remains all-male to this day. At Cornell the men barred the women from campus organizations and excluded them from social events. "Fraternities would not allow their members to speak to women students on the campus, to invite them to parties, or to consider giving a Cornell woman a fraternity pin. The punishment for such transgressions ranged from being forced into the shower, to fines and the removal of fraternity pins from the men."[29] Rejected by the college men, the early coeds found companionship and occasionally love in the ranks of male outsiders. Those college women who were determined to have their own college life created auxiliary extracurricular activities, such as women's pages of the college newspaper; but until the mid-twentieth century these received secondary status. A minority of coeds found a way inside and developed the sorority system with its own set of exclusions.

It is difficult to learn about serious students from conventional sources. College histories tend to emphasize the more spectacular moments in student life, such as the "Dutch War" of 1856 in Ann Arbor when students invaded two favorite German-owned hangouts and stayed to fight townsmen and police.[30] Even primary sources are tainted. Because fraternity men controlled the campus newspapers and literary magazines, the written record reports only their mentality, a fact that has eluded most who have studied undergraduates. In the nineteenth century the sober students had no clear public voice.

One way to get at their perspective is through letters to the editor. Undergraduate publications invariably represented only college life on their news or editorial pages. The outsiders could write letters to the editor, however. For example, in May 1877, one of them complained in the *Yale Courant* about the noise outside his window. "Ingrained into the typical Sophomoric mind," he wrote, was the notion "that inarticulate howling and idiotic, hyaena-like screaming is, at any hour of the day or night, a supremely humorous method of expressing one's feelings." Did not "quiet, unoffending upper-classmen, or even professors, have any rights"? "In the name of all decency, gentlemen, pray act a little more like gentlemen."[31]

Gentlemen might have seemed in short supply at Yale in 1877, but that would shortly change. A new movement was afoot in higher education that dramatically altered not only the curriculum but the nature of the student body. While those under sway of the canons of college life were too preoccupied to notice, the serious students at colleges and universities across the country learned that their institutions offered to them rewards more lasting than style.

In the colonial and revolutionary periods, the curriculum of American colleges had reshaped itself from a sacred to a secular study and had absorbed the intellectual transformations wrought by Newtonian science.[32] To the quite different challenges of the first half of the nineteenth century, however, college professors and presidents responded in diverse—and even contradictory—ways. The inherited course of study served well the needs of students training for the ministry, scholarship, or public life, but it bore little relation to the careers of those interested in business, medicine, or engineering. New schools, such as West Point Academy and Rensselaer Polytechnic Institute, both intent on the application of scientific knowledge, directly challenged the liberal arts college. A few pioneering spirits experimented openly. At the University of Virginia, Thomas Jefferson devised the most radical plan. He divided the institution into eight schools, each headed by a professor, each offering its own diploma, but no degree, to students, who could travel freely from one school to the other. At Union College, Eliphalet Nott established a parallel scientific course that required Greek and Latin in the first year, but then allowed students to study science, mathematics, and the other emerging subjects—such as oratory, modern languages, and law—in the following three. Harvard was willing to try seemingly small, but significant, innovations, and in 1819 George Tichnor began to lecture on modern languages and literature, breaking with both the recitation system and the traditional course of study. In sharp contrast, Yale in 1828 turned its back on change to reassert, in the much-quoted and -followed Yale Report, the enduring value of the received tradition. But Yale as well as Harvard bent halfway to offer the new subjects needed for scientific and technical training. Both created, separate from the colleges, scientific schools whose students were denied the prestige of the B.A. Dragged by the Push-Me-Pull-You, curricular change in the early decades of the nineteenth century took no clear direction.

After the Civil War, new forces intersected and transformed key institutions of higher education. The land-grant colleges founded under the Morrill Act of 1862 were by statute to add to "scientific or classical studies . . . such branches of learning as are related to agriculture and the mechanic arts." State-supported institutions of higher education knew that they had to offer fields, such as education, home economics, medicine, and pharmacy, sought by their citizens. Americans studying abroad came back with a sense of the German university, the value of research, and the power of the European professoriat. Philanthropists founded institutions whose newness opened them to innovation.

In 1866 Andrew D. White presented the plan for a university in New York created jointly by the Morrill Act and the benefaction of Ezra Cornell. By design, Cornell University dissolved the hierarchy that elevated the traditional liberal arts above other courses of study. Along with alternative general programs in the arts and sciences, Cornell offered—as equally legitimate fields for the B.A.—training in the traditional learned professions of law and medicine (not, however, theology) and in the newly emerging fields of agriculture, civil engineering, commerce and trade, education, mechanic arts, mining, and public service. In Baltimore, Daniel Coit Gilman and the trustees of Johns Hopkins' bequest created a university dedicated to advanced scholarship and research. The graduate school of Johns Hopkins University offered to future professors training heretofore available only abroad and certified it with the Ph.D.

When combined, the innovations of Cornell and Johns Hopkins created a new possibility for American higher education—the true university. The university broke the power of the old college curriculum, taught through recitations. It introduced into higher education new fields and pursued them at advanced levels. It employed the lecture system and seminars. It linked research to pedagogy. It required libraries and laboratories. And it insisted that its own faculty be professionally trained, not as ministers, but as scientists, historians, and philologists.

At established colleges, innovative presidents responded to the forces of change and sought ways to transform their organizations into universities. As they did, they altered the basic conditions underlying undergraduate life. They set in motion processes that affected not only their own institutions but every campus. In 1869 one such president took the reins of Harvard College. Neither his proper Boston Brahmin upbringing nor his Harvard education prevented Charles William Eliot from perceiving the essential weaknesses of the institution. Eliot had no reverence for the liberal arts tradition and no respect for college life. Through a series of bold moves over forty years, Eliot re-created Harvard, making it into a great university by the turn of the century.[33]

Eliot's strategy was to blend college into university through an elective system brought about by growth. Eliot greatly increased the student body and Harvard's endowment. With the money generated by philanthropy and by greater numbers of students paying tuition, Eliot made new appointments to the faculty. With one eye on Johns Hopkins, he hired professors with graduate degrees, rather than ministers and young tutors; freed them from the supervision of undergraduate morals; and encouraged them to undertake research. Lectures, largely replacing the discipline of recitations, offered the new scholarship to undergraduate students. Advanced seminars brought to them and to graduate students research methods. As its faculty extended course offerings, Harvard gradually released students from a prescribed curriculum to follow their own interests. By the early twentieth century, Harvard's only course requirement for graduation was freshman English composition.

The elective system and growth in the student body enabled Eliot to reshape his faculty and revise the curriculum and method of study. It also, perhaps unintentionally, drastically altered college life. Electives undercut the remnants of the class system. Whereas earlier undergraduates had moved as a class through daily recitations, under the elective system each student maintained a separate schedule of courses, and no two students had the same program. With the exception of required English, students selected freely from the swelling number of course offerings. The lectures and written examinations that replaced recitations enhanced the possibilities for conveying new ideas and material, but lessened undergraduates' contact with each other. Once the daily testing ground for participants, the classroom became an arena for spectators. The abolition of compulsory chapel ended the last common experience.

A class of 100 in 1860 reciting together sensed their differences in social origin, but they certainly knew one another. Their endless talk about each other reflected their interest in each other. In 1906 a diverse class of 600 had no common meeting ground and felt little sense even of curiosity. The divisions between rich and poor that had marked college throughout the nineteenth century grew more pronounced as new divisions between private preparatory school and public high school, Gentile and Jew emerged. The propinquity of Boston society and its interest in eligible bachelors for its daughters intensified social distinctions. Eliot's disinterest in molding character and his commitment to academic programs caused Harvard to neglect dormitory building and leave the housing of its enlarged student body to the private market. Real estate speculators built the "Gold Coast"—private dormitories that offered elegant accommodations to undergraduates. Residential buildings in the "Yard" retained the standards of a less fastidious era. Students of more modest backgrounds lived in these college rooms. Those unable to afford college rooms commuted from home or rented cheap rooms in Cambridge.[34]

Harvard's story is worth telling not only because Harvard became America's premier university but also because Harvard's metamorphosis serves as

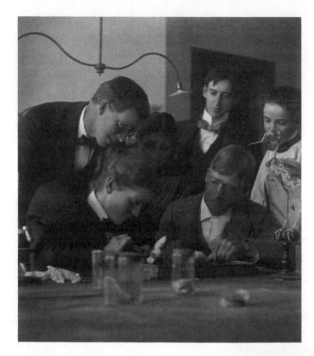

Even on campuses noted for college life, some male and female students found their studies absorbing: laboratory, Stanford University, early 1900s. *Stanford University Archives.*

RIGHT

The laboratory demanded that students solve problems, not memorize the known: laboratory, Stanford University, turn of the century. *Stanford University Archives.*

an archetype for other colleges emerging into universities in the twentieth century. The processes that Eliot set in motion beginning in 1869 found counterparts at old and new institutions all across the country.

Growth in size and change in curriculum reinforced each other. Increasing numbers of students entered, reflecting both a swelling national population and a greater proportion of it choosing to go to college. Although the great days still lay in the future, by 1900 approximately 4 percent of American youth between eighteen and twenty-one attended college. These came not only from the wealthy and the aspiring poor but also from the middle class. They were products of private preparatory schools, the preparatory departments gradually being phased out of colleges and universities, and increasingly of the public high school.

As important to undergraduate culture as the growing and diversifying student body and the elective system was the transformation, at selected colleges and universities across the country, of the inner content of higher education. The creation of Cornell and Johns Hopkins, Harvard's expansion, new institutions such as Clark and the University of Chicago, growth at Columbia and Yale, and the development of the great state universities, such as Michigan and California, fundamentally altered American higher education.

The new scholarship, supported by a trained professoriat, strengthened the forces of empiricism and experimentalism that had long vied in the curriculum with received truth. Knowledge involved the process of discovery. Hypotheses could be tested with the data of the natural and social world. Scholarship became the process of scientific investigation. The student as well as the professor engaged in the examination of data and the building of conclusions. The goal of education became the teaching of methods: the asking of questions, accurate gathering and testing of data, logical reasoning, clear presentation. The claims of scientific scholarship were transmitted through the graduate training of professors and went with them wherever they taught. Thus, while certain elements of university education depended upon scale and intention, the reformation of course content and method was not one of them. Because stability inhibited faculty turnover, in established colleges the process was gradual; but colleges as well as universities experienced the inner transformation of higher education. By the early twentieth century, universities and some colleges provided a place where undergraduates encountered empirical and experimental ways of thinking.[35]

In university settings, outsiders moved into their own. The looser atmosphere of the lecture room, the greater size and diversity in the student body, and the perceived relation of learning to vocation supported those disinterested in college life. By 1896 the University of Michigan, for example, had become a center for research, particularly in the emerging social sciences. In that year the Detroit High School sent Walter Pitkin, the future writer, editor, and professor of psychology and journalism (best known for *Life Begins at Forty*), there on a scholarship of five dollars a week. He quickly found himself an outsider. He was very poor, too poor to consider a fraternity or any social life. He did not drink. He rose early, studied hard in the morning, and generally went to bed around half past eight. Moreover, he came to Ann Arbor for the education. Forty years later the town, the campus, and his companions were a blur, but his recollection of professors and classes was sharp and clear: "Any clever lawyer could put me on the witness stand and prove to any jury that I'd never been in Ann Arbor. But he'd have to stick to questions about the town and my classmates. The instant he asked me about professors and the subjects I studied, he'd lose. For touching these the images multiply and grow sharper as time passes."[36]

As he recalled his professors, he dwelt on their personal characteristics and their manner of teaching. He learned much from the brilliant sociologist Charles H. Cooley, who "never lectured. He sat up in front of us and thought aloud. . . . He wriggled, scratched his head, drummed his fingers, looked away at a point in infinity, dropped his voice to a whisper, and otherwise proved his total detachment from a social environment. Which was an odd way of discussing Social Process, wasn't it?" Pitkin also gained much, if largely indirectly, from the Scotsman Robert M. Wenley, who promoted himself as a "titanic intellect," but who proved to be "totally unoriginal." Pitkin learned to cope with Wenley's cynicism and through him encountered logical analysis and logical thinkers.[37] More than any specifics, what stands out in Pitkin's account is that his professors—with all their foibles—were to him larger than life.

Looking back at the end of his career, Pitkin relished his appellation Social Misfit. Because in college he had not fit in, he had concentrated on his studies. "A year ago I looked up a score of people who were shining lights in college society between 1896 and 1900. Only two of them ever amounted to more than a row of bent pins. They lost the great race on the first lap." In contrast, as a loner, Pitkin had traveled farther and faster. "It wasn't that I was cleverer. It was much simpler. I used my time and energy to better advantage."[38]

One reason for the changed possibility that Pitkin found at Michigan was the impact on undergraduate life of the university's professional schools. As the universities became the loci for professional training, a new atmosphere trickled down. The Harvard Law School both exemplified and reinforced the new system. Training for law had been casual throughout much of the nineteenth century: a legal aspirant read with an established practitioner or went to a law school instead of a college. Under Eliot's appointee C. C. Langdell, Harvard led the way in developing a rigorous case-based curriculum for the study of law that assumed the student already held the B.A. Whatever their earlier collegiate experience, law students took legal training seriously. By the 1880s the most ambitious understood that high rank in class opened the way to a prestigious practice.[39]

College men still distributed prestige according to the canons of college life, emphasizing wealth and style, but in law school only academic achievement counted. As the future artist George Biddle put it, Harvard Law School in 1909 confronted him for the first time with "but one standard of success, the study of law. At the Law School the most arrogant Porcellian snob, or successful college drunkard, or publicized all-American football star, or supercilious North Shore socialite, or eager East Side Jew might now compete and achieve success on the presumed basis of his enrollment in the school—on his honor rating." Biddle learned, too, that success could not be forced. It derived not from one's way of studying or from diligence. Law school taught him that "mental capacity is not the result of method and long hours, as much as it is of mental capacity."[40]

Biddle did not succeed, and turned instead to his real calling, art. By contrast, his brilliant near-contemporary Felix Frankfurter succeeded in full measure. To Frankfurter, the professional atmosphere of law school came as a revelation. He had performed well at the City College of New York, but had not led in undergraduate life. At Harvard Law School he found that excellence mattered, not "your father or your face"—excellence measured by grades. Election to the *Harvard Law Review* came only from academic rank: "All this big talk about 'leadership' and character, and all the other things that are non-ascertainable, but usually are high-falutin' expressions for personal likes and dislikes, or class, or color, or religious partialities or antipathies—they were all out."[41]

Rather than partaking in a peer culture that put distance between teachers and taught, law students openly admired and imitated their law professors. James Barr Ames assumed heroic stature to generations of Harvard law students, the model of a gentleman-scholar-professional. Frankfurter remembered that after talking with him, "you would sort of walk off on clouds."[42]

The law school set the standard for professional training, which not only shaped the field but also affected those newer vocations that aspired to professional status. The assumptions of Harvard Law School students about study, their perception of the relation between training and practice, and their admiration for faculty became normal among students studying in professional schools.

Professional students served as the model for the serious students who saw their college training as advancing them in the world. The composition of these students shifted at the turn of the century as a different group of students entered the new universities—the children of Jewish immigrants. Jews had gone to college in the nineteenth century. But, because they were generally assimilated and their numbers small, they had not formed a clearly recognizable or separate element. The great wave of Eastern European Jews arrived on American shores during a period of growing elitism and intolerance. Impoverished, they huddled in the Eastern cities where they had disembarked. Other immigrants relied on the labor of children. But urban experience in Europe and the Jewish tradition of reverence for the book coupled with the aspirations of parents to see their children attain economic well-being in America led Jews to send their children to public school. Encouraged to learn and excel, some sons took the next step and entered college.[43]

These Jewish sons of immigrants chose institutions close at hand: City College of New York, Columbia, and New York University; Harvard; the University of Pennsylvania; the University of Chicago. By 1918 Jews composed 79 percent of the student body of City College of New York, 48 percent of New York University, 21 percent of Columbia, and 10 percent of Harvard.[44] With the partial exception of CCNY, these schools were emerging into universities. Not only had they changed their forms of organization, method of work, and curricula; they had greatly increased in size and had altered their entrance requirements to become more open to high school graduates. While fraternities and clubs distracted the traditional college men, through college gates came a new contingent of outsiders.

Although admitted as students, on many campuses Jews found no welcome among their classmates. While a country college such as Colgate could tolerate the Russian-born Jew Maurice Hindus because he was a clear exception, at the schools where Jews congregated, they faced sharp discrimination.[45] At universities such as Harvard and the University of Pennsylvania, anti-Semitism poisoned the atmosphere. In a world that valued style, the poverty, dress, and rough manners of the immigrants marked them as distinctive and inferior; but even the most urbane and polished suffered exclusion. Francis Biddle, reflecting on the harsh exclusions of Harvard's club world, recalled that in 1920 when he asked Felix Frankfurter, by then Harvard Law School's distinguished scholar, to speak at the Fly's banquet honoring Franklin Roosevelt, "several of the members of the club would not go to the dinner, and one refused to speak to me . . . I realized how strongly anti-Semitic feeling permeated Harvard clubs."[46] In 1922 following two meetings between prominent Jewish undergraduates and Gentile campus leaders at Harvard, one of the Jewish participants felt that "the most illuminating thing about these discussions" was that "while we had entered them believing that the existent feeling came from the dislike of certain Jews, we learned that it was *numbers* that mattered; bad or good, *too many*

Whatever their status in the larger university, the Jewish members of Menorah could enjoy each other's society: reception, University of Cincinnati Menorah Society, 1921. *American Jewish Archives, Cincinnati Campus, Hebrew Union College, Jewish Institute of Religion.*

Jews were not liked. Rich or poor, brilliant or dull, polished or crude—*too many Jews,* the fear of a new Jerusalem at Harvard, the 'City College' fear."[47]

Where they were barred from entrance, Jewish undergraduates could not travel along the collegiate way. Not only did fraternities and clubs exclude them; they could not join athletic teams in key sports. Even many of the literary magazines, debating societies, college newspapers, and musical clubs refused to allow Jews to work for them.[48]

Did these Jewish outsiders notice? Although overt anti–Semitism cut them deeply, exclusion did not necessarily shape their choices. Like the serious students that preceded them, most of them had, after all, not come to college to play the games of college men. They had imagined Harvard or Columbia as offering, not the competitive struggle of the gridiron or the pleasures of high status confirmed by fraternity or club, but the chance to become somebody in America. The doors that they sought to open were those to the larger society. The key was training, especially professional training. They wanted to succeed academically in college to get into law school or medical school. Others might waste their college years in the games of children, but they had no time for such foolishness. Like the farmers' sons of earlier decades, most immigrant sons did not fight college life; they simply ignored it.

Like others who remained aloof from collegiate canons, many Jews broke the codes that divided students from professors. Interested and eager for good grades, they took their classes seriously. By "hanging around the professor's desk after the lecture with all sorts of fool questions" they appeared to be what an earlier generation of college men called "blues" or "fishermen."[49] Moreover, training in family and yeshiva had fostered an aggressive approach to learning. Mortimer Adler, the future philosopher, did not receive his B.A. in 1923 from Columbia because he could not pass the swimming test required for graduation, but he gained an education. In the College Study in Hamilton Hall books were arranged alphabetically; in his freshman year Adler "decided to circumnavigate the room, making a list of exciting titles for future reference." "It took me months to get around from A to Z. I went to the College Study at every opportunity, after classes and between classes, especially in those hours I had free by cutting physical education." A tenacious student, he knocked on the door of his psychology professor one-half hour before each class. "If he responded to my knock, I would barge in with a list of questions for him to answer or a list of criticisms for him to comment on, based on my reading of the chapter assigned for that day, in which I thought I had found ungrounded inferences, verbal ambiguities, unexplained data, or untested hypotheses." Such intellectual battering persisted until the day Adler arrived with an agenda of thirty-eight items and the gentle professor suggested that the before-class meetings desist. Adler's combative intellectual style pushed a philosophy professor to discourage him from attending his lectures and ultimately caused John Dewey to seek release from Adler's written critiques that pointed out the "inconsistencies and ambiguities" in Dewey's lectures.[50]

Study, inquiry, and persistence worked. Jews won college honors in numbers far greater than their ratio in the student body. At Harvard between 1915 and 1921, "proportionately more than twice as many Jewish regular students" as Gentile received their degrees with distinction.[51]

In the early twentieth century, those partaking in college life linked their ongoing dislike of the poor, ambitious, serious student with mounting anti-Semitism. The growing number of Jews seemed to threaten their world. In 1922, when Richard C. Cabot questioned his Harvard class in social ethics on their feelings about Jews, a significant number of Gentiles perceived them as "governed by selfishness," pursuing "academic knowledge" rather than "social, intellectual, and athletic achievement." As one student put it, Jews "destroy the unity of the college."[52]

Undergraduate anti-Semitism grew to an intense pitch in part because in many institutions, especially in the East, the balance was shifting between college men and outsiders. Manly college life had assumed that courses and study served merely as the necessary entry fee for the real struggles of power among peers. The faculty had nothing to teach worth knowing. The recitations that they conducted merely checked to see if students had memorized the required lines. In the war between college men and professors, the rules allowed no communication with the enemy. These essential elements of the faith remained intact despite the internal revolution that had completely changed the nature of undergraduate education.

College men, encapsulated in the rituals of clubs and athletics, were too busy to notice, but outsiders were attuned to the new possibilities of the university and empirical approaches to learning. They were finding that in this context academic success opened paths to future professional opportunities. Unable to comprehend the changes in the university that made study increasingly pay off, college men found in Jewish students the scapegoat to explain the diminishing power of college life, and they called for quotas. As an editor of the *Yale Daily News* put it, Yale needed an "Ellis Island with immigration laws more prohibitive than those of the United States government" to prevent Yale from becoming a "brain plant."[53]

In 1900 collegiate culture drew careful battle lines between college men and "grinds," lines as sharp as in 1824 at Yale. On the one side ranged the students organized in clubs and fraternities who looked to college life for their essential education; on the other, the serious students who perceived the college as the route into the professions. Between the two, there was little communication and less sympathy.

Owen Wister gives us a view into how the college men perceived outsiders at the turn of the century. In 1901 he published *Philosophy 4*. This slight story is a simple study in contrasts. Bertie Rogers and Billy Schuyler, two sophomores with "colonial names," have hired a bookish undergraduate, Oscar Maironi, to tutor them for their philosophy exam.[54] Bertie and Billy have had an enjoyable spring that seldom included attending lectures. We first meet them in their tennis flannels, struggling to memorize the basic chronology of Western philosophy and to grasp the essential ideas. Prim, black-suited Oscar, with his "suave and slightly alien accent," and his "shiny little calculating eyes," answers their questions with maddening precision and confidence.[55] His careful notes allow him to speak with authority for five dollars an hour. No amount of book learning can hide, however, his steerage origins.

After an exhausting two-day bout, Bertie and Billy escape from their tutor to spend their last day before the exam in the country, searching for the Bird in Hand tavern, rumored to be in Quincy. While Oscar obsequiously knocks on their door each hour, the irreverent and carefree clubbies gambol and feast. When the fateful Thursday comes our heroes write fresh and original answers, but the calculating immigrant merely parrots back the lecture. Wister closes with the delicious irony of their futures: Oscar becomes a minor author and book reviewer; Bertie and Billy assume the careers for which their Harvard days prepared them, successful industrialists in two great companies.

What are we to make of such a parable? Wister, an aristocratic Philadelphian, remembered as Theodore Roosevelt's close friend and the creator of the early Western novel *The Virginian,* has caught in this collegiate tale the mind of the true believer in college life. The world's virtue becomes the college's vice. Attendance, diligence, and care, so valued by Protestant America, are the stuff of which petty pedagogues are made. But carefree abandon, irresponsibility, and good humor are the mark of true intelligence and the sign of future power.

The tale is also one of class and ethnic conflict. The villain is not only hardworking; he is poor and the child of immigrants. Despite his Italian-sounding name, Wister gives to his audience clues that Oscar is Jewish. ("Oscar could lay his hand upon his studious heart and await the Day of Judgment like—I had nearly said a Christian!"[56]) He studies not for its own sake, but only for the power of display that it gives him. He is calculating and manipulative. The heroes are not just playful; they are rich and of old colonial stock. Their sport is the frolic of children. After their night of carousing, they bathe and stride out to take their exam with the "radiant innocence of flowers."[57] For Wister, Bertie and Billy are the true and proper inheritors of the earth.

But they are embattled. With his notes carefully tucked under his arm,

Oscar is smugly superior to his charges. Never for an instant does he recognize their obvious claims to position. He works by different rules. It is Wister's task to demonstrate merely that they are inferior rules. Oscar is a grotesque prig in the present: the distribution of life's awards in the future demonstrates natural justice.

In the mid-1980s *Philosophy 4* seems a nasty little book, filled with venom and false values, but its readers in 1901 thought it delightful. The Oscars must not have read it. The Berties and Billys who did found in it reassurance that the future as well as the past was theirs for the taking.

But they were wrong, at least in part. In the mid-1870s everyone surrounding Theodore Roosevelt at Harvard had moved quickly to high positions: the first caller to his college rooms became president of the Eastern Railroad in 1888; his five freshman tablemates became the judge of the New York Court of Appeals, a Boston banker, a Boston lawyer, a partner in a Boston lumber company, and a vice-president of a New York bank.[58] But American society was changing. Undoubtedly college life in the early twentieth century still fostered business success through leadership, style, and contacts, but professions demanded competence proven through disciplined training. Some Oscars were becoming lawyers, doctors, engineers, and college professors, as well as minor book reviewers. The *Fiftieth Anniversary Report of the Harvard Class of 1907* profiles such *cum laudes* as Isaac Gerber, a physician who introduced radium treatment to Rhode Island; Gilbert Julius Hirsch, the chief of the Foreign Reference Service in the Library of Congress and the head of the Library of the United States Supreme Court; and Mark Linenthal, a partner in the engineering company Linenthal & Becker, who pioneered in the design and construction of reinforced-concrete ships.[59] College-educated Americans were finding two routes to prosperity, an old and a new. As the twentieth century progressed, the outsider's path turned out to lead to an inside track.

How did the undergraduate experience of the outsiders prepare them for the future? In college they lived in an oppositional culture, in the shadow of the dramatically visible fraternity and club structure. They learned a sharp lesson that served them well about the location of wealth and power. As they coped and struggled outside the prestigious world of the insiders, they found the kinds of rewards open to brains and to sustained effort. Good grades, which the college man scorned, emerged as a means to graduate fellowships and to professional training. It was not a glamorous life, but its hardness, cruelties, and achievements had a tangible quality that ultimately paid off.

# Rebels: The Idol Breakers

The divide that separated the college man and the grind was extraordinarily wide at the beginning of the twentieth century. Reports from colleges and universities all over the country testify to two kinds of students, one playful, the other serious. The strength of the two parties at different schools varied, as did the specific qualifications for entry into the ranks of collegiate life. Harvard clubs cast all public school graduates beyond the pale, unlike the University of California, to which few private school alumni even came. Yale assimilated some public school types, especially Westerners who played football. But, as at the time of the fraternities' founding, exclusion of outsiders, however defined, remained a guiding principle.

Vincent Sheean has provided a fascinating glimpse into this world at the University of Chicago around World War I. Despite Chicago's important place in the history of higher education, Sheean learned very little as a student. He preferred "snap" courses with little challenge. He had a few great teachers, but little penetrated: "the social system of the undergraduate world in which I lived was the villain of the piece. No teacher could have compelled full attention from a mind preoccupied with elaborate details of social relationship." He described his fellow students as "a couple of thousand young nincompoops whose ambition in life was to get into the right fraternity or club, go to the right parties, and get elected to something or other." There were two Universities of Chicago, but only one mattered, the minority that "thought itself a majority, thought itself, in fact, the whole of the University. And it was to the frivolous two thousand that I belonged."[1]

A budding journalist, he sought out the offices of the *Daily Maroon*. And he rushed for a fraternity. His singular innocence revealed to him an element of fraternity life generally shaded from view. He entered the university with no knowledge of the Greek system. One congenial group invited him to lunch. He admired some of the upperclassmen, especially A.B., the editor of the *Maroon,* who seemed to him a "supreme god" who dwelt above all the rest "in a kind of hazy splendour like that which crowns a high mountain in the sun." Sheean agreed to pledge. But on the day of his initiation, a young coed whom he admired gave him the bewildering news that her friends considered the fraternity he was joining to be Jewish. Sheean, who knew Jews only from Rebecca in *Ivanhoe,* was stunned by her revelation that he was about to doom himself. "It's that damned fraternity," she told him. "You can't possibly belong to it and make anything at all out of your college life. You'll be miserable in another year, when you know where you are. No girl will go out with you—no nice girl, that is. And you're barred from everything that makes college life what it is."[2] By joining the fraternity, he would be marking himself as a Jew and an outsider.

Sheean and his roommate had little time to think, for the initiation began that afternoon. The two of them let themselves be branded by the brothers, and then escaped through the window of their dormitory to avoid the final stage of the initiation that would make them Jews in the eyes of the campus.

When he returned to the university, Sheean entered the world of the outsiders, or "Barbs." These "included most of the Jewish students, who were a majority of the total enrolled; the 'grinds' and 'Christers' among the Christian students; and a few notably 'queer' ones who were too violently unlike the average to be desirable recruits to the campus life." Campus codes kept all fraternity members from so much as speaking to one who had de-pledged. Sheean joined the Poetry Club. There he met Glenway Wescott, right off a Wisconsin farm, who "frightened most of his classmates with his waving yellow hair and his floating black cape and his weirdly literary manner of speech." And Elizabeth Roberts, "serious with a terrifying concentration," who "never showed the slightest interest in the frivolities of the ordinary undergraduates." These and the other Barbs were actually learning something at the university. "Scornful of the 'campus life' that preoccupied the rest of us, they grew into intellectual maturity more rapidly than their fellows, and their interest in general ideas was aroused before most of us knew what an idea was."[3] But Sheean wanted the collegiate way, and when he had lived through the required term of ostracism, he pledged a good Gentile fraternity.

At graduation what had he learned? "Not much," he felt. He had not gotten to know Chicago, because despite its attractions, he stayed "walled up in a world self-contained, self-governing and self-sufficient, the world of college undergraduates." Of academic subjects, he came away with only modest acquaintance. "I had learned a good deal about snobbery, cruelty, prejudice, injustice and stupidity. I had acquired half a dozen friends—perhaps. I had learned how to dance the fox trot."[4]

It was Vincent Sheean's unique experience to have been both Jew and Gentile, Barb and Greek. He felt trapped between a vital life that he did not want and the useless one that he chose. In the same years, others were feeling equally trapped; but unlike Sheean their social position did not allow them to choose the college way. They did the next-best thing: they created a new world.

Walter Lippmann entered Harvard in 1906, eager for all that it offered. The son of New York German Jews, he had led a sheltered life in a prosperous, cultured home. He prepared for Harvard at the Sachs School and Collegiate Institute. He came to college with every expectation that he would move from success to success.[5]

He quickly learned that, as a Jew in the twentieth century, he could not win in college life. In contrast to Bernhard Berenson's experience at the more open Harvard of the 1880s, Lippmann was blocked from Harvard's final clubs and from major campus organizations. As Van Wyck Brooks' reminiscences of Harvard during this same period clarify, Harvard was a complex undergraduate society in which there were worlds within worlds. Perhaps Lippmann might have been welcome in Brooks' aesthetic circle with its adoration of Walter Pater and its fascination with the poetry of William Butler Yeats (although Brooks mentions no Jews among his Stylus Club friends), but despite his literary interests, Lippmann sought to lead.[6] Such a talented and ambitious young man could not be daunted for long. In 1908 Lippmann helped form Harvard's first Socialist Club. It broke the code that barred outside politics from college gates, and it committed students to social causes. It also fought inside to remove the "suffocating discretions, the reservations, and the bland silence" of college life. In 1910, through the Debating Club, Lippmann turned to disclosure, staging a debate on "The Yard and the Street," in which he openly attacked a key element of Harvard's club system, the Institute of 1770, for the divisions it created among undergraduates. He and his friends joined the successful campaign of the Yard against the right of clubmen to control class offices. As John Reed later recalled, "The result of this movement upon the undergraduate world was potent. All over the place radicals sprang up, in music, painting, poetry, the theatre." Although the clubmen and the athletes probably "never even heard of it. . . . it made me, and many others, realize that there was something going on in the dull outside world more thrilling than college activities."[7]

Lippmann made the connection between his battles on campus and the intellectual ferment of his day, giving him allies and a sense of mission. When he wrote for a student publication a criticism of the elitist *The Privileged Classes* by the conservative English professor Barrett Wendell, one of Harvard's upholders of gentility, the philosopher William James— ever open to new ideas in the young—knocked on his dormitory door to congratulate Lippmann on his good sense. The young student gained a

The *Harvard Monthly* staff, 1910 (Walter Lippmann, standing, third from left; John Reed, seated, second from left). *Harvard University Archives.*

weekly invitation to tea at the James house and a new conception of himself as an intellectual. James encouraged Lippmann's iconoclasm, hopes for reform, commitment to action, and belief in the power of science. Lippmann broadened his acquaintance among the faculty and, with his course work complete, remained at Harvard a fourth year to become George Santayana's graduate assistant.[8]

Lippmann at Harvard was among the first, but within a decade others like him across the country were breaking through college codes to shape a third kind of student life. Although it appeared to most that only two options were open—college life and the world of the outsider—the more daring were creating a third, rebellion. Unlike the clubmen, the rebels perceived that the campus was not all. Outside its gates stood a vital world of economics, politics, and the arts, more real than the fun and games of football. But unlike the outsiders, the rebels fought back. They challenged the college man on his own turf. The rewards were the college newspaper and campus government. But in fighting for power, they did not forget the purposes of the university. They tried to make real contact with the minds of the professors, in class and out. Although sometimes negligent about assignments and cavalier about exams, rebels took ideas and their consequences seriously.

At a certain level, rebellion had long been a possibility. At Williams College in the 1840s James Garfield and other Delta Upsilon men—uncomfortable with the existing fraternities and perhaps unwelcome in them—were not content to be quiet outsiders. They created their own organization and vied for power in campus elections. Once the non-secret fraternity lost its distinctive quality, however, men in the New England colleges were left with only two options.

As a result, when Max Eastman, the future socialist and writer, entered Williams in 1900, he had "one firm and clear ambition: not to lead my class." That he had done in preparatory school. In his college diary he recorded his freshman attempts to "live life," by which he meant become a college man. Sponsored by the wife of a powerful alumnus, he joined a fraternity known at Williams for its "wealth and sporty polish."[9] There he made good friends among the high-spirited, schemed up ingenious college pranks, and, under the influence of a generous lush, became lazy and somewhat dissolute. Fortunately he also discovered poetry and the company of college poets.

After three years of college life that produced a sizable debt, Eastman took a year off to save money and recuperate from back trouble. He returned for his senior year with "the odd notion of using Williams College as an institution of learning." In recalling this he noted that for the first time his college diary mentioned professors, classes, and ideas. He began not only to study hard but to seek out his professors as friends, to learn from them that ideas were not confined to the classroom. Caustic, witty Asa H. Morton brought him into the world of contemporary culture. In his studio, after dinner, he introduced Eastman to European painting and lent him a copy of the French newspaper *Le Temps* that contained a speech by the socialist Jean Jaurès.[10]

In his final incarnation at Williams, Eastman ultimately rejected the worlds of college man and dandy, but he lacked a language for what he was becoming. And he appeared alone in his quest. In another place or at another time, he might have found others like himself and taken on the role of college rebel.

State universities traditionally offered a more hospitable setting for dissent from college life than the small, homogeneous Eastern colleges. At least until the 1920s their more varied student body created a relatively tolerant atmosphere. At the University of North Carolina, for example, Thomas Wolfe's sheer energy and raw talent commanded respect during his student years (1916–20), and he edited the *Tar Heel*. In this all-male undergraduate world, accepting classmates excused his messy appearance and his unshaven face because they recognized a genius.[11]

Wolfe was a loyal son of the university. Throughout his four years he treasured the memory from his freshman year of the Thanksgiving Day football game in Richmond at which North Carolina defeated Virginia. Becoming a university student also meant his initiation into the secret world of the brothels of Durham and Raleigh. He confided to his diary that his first sexual encounter with a prostitute had "all the passion and the fire." On his first visit, two older freshmen accompanied him. With his regular returns, he went alone, if necessary borrowing the two dollars for the prostitute and the dollar for the round trip to Durham, his usual haunt. His journal entries of these experiences were sharp: he wrote of going to Raleigh, where he patronized "Lillian Price, the priceless and motherly whore—'Lillian, Let me in.' The grinning negress; the strong odor of antiseptic—The chained blinds and the lattice work." Turning to black prostitutes for sexual expression did not provoke feelings of guilt. In the world of double standards, Wolfe accepted it as normal. What would have been unthinkable in the 1910s in Chapel Hill would have been a sexual affair with a white young woman of marriageable age.[12]

As he wrote in his journal of the intense emotions and sensations of becoming a man, Wolfe created raw material that he later used in *Look Homeward, Angel*. His self-presentation in college, however, was shaped by the double standard. Although Chapel Hill allowed personal eccentricity and private dissipations, there were clear standards for public behavior that Wolfe learned not to breach. While he occasionally misjudged the occasion and embarrassed himself by saying the wrong thing, in his speeches and *Tar Heel* pronouncements he normally assumed the mantle of the college man. Untouched by modernism in this Southern collegiate setting, Wolfe never

Thomas Wolfe in expressive and conventional roles at the University of North Carolina, 1919: (LEFT) leading man in the *Return of Buck Gavin* and (BELOW) member of Pi Kappa Phi, front row, second from right. *North Carolina Collection, UNC Library at Chapel Hill.*

perceived that he might give his lusty and private writings public creative expression. During his university years, he maintained a public posture as a North Carolina booster and as the defender of conservative morality.

At certain state universities, such as the University of Michigan, where the Greek system commanded the loyalty of a minority of undergraduates, Barbs never completely retreated. They sustained an independent mentality quite close to that of collegiate rebellion. In 1905 Paul Scott Mowrer, who later distinguished himself as an international correspondent, entered the University of Michigan as a special student. He had already spent a year on the Chicago *Daily News* and knew from the beginning he wanted to avoid the juvenility and the conformist pressures of college life. "I liked to wear what I liked, when and as I liked. My theory was that if anyone really cared about me, he should be happy to accept me just as I was."[13]

Although a man who took his pleasures, he had come for courses and classes. In Professor Fred Scott's seminar on criticism, he encountered Plato. As Scott read to the class from the *Phaedrus,* Mowrer experienced a revelation. The words of a man "centuries out of date" were "as much alive as William James or the author of the last best-seller. . . . This Phaedrus—he was still a young man like me, enjoying a good talk with an older man, Socrates, a man maybe not unlike Scotty. And they were dealing between them with the same questions we had been working at. It was miraculous, as if the earth had taken on a new dimension."[14]

Unencumbered by fraternity rules that required tuxedos and drinking bouts and prohibited dating coeds, Mowrer conducted a free and easy social life and courted Winifred Adams, who became his first wife. He reported for several campus publications and even served as a music critic to get free tickets to concerts. When he became the editor of the *Michigan Daily,* he took the paper from "the football crowd," to report a wide range of college activities and to use the editorial page to challenge professors on social questions.[15]

Even at Yale this independent mentality was possible. When Robert Moses (class of 1909), the future planning czar, found himself barred from certain sports and the *Lit* because he was Jewish, he did not give in. Moses turned to the less prestigious swimming team and created the Minor Sports Association to raise funds for support. He joined the lively *Yale Courant.* Cut from senior society lists, he became president of the Kit Cat Club, whose very name, taken from the group surrounding the eighteenth-century English author Samuel Johnson, expressed its members' literary aspirations.[16]

Eastman, Wolfe, Mowrer, and Moses each developed an independent stance to the college world, but true collegiate rebellion involved more. It required both the creation of a social group, no matter how small, and an explicitness, a consciousness. Rebellious individuals, set against college life, had long existed on college campuses. But until there could be interaction and ferment, they remained lonely and isolated or campus phenomena, somehow tolerated but hardly understood.

Moreover, college rebellion remained only latent or partial until it could be linked with a coherent ethos. This awaited the early twentieth century. Critical to the emergence and sustenance of an aggressive alternative to college life was the rise of the university and of modernism. Rebels needed a way to link their opposition to collegiate culture to new currents of thought. In its questioning of authority and emphasis on creativity and individuality, modernism provided the perfect support to rebellious undergraduates as they fought against college life. Although they might see their particular institutions as hostile to real learning, they had to perceive the potentialities that the university offered. Finally, they needed to feel that they joined with others outside their individual college in a common cause.

In the high time before World War I, undergraduates first put all these elements together to create collegiate rebellion. One can see this in the texture of one of its earliest statements, with its mingling of the critique of college life with social radicalism and aesthetic modernism. Lee Simonson, Lippmann's close college friend and later a noted stage designer, lambasted his classmates in the *Harvard Advocate.* Despite his position in college as "an outsider"—belonging to no organization—Simonson chose to speak out in opposition. What galled him about Harvard students was their lack of engagement in the life of their time and their false sophistication. At Harvard, he found "no effective sign . . . of the boisterous virtues of youth, of those for whom life is tense with secret possibilities and surprises— revolutions, rejuvenations, and catastrophes." He accused his colleagues of mimicking middle age. He called on them to claim "reckless enthusiasm, the eagerness to find out new causes and fight under them, the conviction that life must be changed somewhat and strained into newer and finer shapes, the willingness to be used for a purpose and to be thrown upon the scrap heap in its service, in a word the radicalism and impatient idealism which should be the *panache,* the inherent and appropriate mark of youth." Harvard concerned itself more with manners than with issues: "We reserve our horror chiefly for the parvenu. The fellow who talks in a loud voice worries us vastly more than the notion of upwards a million or more children warped and blighted in sweatshop and factory." Most of all, he missed at Harvard any serious appreciation of contemporary social criticism or litera- ture. To counter this, Simonson proposed that students create a dramatic club, to produce the new works of Synge and Yeats and undergraduate dramatists, and a reform club, to bring socialists and single-taxers to campus.[17] His perception of the problem, his solutions, and his prose demonstrate the connections between modernism and the invitation of undergraduate rebellion. Identifying college men with conformity with the world as it was, he claimed for the opposition new movements in the arts and in politics. He identified youth with the *élan vital* that opposed given forms and promised a new and better world.

One of the first to articulate a general program for collegiate rebellion, separate from a specific college, was Randolph Bourne. His face misshapen and scarred by injuries at childbirth and his body hunched and stunted by spinal tuberculosis at age four, Bourne did not enter Princeton in 1903, as he had hoped. His alcoholic father had been banished from the family. His uncle, upon whom he depended for support, insisted that Bourne go to work instead.

Six years later, on full scholarship, Bourne entered Columbia College. Both the delay and the change in college were fortunate, for at Columbia he found intellectual companions among students and challenging mentors on the faculty. Bourne made friends among a wide range of students in the college, the law school, and the graduate school, friends who could ignore his physical deformities because of his broad-ranging and stimulating conversation. He did well in his courses, read widely, wrote for the *Columbia Monthly,* and found his voice. In his sophomore year, when his philosophy professor asked if he might send an essay by Bourne to the *Atlantic Monthly,* his literary career began. Encouraged at every turn by the editor Ellery Sedgwick, Bourne became, while an undergraduate, a regular contributor to the *Atlantic.* His Columbia years were remarkably happy, filled with success and good talk; but, as an incipient radical, Bourne cast himself in opposition. He turned against President Nicholas Murray Butler, whom he called "Dr. Butcher," defended university scrubwomen, and set himself against college life. As he wrote to a correspondent, he perceived that his "path in life will be on the outside of things, poking holes in the holy. . . . howling like a coyote that everything is being run wrong."[18]

In "The College: An Undergraduate View," initially published in the *Atlantic Monthly* in 1911 and reprinted in *Youth and Life* in 1913, Bourne outlined what he saw wrong. College was torn between the conflicting worlds of scholarship and the extracurriculum. Scholarship was "fundamentally democratic"—we would say meritocratic. "Before the bar of marks and grades, penniless adventurer and rich man's son stand equal." In contrast, the extracurriculum took account not only of ability but also of "the undefinable social prestige" that a student brought with him into the college world. The result is a "division of functions,—the socially fit take the fraternities, the managerships, the publications, the societies; the unpresentable take the honors and rewards of scholarship." Although "each class probably gets just what it needs for after life," the intellectual life of the college suffered because of the "invidious distinction" attached to extracurricular activities.[19]

Bourne did not criticize only the college man; he also took on the outsider. The student who was too eager to get on to professional school weakened the college as well. "In his headlong rush he is apt to slight his work, or take a badly synthesized course of studies, or, in an effort to get all he can while he is in the college, to gorge himself with a mass of material that cannot possibly be digested." Caught between the "listlessness" of the college man and "impetuosity of the prospective professional man who wants to get at his tools," the real scholar was left alone to work out his "own salvation."[20]

Without real hope, Bourne called on the colleges to cease their support of athletics and to reform and democratize the fraternities. More to the point, he challenged the undergraduate to take "the risk of being considered a traitor to his class . . . and ally himself with his radical teachers in spirit and activity." This new collegian could then partake of the "new spirit" of the colleges. Tradition, which had long dictated a narrow classical curriculum, had now been toppled. In its stead had come the social sciences that united "the humanistic spirit with the scientific point of view." Herein lay the real hope for the future.[21]

Margaret Mead was one of the first to live out Bourne's prescriptions to the full. Initially, however, she experienced the harsh loneliness of the outsider in a crowd. In 1919 she entered DePauw College. The daughter of academics, she had approached college with keen anticipation. She expected college to be "an intellectual feast. I looked forward to studying fascinating subjects taught by people who understood what they were talking about. I imagined meeting brilliant students, students who would challenge me to stretch my mind and work. . . . In college, in some way that I devoutly believed in but could not explain, I expected to become a person." Instead, DePauw in 1919 was "a college to which students had come for fraternity life, for football games."[22]

Eager to join the life around her, she rushed for a sorority. She arrived at the Kappa party in a dress designed to look like poppies blooming in wheat. The sorority sister who invited her "turned her back on me and never spoke to me again. I found the whole evening strangely confusing. I could not know, of course, that everyone had been given the signal that inviting me had been a mistake." She did not receive a bid. The rest of the year Mead spent as an outsider, holding herself aloof in the hope of being sought at a later time. She began to feel herself "an exile." Sitting in the library, reading the drama reviews from *The New York Times,* she longed for New York City. She persuaded her parents to let her transfer to Barnard.[23]

Margaret Mead as graduating senior: *Mortarboard,* 1923.
*Barnard College Archives.*

At Barnard she "found—and in some measure created—the kind of student life that matched my earlier dreams." She lived outside the dormitory with talented young women, half Jewish, half Gentile, from different classes. This lively group took as its name the epithets thrown at them or Barnard students at large: "a mental and moral muss," "Communist morons," and finally the one that stuck, the "Ash Can Cats." They thought of themselves as radicals and licked envelopes for the Amalgamated Clothing Workers. They supported Sacco and Vanzetti. They learned about sex and Freud and chose mottos from the heated poems of Edna St. Vincent Millay.

They went to the theater. That one of them—Léonie Adams—was a published poet added a certain piquancy to their life. Mead and her Barnard friends "felt extraordinarily free" as women, free to choose not to marry or to marry.[24]

At Barnard she connected to the faculty, especially William Fielding Ogburn, Franz Boas, and Ruth Benedict. Boas remained a distant, frightening figure who generated awe, but Benedict reached out to Mead. At a lunch in her senior year Mead discussed her future with Benedict: should she go into sociology or psychology? Benedict responded: "Professor Boas and I have nothing to offer but an opportunity to do work that matters." But in fact, she offered more, her friendship. When Mead could not save a friend from suicide, Benedict gave her honest counsel. As Mead herself admitted, "by electing anthropology as a career, I was also electing a closer relationship to Ruth." As the friendship between former student and teacher grew, the two "read and reread each other's work, wrote poems in answer to poems, shared our hopes and worries about Boas, about Sapir, about anthropology, and in later years about the world."[25]

As Margaret Mead's experience clarifies, the rebel is both he and she. Two of the codes that the rebels broke were the absolute distinction between men and women on campus and male presumptions about the place of women in college life. At many institutions college women had been relegated to the role of outsider. This fit the serious, strong-minded women of the late nineteenth and early twentieth centuries who used the college to attain a professional position. But it hardly fit the more conventional daughters who came to college in growing numbers in the early twentieth century. These women generally took a path complementary to that of the college man, becoming sorority sisters whose primary interest revolved around campus social life and dates. Margaret Mead originally thought she wanted this world at DePauw. As she became a rebel at Barnard, she found herself in the company of other women—and men—like herself.

In the early nineteenth century, collegiate styles were linked to temperamental differences among socioeconomic and religious groups. One hundred years later the creation of a third possibility for college students—rebellion —derived from the emergence of a new mentality. Adolescence may be a biological fact, but the forms that it takes spring from culture. The early-nineteenth-century college received adolescents largely shaped by two diverging temperaments, the hedonism and recklessness of the genteel and the anxious spirituality of the evangelical. In the early twentieth century, a new kind of adolescent entered college, one who rejected parental ways and questioned the broader society. College rebels claimed much that college life had guaranteed: its pleasures, commitment to the present moment, and intensity. To this rebels added repudiation of conformity and belief in youth's special ability to perceive social and aesthetic solutions to contemporary problems.

Although no clear class difference divides those students who turned to collegiate rebellion from their more conformist classmates who became college men and women, the rebels normally had two elements in common. They sprang from nurturant roots. Just as wealthy mercantile homes and plantations had been the ideal setting for producing the college men of the early nineteenth century, so did the most sensitive, child-conscious elements of the middle class become the breeding grounds of college rebels. Because, as the case of Max Eastman illustrates, the fraternity could absorb many spirited youths, collegiate rebellion normally required a necessary, as well as a sufficient, cause. Rebels generally came from nurturant families whose histories barred their young from the collegiate way. In certain cases, such as that of Randolph Bourne, the family confronted a sharp reversal of fortunes. In others, such as that of Margaret Mead, the family sustained a quiet nonconformity. In many, the trigger was the mere fact of being Jewish.

The majority of Jewish students, especially those whose families had immigrated recently, came to college as preparation for rising in the world and eschewed the organized worlds of clubs and sports; but some—especially those from German backgrounds—wanted what they could not have. Growing up with privilege rather than want and sheltered from discrimination in private schools, these assimilated Jews had assumed that all paths in America were open. They had a rude awakening in college. At Harvard and Yale, they learned that they were different. They aspired to the success of college men, but their Gentile classmates linked them to rough-mannered immigrant Jews and were indiscriminate in their discrimination. Exclusion cut deep. As they sought for alternative paths to success, some assimilated Jews became college rebels.

College rebellion allowed its adherents to reject at the same time their intolerant classmates and their homes. In their stance as radicals they could ignore social slights while projecting futures for themselves more imaginative than the bourgeois worlds of their parents. Rebels envisioned a society open to all talents, including their own, and one that accepted their libidinous energies. If it were a just world, then their achievements would not be at the expense of others' starvation. Elsewhere such a dream has fueled revolution. In America it has fostered collegiate rebellion.

Undergraduates, such as Walter Lippman and Margaret Mead, came to revel in, rather than suffer from, their differences from other undergraduates.

The written record of their lives contains their joyful discovery of the life of the mind and of the world of politics. These were exciting years in which rebellious students took all knowledge and all society as their province. Such students broke with the canons of college life to engage their teachers in lively debate. They refused to limit their friendships to their own social and ethnic groups. College became a time of coming alive, of breaking with the limitations of their origins to discover the world.

In some places the university was ready to greet them, at least intellectually. As they reached out to encompass the world, college rebels discovered, sometimes to their surprise, the profound changes that had attended the emergence of the university. Some of the great minds of the early twentieth century were available to them both in class and out, as hungry for good students as these students were for mentors.

In contrast to the conformity of the clubmen or the deference of the serious students, rebels such as Lippmann and Mead adopted an iconoclastic style. They took their cues less from faculty than from radicals and artists outside the academy, breaking with tradition in their lives and work. Although rebels felt a special kinship with the occasional professor open to modernist possibilities, they needed no on-campus presence, for they felt their ties with the creative currents sweeping America. It took only access to *Seven Arts* or to pirated copies of James Joyce's *Ulysses* or membership in the Intercollegiate Socialist Society to establish one's identity as a rebel. An argumentative style, a willed nonchalance about grades, artistic dress, and self-proclaimed identity gave the necessary clues to the outside and enabled the rebels to find each other. As champions of the new sensibility, they turned to the newspapers and literary magazines that became their first base of power.

Unlike the outsiders, college rebels did not withdraw, but entered the fray. They fought with the fraternity leaders for control of campus organizations, running slates of independents. Where existing organizations barred them, they created new ones. On many campuses they became reporters and editors of the college newspapers and literary magazines. The iconoclasts brought a new spirit onto campus, insisting that students confront the conflictual issues of the broader society. The college press ceased to be a sports page and became the sounding board for controversy. Editors took on college life, questioning the worth of fraternities and clubs and wondering in print if there were not virtues to academic achievement. Student rebels sought to overturn college life. In this they failed. But through the effort they created a vital alternative, appropriate to the new century.

What did the rebels learn from their countercultural life? Excited by ideas, they began to associate informally and formally with those who were making the same discoveries. Many of the twentieth century's most challenging theories and programs originated in college bull sessions. New journals appeared, old ones were infiltrated. Undergraduates learned the techniques of organizing and writing that they later employed as America's premier writers and intellectuals.

Like the initial emergence of college life in the early nineteenth century, this alternative threatened college authorities. However alien the fraternity and club world from academic purposes, by the early twentieth century college administrators understood it and believed that they could contain its potentially destructive elements. The shape of rebellion, however, had no familiar form. What is more, it trespassed the boundaries that separated town and gown and cordoned off student high jinks from the politics of alumni. As students began to engage in politics—of suffrage, the labor movement, and socialism—they moved off the campus or brought in the outside world. College men predictably staged a violent drunk after a football game. But what might those young whippersnappers at the *Daily* cook up next? As intriguing and appealing as were many of the rebels, they challenged their institutions with the unknown.

# 5

## The Sideshows and the Circus

In 1912 Owen Johnson published *Stover at Yale,* the best-known depiction of college life. In the years that followed, secondary school students supposedly read it in preparation for the manly trials to come. But despite its reputation for celebration, *Stover at Yale* is a deeply ambiguous, unresolved work. It can be seen as an early volley in an emerging debate about the relation of college life to education in the twentieth century.

Johnson's portrayal of Yale focused on the young hero Dink Stover, who arrives in New Haven ready for full immersion in college life: "Four glorious years, good times, good fellows, and a free and open fight to be among the leaders and leave a name on the roll of fame."[1] A Lawrenceville man, Stover lacks the political muscle of the Andover crowd, but he has grit and a friendly, open manner that take him far. At the opening freshman-sophomore rush, he rips off his shirt to stand as champion for his class. He tries out for football and scores well.

But midway to becoming the biggest man on campus and a member of Skull and Bones, the senior society of fifteen chosen at the end of junior year, he stops. Seemingly secure in his success on the gridiron and as a member of a sophomore society, Dink Stover begins to wonder why he is struggling so hard. He has locked himself into a tight discipline, but at the expense of his personal life. He asks himself, "In one whole year what have I done? I haven't made one single friend, known what one real man was doing or thinking, done anything I wanted to do. . . . I've been nothing but material—varsity material—society material."[2]

A classmate named Gimbel leads an anti-society movement to block club members in college elections. Stover does not join, but in his quest to find himself, he seeks out the "flotsam and jetsam" of the class, the outsiders whose serious talk about politics and life opens his eyes to a different Yale.[3] Johnson's fictional outsiders are country boys and scruffers, Protestants all. They come to college to get an education, to become someone in the world. Grotesque in body and lacking any pretensions to style, they take their studies and ideas with total seriousness.

Ultimately Stover cannot manage to live excluded from the society world that gives him his moorings. He becomes bored by the outsiders and longs for "the men of his own kind" who spoke "a language he understood."[4] Depressed and isolated, he turns to drink and games, only to bring himself up short when he realizes that he is confirming the judgment of his enemies that there is no manly alternative to the sophomore society system.

His solution is that of innovative students on actual campuses throughout the country. He seeks out the more independent society men and creates with them a political forum for serious discussion, similar to Walter Lippmann's Debating Club at Harvard. This attempt to transform college life is met in fiction with full acceptance, and Stover receives the all-important tap by Bones.

But Stover's is not the only possibility. Sidney Brockhurst, an independent classmate who from the beginning has challenged the collegiate way, offers the alternative of bohemian rebellion. He argues for a Yale open enough to allow the cultivation of the spirit. Speaking for the free play of the intellect, Brockhurst poses the elusive possibility that has tantalized generations of college rebels: "I dream of . . . something visionary, a great institution . . . of men of brains, of courage, of leadership, a great center of thought, to stir the country and bring it back to the understanding of what man creates with his imagination, and dares with his will."[5]

Johnson does manage to create a true hero who appropriately follows the Yale fictional tradition of the burly Westerner. Mature, physically powerful, Tom Regan moves through college letting his own judgment distinguish between the important and the trivial. He studies hard to ensure his grades, using no ponies—though no hint of intellectual excitement emerges. He plays football because it is the true challenge to a man. He joins the outsiders' bull sessions because, as a future politician, he needs to understand the people. He has nothing to do with hazing or societies, but, unlike Gimbel, chooses merely to leave his room rather than confront his opponents directly. He is decent and fair, and his offer of friendship gives Stover the solid base upon which he might build a self.

But despite Regan's almost magical presence, the book, like Stover himself, remains unresolved. Stover's final victory, when he receives the

Bones' tap, "Go to Your Room," only obscures the contradictions that Johnson has posed. Stover has confronted neither the deep divisions of the college community nor the pressure of "doing for the college." *Stover at Yale* merely poses the issues.

The reality behind the fiction: Frederick J. Daly, class of 1911, captain of the Yale football team, 1910; *Yale Banner and Pot Pourri,* 1910–11. *Manuscripts and Archives, Yale University Library.*

Others waged the debate about college experience in speeches, essays, and policy decisions, rather than in fiction. In the nineteenth century the revolution in knowledge and the way it was organized fundamentally reshaped higher education. The process of curricular change continued in the twentieth century. In addition, however, a new force entered. Educators concerned about the larger education of undergraduates attempted to reshape college life.

Once set in motion, curricular change has been ongoing.[6] It has been estimated that in the twentieth century the curriculum has quietly reworked itself every twenty-two years.[7] Reaction from the excesses of the elective system has sparked the most heated debate and some efforts at reconstitution. Under the elective system's purest forms, carefree students specialized in elementary courses promising no challenge, while the tunnel-visioned pursued their interests in a single direction. Educational reformers of the twentieth century restructured requirements to insist that students both undertake intensive work in a major and sample a variety of other fields. Profound critics, however, realized that to set limits on students' choices within the existing offerings did not really confront the fragmentation of knowledge created by the intellectual specialization of academic disciplines organized in departments. While most institutions remained passive in the face of powerful departments, some attempted to create courses in general education that either synthesized knowledge or introduced the methods and questions of the sciences, social sciences, and humanities. Led by Columbia after World War I, by 1926 there were over a hundred general education courses in American colleges. Although the movement gathered followers, the specialization and intellectual assumptions of academic scientists generally prevented them from participating and thus limited general education to non-scientific fields.

A few educational reformers challenged intellectual specialization in whole cloth, to produce at the University of Chicago, St. John's College in Annapolis and Santa Fe, New Mexico, and Scripps College in California required programs of study that attempted to offer to undergraduates all the necessary ingredients of what an educated person should know. As vital as these efforts were to students who chose to submit to them, because intellectual integration went against the grain of both the professoriat's academic training and its principal routes of professional advancement, these programs remained the individualized creations of mavericks, admired abstractly but seldom flattered by imitation. In other places, the word *curriculum,* which in the nineteenth century had meant a common course of study—both content and form—lost anything other than an institutional meaning. In the twentieth century it became simply the term for the sum of the course programs of individuals, who selected, under some restrictions to be sure, courses from among the vast array of offerings in the catalogue. It had the same relation to the curriculum of the past that a cafeteria tray at the checkout counter bore to the family meal.

Although they won some skirmishes, reformers of higher education in the twentieth century essentially lost the war with the curriculum. They con-

78148

fronted a well-organized army of professionalized academics organized in departments. When reformers challenged undergraduate life, however, they had a real chance, for the direction of change was on their side. Yet along the way, some reformers became so sidetracked by false issues that they devised limiting, destructive remedies.

Those who attempted to reshape undergraduate experience were less interested in the question of what an educated person ought to know than in the even more rudimentary one: How can we get the undergraduate to have any interest in knowing at all? The answer of the protagonists depended a good deal upon the kind of undergraduates they themselves had been and the type of contemporary students they hoped to reach. Abraham Flexner, who had known only undiluted intellectual effort at Johns Hopkins, saw students of the early twentieth century in a block: he judged them to be "flighty, superficial and immature, lacking, as a class, concentration, seriousness and thoroughness." In his influential *The American College,* published in 1908, he explored the causes of student failings and called for change. He did not perceive an undergraduate culture that lived by its own rules, for he had never encountered it. Rather he located the problem in college administration and faculty. He opposed the college's reliance on the lecture system with a separate grading staff. He criticized higher education's failure to build an undergraduate curriculum that encompassed basic subjects. Flexner assumed that colleges could make students serious and graduates wise by changing the content and improving the quality of instruction.[8]

Woodrow Wilson, from his president's desk at Princeton, saw the problem in different terms. He had his eye on the college men, whom he perceived as "the natural leaders and doers," "the finer, more spirited, more attractive, more original and more effective" students on campus. He knew the type well, for he had been a Princeton student leader in the 1870s. In the years that followed, as he moved from student to professor to college president, his view of the value of college life shifted. In their engagement in athletics and activities, men caught in the collegiate way were essentially lost to the fundamental purposes of the college, which was, in Wilson's mind, "the association of men, young and old, for serious mental endeavor and also, in the intervals of work, for every wholesome sport and diversion." College men could be made to study and perform on examinations, but their spirits were elsewhere: "The side shows are so numerous, so diverting,—so important, if you will—that they have swallowed up the circus, and those who perform in the main tent must often whistle for their audiences, discouraged and humiliated."[9] Yes, colleges had scholars. Wilson recognized the serious student who kept "modestly to his class-room and his study."

But these young men stayed outside the game and thus remained "withdrawn and ineffectual."[10]

One of Wilson's first acts as president was to establish a tutorial system, staffed by forty-five preceptors. More controversial was his plan to create residential quadrangles to supplant Princeton's exclusive eating clubs as the focus of undergraduate life.[11] Defeated by faculty, alumni, and trustees, in 1909 Wilson took to the stump with his critique and the dream of restoring the college to an intellectual community of students and teachers.

Woodrow Wilson continuing his life as a college man in law school: Jefferson Literary and Debating Society, 1879–80, University of Virginia; Wilson is at the left. *University of Virginia Library.*

Early in his presidency, when Wilson spoke to Harvard's Phi Beta Kappa on this theme, he was surprised at the enthusiasm of his audience. Former Harvard president Charles William Eliot, however, "showed very plainly that he was disturbed both by what I said and by the reception given it there where he had been king." Wilson recognized that his emerging scheme "would undo half the work Mr. Eliot has done."[12] The issues no longer lay outside Harvard. During Eliot's last decade A. Lawrence Lowell, a member of his faculty, challenged key changes during Eliot's presidency and in 1909 became his successor. It is normally said that Eliot did not interest himself in the lives of undergraduates. This has been wrongly put. Once quite elitist, Eliot came by the end of his tenure to accept the range of students his university drew, including the "other Harvard" of the Yard. By expanding the student body he opened up the university to great numbers of high school students, many of them the children of immigrants. Nothing he ever said suggests that Eliot regretted the infusion. In 1915, when he addressed Harvard's Menorah Society, he rejoiced in the liberty that Jews had found in America, and he exhorted his audience of Jewish college students to use that liberty well. The mission of American members of the faith, he felt, should be to abjure the temptations of materialism and luxury to "hold fast to its [Judaism's] social and artistic idealism, and press steadily towards its intellectual and religious ideals."[13] Eliot must have seen as one measure of the success of his reforms the growing number of outsiders using the university as he intended it to be used.

But Lowell saw something else. His eye, as that of Wilson, was trained on the clubmen. Like his cousin Charles William Eliot, Lowell sprang from Brahmin stock. As a Harvard undergraduate in the class of 1877, he had distinguished himself as a runner and scholar. Although he had enjoyed the friendship of the similarly wellborn, he did not make one of Harvard's socially prestigious final clubs, possibly because he was a serious student. Rather than Eliot's nineteenth-century Brahmin confidence, Lowell typified its twentieth-century embattled pessimism. He mourned the relative decline of Anglo-Saxons within the American melting pot and fought their failure of leadership. He believed Harvard had a mission to arrest the decline. The problem was not that there was an absence of scholars, but that the scholars were not the right men.

Lowell understood, as did few others, that academic achievement had a direct relationship to success both in professional school and in future careers. In 1903 he and his colleagues had studied the law school. They found that only in myth did the " 'sports' in College pass the 'grinds' " in law school. Rather, students in law school "who do distinguish themselves there are drawn mainly from the holders of degrees *cum laude,* and that the chance of distinction in the Law School increases in proportion to scholarship in College."[14] How could college men be convinced that, unlike Bertie and Billy, their future lay in imitating Oscar?

Moreover, the right kind of students did not go to graduate school. Instead, scholarship attracted men who were "good but docile . . . with little energy, independence, or imagination." This "industrious mediocrity" of those "not of first-rate quality" he called "soft metal."[15] How could Lowell change this, how could he interest the future leaders—the clubmen—in the curriculum?

Lowell spent his long career at Harvard devising solutions. Unlike Wilson, he did not put forward his plan in whole cloth for it to be knocked down by the opposition. Rather he implemented it gradually over several decades. He built freshmen dormitories, created the Harvard House system with its masters and resident tutors, set up the tutorial system, directed electives into concentrations, established a reading period, and set the general examination as a graduation requirement. By his retirement it was said that studying had become Harvard's indoor sport.

As Lowell began, one element seemed to stand in his way. College men at Harvard saw all scholars as "grinds" or outsiders, and in the early twentieth century they identified "grinds" as Jews. Rather than confronting college divisions as undemocratic or dealing with ethnic stereotypes, in 1922 Lowell proposed to imitate Columbia and reduce the number of Jews.[16]

Students do not have a monopoly on shortsightedness or bigotry. One of the curious elements of the university that make for myopia is that professors and college presidents were themselves once students. The universities of the future that they seek to construct often bear strong resemblances to the colleges of their past. Although it gratified many professors to have large numbers of outsiders and rebels who raised penetrating questions, it profoundly disturbed others that many of these did not come from white Anglo-Saxon Protestant stock. Conscious of the clubmen's growing anti-Semitism, some college presidents worried that the gap between Jew and Gentile was growing unbridgeable. What would happen, they wondered, if the outsiders continued to grow in numbers: would the insiders simply withdraw to find in Williamstown or Hanover an atmosphere more congenial to their tastes? City College with almost 80 percent of its student body Jewish and New York University with almost 50 percent suggested this scenario. What would then be the fate of Columbia or Harvard?

President Nicholas Murray Butler of Columbia had asked these questions in the 1910s. President A. Lawrence Lowell of Harvard confronted them in the 1920s. Both found the same answer: limit the number of Jews.

Ironically, neither Butler nor Lowell admired the mindless competition and status-seeking of the clubmen. At Columbia and Harvard, the two presidents were trying to create a more genuine scholarly environment. But like the clubmen, they could not accept academic success falling into the hands of outsiders, and they may have been threatened by the deepening iconoclasm of campus intellectuals. Both saw their mission as converting the insiders.

Butler turned to a new admissions policy, creating at Columbia many of the elements of current admissions practice. Lowell proposed a quota on Jewish students. Enough members of the Harvard faculty opposed open discrimination to force Lowell to shift his battle underground. He imitated Butler and imposed a limit on the growth of the undergraduate college, making admissions competitive. To the already existing academic standard, he introduced new criteria designed to limit the number of entering Jews: appearance, background, extracurricular achievements, and character, all judged by alumni and admissions personnel. As at Columbia, these measures worked as effectively as any numerical quota. In 1926 the chairman of Harvard's Committee on Admissions noted to Yale that the new system would bring the proportion of Jews in Harvard College down from 25 percent to roughly 15 percent.[17]

Not all faculty approved. Harry Wolfson, the brilliant immigrant who became the first Jew in modern times to join the Harvard faculty, retorted that although such matters as appearance might be appropriate qualifications for "book agents, bond salesmen, social secretaries and guests for a week-end party," they served as no basis for "the selection of future scholars, thinkers, scientists, and men of letters."[18]

Few universities had either the inclination or the resources to imitate Lowell's curricular and building reforms, but the quota on Jewish admissions proved both inexpensive and congruent with rising anti-Semitism. Quotas became widespread, especially in private institutions on the East Coast in the interwar years. Professional schools followed suit, drastically limiting the access of Jewish youth to law and medicine.

While Wilson, Lowell, and Butler sought to bend college men into serious students, a few reformers took an even harsher line and determined to wipe out college life entirely. William T. Foster, a former student of Charles William Eliot and a professor at Bowdoin College, was thoroughly disgusted with the undergraduate culture that he knew—the "laziness, superficiality, dissipation, excessive indulgence in what we are pleased to call college life." An established college was hampered by the collegiate traditions revered by alumni, but a new college in a distant region offered the chance to start afresh. Foster's declaration of war on college life warned the trustees of the Reed Institute in advance of the unconventional notions of the man they chose in 1910 as the first president of Reed College in Portland, Oregon.[19]

In office, Foster constructed his college carefully. He hired a young, energetic, well-trained faculty with high credentials and firm experience in prestigious Eastern institutions. In contrast to the lax requirements of even the most prestigious colleges, Foster insisted that all students be fully prepared for college work. He prevented the formation of college life by eliminating intercollegiate athletics and the Greek system. In recruiting students, he insisted that applicants be fully cognizant of the distinctive nature of Reed. As he wrote in the first catalogue—adopting the simplified spelling that he advocated—"Intercollegiate athletics, fraternities, sororities and most of the diversions that men are pleased to call 'college life,' as distinguisht from college work, have no place in Reed College. Those whose dominant interests lie outside the courses of study, should not apply for admission. Only those who want to work, and to work hard, and who are determined to gain the greatest possible benefits from their studies, are

Reed College students developed their own kind of pleasures: Biology Club, 1923. *Hauser Memorial Library, Reed College.*

welcomd. . . . Others will be disappointed."[20] Finally, he prevented the possibility of the "gentleman's C," the student working only to stay in, by imitating the graduate school and requiring both a comprehensive examination at the end of the junior year (to qualify for the senior year) and a thesis supported by an oral examination.

In 1919 Foster submitted his resignation. Reed College was besieged by financial difficulties and internal conflict that the president's unpopularity only exacerbated. However, Foster's experiment proved to have staying power. Under his successor, Richard F. Scholz, and new senior faculty appointments, the college moved even farther along the path of intensive intellectual immersion and adopted a required humanities program.

Reed College created and sustained a new kind of college. Though the college had severe financial problems and suffered community disapproval, its commitments remained unchanged. Its original purposes attracted students who worked far harder than those at other institutions and who disdained organized activity. By one measure, Foster's vision was a success: a high proportion of its graduates became Ph.D.s, among the highest of any college or university. By another standard, however, the enterprise was deeply flawed. Roughly two-thirds of those who entered as freshmen failed to finish, in contrast to the 25 percent attrition rate of Swarthmore or the 10 percent of Harvard.

Starting with a clean slate, other new twentieth-century colleges—such as Bennington and Sarah Lawrence—could imitate Reed in creating forms to eliminate or discourage college life. But what of existing colleges and universities, who inherited the panoply of customs and institutions that undergraduates had created over the preceding hundred years? By the 1920s the administrators of most colleges and universities had come to an accommodation with college life.[21] Not only was it assumed to be normal; its long-term benefits were now clear. Alumni with fond memories of college days emerged to endow alma mater. Football games cultivated undergraduate loyalty, especially when the school had winning teams. Moreover, the codes of college life—however hostile to the academic enterprise—served to govern student behavior. As colleges and universities grew to a larger size, their administrators perceived the value of communal order, even one patrolled by students. The trick was to harness college life, to limit its hedonism and more destructive elements, and to emphasize its relation to citizenship and service.

Colleges created student governments whose officers were elected by undergraduates. The official college thereby gave recognition to the students' own system of prestige. Its purpose, however, was not to empower college leaders, but to foster communication with them and to co-opt them. Self-government normally meant that while undergraduates might give opinions and advise, they could not make the rules, or at least not the important ones. In return for office, heads of college government were given the responsibility for influencing their following and, where there were student courts, for acting as judge and jury. Student government was part of the effort to harness college life to official ends.

Colleges created a new job. Quite early on a number of institutions enlisted specific members of the faculty to supervise students' manners and

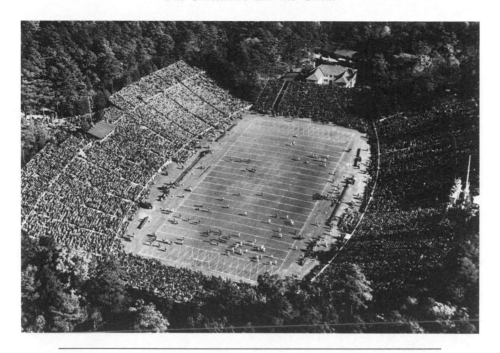

Football gathered the faithful on campus and off: Carolina–Duke game, 1946, Kenan Stadium. *North Carolina Collection, UNC Library at Chapel Hill.*

For many undergraduates, victories on the football field sealed their loyalty: Northwestern Rose Bowl rally, 1949. *Courtesy Northwestern University Archives.*

Institutions of higher education absorbed the activities and organizations of college men: Longhorn Band, University of Texas, undated. *Eugene C. Barker Texas History Center, The University of Texas at Austin.*

morals. New coeducational universities, such as the University of Chicago, felt a need for a prominent woman to oversee female students, founding the office of Dean of Women. When the University of Chicago opened, President William Rainey Harper appointed Alice Freeman Palmer, former president of Wellesley College, to the position. In 1901 the University of Illinois established the position of Dean of Men with the appointment of Thomas Arkle Clark, who became the legendary undergraduate dean.[22] By 1930 a textbook on college administration assumed that in a college of more than three hundred, a dean existed to supervise the non-academic life of students and to advise and inspire them. The dean "is assumed to be competent to give advice on almost any phase of a student's life from the choice of a vocation or life mate to the selection of the best shoe store or haberdashery in town." The deans' most important task was to make college life compatible with the administration's goals. Working with student leaders, they helped plan and coordinate student activities.[23]

As colleges and universities harnessed and co-opted college life, the particular institutions and traditions of a segment of the student body became established as the official institutions and traditions of the college. Just as athletic teams came inside under coaches who belonged to the faculty, so did other elements of the extracurriculum. Male singing groups that had hired local musicians to aid them became college choral societies led by members of the music faculty. Their songs became the college's songs. Yearbooks, once the preserve of particular clubs, evolved into official student yearbooks. Secret societies emerged as honor societies, their tap days campus-wide occasions.

The sharp distinctions that had once existed between the official college and college life disappeared. As students sat on disciplinary councils and deans crowned homecoming queens, the two seemed to be partners in promoting the good of the school and in developing school spirit. By the 1920s, college life—while still hedonistic and hostile to intellect—had lost much of its oppositional stance. To outsiders and rebels, its outlines could become blurred with those of the administration: in many cases, both seemed to represent establishment and conformity.

At all but a few places, the agreement to help shape college life rather than oppose it involved a full acceptance of the Greek system. At one level, the issue was a thoroughly practical one. Many universities needed fraternities to house and feed students. At the University of Illinois, where they had been banned until 1891, the administration did an about-face to encourage them. At the turn of the century the university listed eighteen approved fraternities and five sororities.[24] By 1915 eleven of the houses had built and owned their own property, and others leased houses from real estate dealers, providing, in all, housing for a thousand men. Dean Clark became one of their chief propagandists. He argued that fraternities provided the comforts of home, taught manners, helped form good habits of study. Most important, the fraternity bound the alumni in loyalty to the university: "The fraternity more than any other agency . . . helps to tie a man to his old associations and to anchor him to the college."[25]

But a few others had their doubts about the sideshows. Clarence Cook Little, president of the University of Michigan between 1925 and 1929, was unmitigating in his scorn. A research scientist trained at Harvard and the former president of the University of Maine, Little shared many of Lowell's approaches to higher education. He tried to create a University College to offer to freshmen and sophomores a common curriculum. He wanted to establish character as a criterion for admissions. And he tried to bring under university regulations the social life of students. Little saw the fraternity system as a bar to change. It worked for its own purposes in opposition to university ideals, "surrounded by a smooth, cyst-like wall of selfishness." It fostered the wrong ideals, sheltered the cheater, bred mediocrity in scholarship, encouraged drinking, created false class distinctions, and soured college politics. Although Little did not propose abolishing fraternities, he wanted them delayed until sophomore year and brought under strict regulation. And he campaigned for dormitories with faculty residents to serve as small residential colleges within the university.[26]

Little's temperament, rhetoric, and goals went against the grain of the diverse state university. After four years of conflict, he resumed his scientific career, with few concrete achievements. A more limited effort, but more successful, was that of Alexander Meiklejohn at the University of Wisconsin. Forced out of the presidency of Amherst College because of his innovative approaches to education, liberalism, and fiscal irregularities, in 1926 Meiklejohn came to Madison as chairman of the Experimental College. Within the large, heterogeneous university, the college created a new option for young men: a two-year program of informal, but intense, study combined with communal life. No syllabus or formal classrooms shaped the work. Individually and in groups, students and professors shaped a discourse on ancient Greece and contemporary America. To encourage informal faculty-student contact, the students lived apart from the university in a dormitory that also housed professors' offices. Although the college was killed after five years by an array of external political forces that included fraternities, anti-Semites, and conservatives, its short-lived, but real, success demonstrated that although it may have been impossible to transform a large state university in a few years, a daring educator could rather quickly create an enclave that changed the college experience for the small number of students willing to try something different.[27]

Perhaps the most effective effort to confront undergraduate life came not at a large institution that contained diverse student groups, but at a small, uniform college dominated in the early twentieth century by the ethos of college men—Swarthmore. In 1921, when Frank Aydelotte became presi-

Intellectuals on the way to becoming Swarthmore campus heroes: honors seminar in philosophy, taught by Prof. Roderick Firth, 1940s or 1950s, students unidentified. *Friends Historical Library of Swarthmore College.*

dent, the college had moved far from its early Quaker austerity to become a well-endowed coeducational liberal arts college that provided its students with one of the most enjoyable extracurricular lives available.[28] Its well-financed football team played against Ivy League contenders. Fraternities and sororities dominated campus social and political life. Relatively lax standards meant that the faculty did not interfere significantly in the pleasant round of college days.

For twenty years Aydelotte gradually worked to transform Swarthmore.

He began by introducing the Honors Program for upperclassmen, designed "to separate those students who are really interested in the intellectual life from those who are not" and to demand of the former higher standards.[29] To this he added Open Scholarships, modeled after the Rhodes Scholarships, awarded to five entering men through a national competition on the basis of intellectual ability, character, and leadership. The recipients set a high standard for the rest of their class. As national publicity enhanced Swarthmore's reputation, admissions became increasingly competitive, allowing the college to select intellectually promising students.

Aydelotte made changes at the other end as well. By measured steps he brought football under the college's control, first by ensuring that its coaches joined the regular staff and then by financing the athletic program through the college's regular budget rather than by gate receipts. Swarthmore stopped playing Ivy League teams and substituted the small-time. All the while Aydelotte sought to temper Greek life, then enjoyed by three-quarters of the student body, barring hazing and opening up college activities to independents. In 1925 Aydelotte initiated an explicit campaign. Swarthmore, he got his Board of Managers to agree, was "a college and not a social club." Following eighteen months of serious debate, a primary step in breaking up college life came in 1934: after the Women's Student Government voted two years in a row to abolish Swarthmore sororities, the college did so. Though fraternities remained for decades, the lack of a female counterpart put them on the defensive. The senior men's honorary society, Book and Key, modeled after Yale's Skull and Bones, found itself without student support, as juniors, "repelled by its exclusiveness and its secrecy," refused to be tapped.[30] By 1932 approximately 40 percent of the senior class opted for the Honors Program, and the intellectual began to emerge as the campus hero.

The words and deeds of some college presidents engaged in the debate over college life reshaped the attitudes of some undergraduates. Changes in the economy affected others. In 1922 a Yale man might have responded to the advice that the college man "need not worry about the future" because he faced "large opportunities and possibilities at the top" of all callings, opportunities "big enough to command the most ambitious efforts of any man."[31] But a decade later, he might not have been so sure. The Depression brought a marked change in college atmosphere. Not only were fewer students able to afford Greek life; many more worried about life after college. Observers noted a new seriousness of purpose and maturity among college students.[32]

A critical element affecting students' attitudes was a shift in their perception of what led to future economic success. Some undergraduates and college administrators had believed that the big man on campus was on a sure path to wealth and power. The "grind," through hard work, memorization, purchasing notes, and "jollying the professor," had overstretched his abilities. His grades gave no evidence of the quality of his mind and no prediction of his future prospects. But evidence coming in in the 1930s from a variety of quarters led to a questioning of that assumption.

Opening ceremonies on some campuses clarified academic purposes: placement exam, University of Chicago. *Special Collections, Regenstein Library, University of Chicago.*

One of the most intriguing is that by a Harvard alumnus, the sportswriter John R. Tunis. As a Harvard undergraduate, he had drifted, disappointing his mother by his failure to take advantage of his opportunities. He later recalled: "I stubbornly resisted all attempts at that period to educate me. . . . I possessed no intellectual disciplines, being ignorant, lazy and uninterested. . . . I was immature, shy, all too often . . . frightened of my professors, especially the great and learned pundit who gave the course on Francis

Bacon, a course I must have taken because it did not come at nine in the morning." His real education came from the Boston theaters that he attended with far greater diligence than classes that he often missed by oversleeping. Put on probation in the fall of his freshman and sophomore years, he worked hard in the spring only so that he might play on the tennis team.[33]

In 1936 Tunis published *Was College Worth While?,* a distillation of his Harvard twenty-fifth reunion book. It compared the worldly success and reputation of members of the Harvard Class of 1911 with their careers in college. Tunis found to his surprise that the athletes, who in his years had come from the wealthiest families, had failed to measure up to their early promise. With only one or two exceptions, the football team had not led to the job or the partnership in the firm; most college athletes had not become big money-makers or achieved eminence. In contrast, the Phi Beta Kappas had done very well: 30 percent of them had found their way into *Who's Who,* and they commanded incomes well above the class median. Although the clubmen had not failed, neither had they shown any marked success, as measured by income or prominence. Inexplicably, the "unknowns," those who had not been in any clubs or on any teams nor been active in any extracurricular activities, included the greatest number of distinguished alumni.[34]

Because the author questioned whether Harvard had actually educated not only John Tunis but the class of 1911, his book infuriated many in the Harvard community. "The Old Freddies at Cambridge furiously raged at this volume of mine. When I went to my reunion that June, my classmates looked the other way, as you'd expect." Yet the book "attracted attention, four pages in *Time* under Education . . . was well reviewed" and was condensed in *Reader's Digest.*[35] In addition, college students and their parents had other means of learning its message. As they read newspapers and alumni magazines, they must have been struck by the unexpected prominence or affluence of outsiders and rebels. No one who had gone to Harvard or Yale in the first decade of the century could have missed noting that Walter Lippmann had emerged as a major opinion-shaper and that Robert Moses wielded enormous power. Alumni magazines in their class notes recorded the lesser triumphs of unknowns who began to surface with news of distinguished careers.

One could hardly argue that in the America of the 1930s Oscar had overtaken Billy and Bertie; but at least he was no longer necessarily a minor book reviewer. The new broadened curriculum, the rise of the professions and specialized training, and the growth of empirical modes of thought altered both the education of college students and their future opportunities.

Those rejected by the insiders had been the first to perceive that they could rise in the world by academic distinction in college, but by the 1930s significant numbers of potential insiders began to take note.

As these undergraduates responded to clues from the broader society, they began to have questions about college life. College students may at times be bigoted and self-involved, but they are not stupid. They are attuned to their own self-interest. In the 1920s some of them remained under the delusion that only by becoming college men could they gain future wealth and power in business America. Changes in the twentieth century threatened them, and they turned the Jewish outsider into a scapegoat. But within a few years, as they learned that they had been at least partially mistaken, some of them began to question their own narrowness and their devaluation of serious study. This did not lead to any immediate abandonment of traditional college life, but it did lead to some erosion and some questioning of discrimination.

On some campuses, particularly at the larger universities, the balance between collegians and outsiders shifted in ways which threatened the hegemony of college men. Rebels found new recruits among disaffected clubmen and fraternity brothers. At smaller colleges, some of the divisions between students began to soften, and key undergraduates started questioning the racial and ethnic discriminations built into the fraternity structure. Although students remained separated into different worlds, the boundaries between them became less stable and certain. By 1960 the stage was set for the more extensive debate about college experience—this time waged among undergraduates—that helped fuel the conflicts of that turbulent decade.

# The Organized

The remarkable thing about college life from the 1920s through the 1950s was its persistence. It survived despite wars, depressions, student strikes, administrators' meddling, and the growing awareness that professional training requires hard study and high grades. Numbers and relative power on campus shifted in different places and periods, but the phenomenon itself remained. What explains this tenacity?

Undoubtedly college life felt right to some male adolescents leaving home to find themselves at the mercy of professors, deans, and college presidents. Administrative rhetoric about student participation in governance aside, students remained a subject people. They entered a society in which they did not make or enforce the rules—at least not the important ones. In this way they had much in common with workers, slaves, and prisoners. Some students submitted fully—or at least appeared to do so. Others rebelled openly. Still others sought a collective form of covert protest and escape. College life was the subculture that this third group of students created to protect themselves from the harsh and seemingly arbitrary power of their masters. It provided a channeled means of expressing hostility to college authority and became a partially accepted form of adolescent rebellion.

Part of college life's appeal was that it allowed male adolescents the full expression of their youthful high spirits and their hedonism. It opposed not only the faculty but also the ethos of serious students willing to defer gratification until graduation. It insisted on the primacy of the present, the right to enjoy the here and now. Unlike scholastic success, which seemed to benefit only the individual, college life appealed to the college man's sense of loyalty and collective responsibility to the group.[1]

College life also gave shape and meaning to certain students' sense that they were on the verge of an important future. As they looked toward the society they were about to enter and hoped to conquer, they saw the institutional side of college life as the appropriate staging ground for adulthood. The open competitions, the power struggles among fraternities, and the battles in which the strongest rose quickly to the top presented the right kind of challenge to some young men gearing up for the trials of American capitalism.

By the 1920s there were many more such men. American colleges and universities were attracting not only those heading for the professions but also middle-class youth hoping to enter business. Spokesmen for the business community, once hostile to college education, now insisted on its advantages. They stressed the benefits, not of disciplined training in a field, but of general culture and college life. The collegiate culture created by the wealthier students of an earlier era had great appeal to aspiring middle-class young men hoping for business success. In college they might make connections, learn how to lead, and assume the manners and appearance of the American elite. For them college was instrumental less for learning skills than for acquiring contacts and style.

Despite its oppositional stance to the purposes of the faculty, in the period between 1920 and 1960 college life assumed a new authority on campus. As administrators shifted from confrontation to accommodation, they officially recognized student organizations. Athletics became public relations events to bind to the school the larger community of students, alumni, friends, and politicians. Football and basketball emerged as communal rituals of struggle and conquest that renewed loyalty and confirmed prestige. Fraternities grew in numbers and wealth. It has been estimated that by 1929 slightly under 4,000 chapters owned total property worth $90 million. The customs of college men became the official campus customs, linked with the unique history of the institution. As deans of men and women cooperated with the leaders of student society in planning events and enforcing codes of conduct, the apparent distinctions between institutional goals and those of college life faded. Whatever the realities of real power, in students' eyes college life was in the saddle.[2]

For a certain kind of middle-class youth in the twentieth century, college life could completely fill his four years, with no room to spare. Such a collegian was future reporter Frank B. Gilbreth, Jr., the son of efficiency experts who later immortalized his family in *Cheaper by the Dozen.* In 1929 young Gilbreth left for the University of Michigan filled with the high expectations of his brothers and sisters. As they put him on the train, they glibly spoke of the best fraternity, football greatness, and Phi Beta Kappa; but Gilbreth worried whether he would be able to stay in school or make any friends.

Young men in line at the movie theater in Chapel Hill for the first afternoon show, "Smith's 2 o'clock class," 1930s. *North Carolina Collection, UNC Library at Chapel Hill.*

His older sister and her husband had actually eased his way, for both had been prominent at Michigan. Gilbreth made a snobbish fraternity. Then came his trials to become a college man. After a body-bruising workout convinced him that college football was beyond him, he followed the advice of the brassy upperclasswoman who had befriended him and headed for the *Daily.* He quickly learned the double-edged rule of success: stay in the good graces of the dean and at the same time manage to be a critic of the university. Gilbreth was lucky. Two events early in his freshman year established his reputation among undergraduates. A typo made him a student champion: when he reported how the dean had hurt his back in forcing a window in his office, the paper left out a critical *n*. As a result, Gilbreth accused the dean of moral improprieties against a widow. While he was recovering from the dean's wrath, a blind date landed him in the Detroit police station as a suspected bootlegger. The escapade established his reputation for derring-do among his peers, and the dean—tolerant of errant college men—neither expelled him nor removed him from the *Daily*. [3]

After a more sober three years, Gilbreth became managing editor of the paper and thereby a member of all the prestigious undergraduate societies. One final escapade almost cost him his degree, however. In his senior year, devoted to the *Daily* rather than to the few courses required for graduation, he and a good friend found themselves in the same arts class, known as "a comfortable and illustrated loaf." To relieve the tedium of the lectures, especially the professor's recurring request that the students learn to appreciate the aesthetic qualities of the nude, his friend arranged to switch slides. Instead of the Greek statue, introduced appropriately as a "magnificent specimen of technique," a full-color photograph of a seductive "buxom and uninhibited young lady . . . on a leopard skin" appeared on the screen. Gilbreth's snickers and his prominence as editor brought professorial wrath on his innocent head. Loyalty to his friend kept him from telling the truth. Barred from the class, Gilbreth appointed his friend as his mentor. Each afternoon after class they studied together and even did research on the works of art. Gilbreth landed a B plus in the course; his friend, who had failed to pass a good number of his courses, an A plus. Gilbreth graduated, and his friend unexpectedly saved his previously stunted college career. His high mark, of no importance itself, made him eligible for the track team. [4] Gilbreth's account of his experience with fine arts is his only mention that, along with the *Daily,* the fraternity, undergraduate organizations, and social life, the University of Michigan also offered courses.

How have successive generations of Gilbreths learned the collegiate way? It has been argued that many young men were primed when they entered —that they came to college with the knowledge already passed on by fathers, brothers, and a close reading of *Stover at Yale*—but actually their appetites were only whetted. To finish secondary school and get into college, a fair number of future collegians had to work very hard. The information from admissions offices which they studied emphasized the high academic quality of prospective colleges, course offerings, and formal requirements. A careful social scientist observed and tested an entering class of a small Midwestern college in the early (and pre-radical) 1960s. He examined how incoming students learned to become undergraduates. The college took pains to select bright, capable, and highly motivated students and tried to socialize

# FROSH DEATH NOTICE

## Twenty-Two Wants Blood!!

Class of Misery, Peruse and Obey These Fourteen Points of the MIGHTY SOPHOMORES Lest Thy Sins
Be Washed Away in Muddy Searsville (2.75% Sulphuric Acid)

**W**ASH THY SIN AWAY, you uncracked nuts of 1923, lest our unmitigated wrath descend in violent fury on your measly carcasses.

**A**LL Frosh inhale the filthy water, who queen on the quad or at large. This privilege is accorded only to us who have brains.

**S**MALL brains and ivory skulls are poor soil for the cultivation of intelligence. Therefore study constantly and avoid the axe.

**H**UMILITY greatly lessens punishment. Speak when spoken to, come when called. Implicit obedience alone averts the tortures of the drowned.

**T**UBBING is our specialty. Beware of smoking. Tobacco is made for man, not for unsophisticated weaklings. Pipes and pills are strictly prohibited.

**H**OLLOW-HEADED simps must show proper respect to the "POWERS THAT BE." Remove your dink when passing a superior.

**Y**OUR presence is never required at theaters on school nights. Saturday is children's day. You couldn't get the deep stuff anyway.

**S**LEEPY-HEADS, wake up! Stanford democracy demands continual acquiesence. Get the habit of "'Lo Gents" like a regular fellow.

**I**DIOTS! Cultivate no hair on your mouthpieces. Heed this warning, lest your masters, the Sophomores, wash it off with slimy Searsville.

**N**UMSKULLS! Seek education. You are required to attend all campus activities. You are tolerated there but not elsewhere.

**A**LWAYS wear your dink, to keep your backbone from unravelling. Later you may develop a head which will take its place.

**W**ATER washes clean. America has nothing else. The class of 1922 rule. "If some is good, more is better." Senseless imbeciles, use the berry.

**A**WAY with that Prep school stuff. We know you are nothing without being labeled like an arsenal. You may wear gas masks to Frosh class meetings.

**Y**OU yellow streaked lumps of putty, listen. WE ARE THE ITS, YOU ARE THE NITS. You are the buck privates in this man's army, permanently assigned to K. P.

—— THOSE OFF THE BOAT ARE IN THE WATER

Babes of the "Skidoo" class of 1923, fail not to appear on the football field at 4:30 this afternoon, and the Sophomores will tolerate your presence long enough to wallop you to a frazzle.

Stanford freshmen of the class of 1923 served notice by sophomores. *Stanford University Archives.*

Hazing served as an initiation ritual for some undergraduates: Berkeley, ca. 1920. *University Archives, The Bancroft Library.*

them into faculty standards, only to see them turn away from their studies to value well-roundedness in sports and extracurricular activities. It took only seven weeks in the fall for the bulk of entering freshmen to lose the "grades orientation" with which they entered.[5]

New students did not learn from each other. They directed their gaze upward to those older students willing and able to guide them. Thus peer pressure was oddly slight: the behavior and standards of other freshmen did not affect new students. They learned through a foreshortened generational process as older students offered direct counseling and opportunities for imitation. Fraternity rushing intensified the acculturation of freshmen as students looked closely at the members of desirable houses for cues. Pledging brought clear lessons in right thinking and acting.

Thus freshmen did not re-create college culture; they received it. The process of becoming a student involved the *"transmission* of culture from one generation to the next."[6] In this small college, only exceptions remained impervious to this process—the outsiders. The bulk of the students moderated their ambitions for high grades and threw themselves into the world of fraternities and extracurricular life.

As college life has persisted through successive transmissions, certain elements have remained remarkably stable. When social scientists began to study it in the 1920s, they delineated a world that in some respects could have existed in 1840, 1880, or 1910. Thus, while individual researchers have generally framed what they have to say by carefully pointing out the specifics of time and place, their research is applicable far beyond its particular context.

In the twentieth century several aspects of college life, however, altered significantly. The most dramatic transformation involved undergraduate sexuality. Changes in attitudes about sex and in sexual practices reshaped the form and content of college life for both men and women.

In the nineteenth century, those men who had gathered in undergraduate fraternities and clubs had believed that only men mattered—or, at least, that only men ought to matter. Success, rewarded to be sure with an admirable woman upon graduation, came to the individual who competed successfully in the manly worlds of the gridiron or the newspaper. While Yale stories might have some courting scenes in proper New Haven parlors and a prom in the junior and senior years, a hand or a cheek was all a fictional unbetrothed virgin might offer. In coeducational colleges and universities, codes governing the relations between the sexes differed depending upon the strength of the collegiate tradition and the on-campus ratio of college men to others. At Oberlin or Earlham, where religious commitment and an ethic of simplicity dominated, men and women students enjoyed an informal social life, unencumbered by the college way. At Cornell and the University of Michigan, coeducational sociability was partially supplanted by an overlay of male college life that until the 1910s insisted that the right kind of man lived and worked only among men. Such college men gained status if they imported women to campus for the important dances.

Given the traditional college man's commitment to the indulgence of his appetites for food, tobacco, and alcohol, it is unlikely—despite the absence

Freshmen in the 1950s at the University of Virginia directing their gaze upward during freshman orientation. *University of Virginia Library.*

of sex in reporting, memoirs, and fiction—that he remained sexually continent during his undergraduate years. Thomas Wolfe's private journals written when he was a student at the University of North Carolina in the late 1910s offer a glimpse into what must have been the typical recourses of college men—frequenting prostitutes and masturbation. Although Dink Stover played around innocently with town girls from New Haven, his real counterparts probably took more liberties. The relative absence of sex in the public record of nineteenth- and early-twentieth-century male college life is significant. The code of the college man of that era insisted that sexual drives, however urgent, were to be satisfied on the sly. Romance might enter for a moment at the prom, but sex was to remain outside the fields of public undergraduate conquest.

Beginning in the 1910s in some places, the 1920s elsewhere, sex entered openly into the realms of the college man. In 1920 F. Scott Fitzgerald's *This Side of Paradise* informed a postwar generation of the new possibilities. The novel itself is a complex work that takes Amory Blaine from childhood to adult crisis, but undergraduates read it for what it told them about college life. Set in prewar Princeton, it is in some ways a reworking of *Stover at Yale* through a new sensibility. Blaine is no Dink Stover, for he verges at times on being an anti-hero, but he comes to Princeton determined to be a "Big Man," succeeds, then falters, and ultimately finds his way again in a more questioning, open Princeton that allows dissent.

What appealed to—and shocked—a new generation of readers was not the novel's references to the past, but its new elements. Blaine and his contemporaries not only flunk courses, spend a lot of money, divide into snobbish cliques sanctioned by clubs, judge each other on appearances, and drink—part of the standard repertoire of college fiction; they drive fast cars and they pet. As Amory takes to the rails with the Triangle Club presenting its musical on an annual Christmas tour, he comes "into constant contact with that great current American phenomenon, the 'petting party.'" Through Blaine's consciousness, Fitzgerald announced that American mothers, who associate sexual freedom with servant girls, have no "idea how casually their daughters were accustomed to be kissed." In what became one of the most-quoted passages in modern fiction, Fitzgerald elaborated: "Amory saw girls doing things that even in his memory would have been impossible: eating three-o'clock, after-dance suppers in impossible cafés, talking of every side of life with an air half of earnestness, half of mockery, yet with a furtive excitement that Amory considered stood for a real moral letdown. But he never realized how widespread it was until he saw the cities between New York and Chicago as one vast juvenile intrigue."[7] Although Blaine witnesses a friend dead after an automobile crash and, in the company of a loose woman, runs from his ghost, the somber tones of the book did not capture the undergraduate imagination as much as did its erotic promises. *This Side of Paradise* set some American youth to dreaming about becoming college men.

Sex came onto campus both in fact and in consciousness. The changes were sharp. In 1922 an Illinois alumnus reacted in horror to the new situation: "Men of Illinois have ceased to strengthen themselves through association with their fellow men; they must have the company of women, and through over-indulgence in their society, they are losing their energy

College cartoonists helped create an image of the worldly college man of the 1920s: *Corks and Curls,* 1924, University of Virginia. *University of Virginia Library.*

"Spring Neckwear": Northwestern University, *Purple Parrot,* April 1927. *Courtesy Northwestern University Archives.*

and their spirit." Gone were the days that he remembered, when one could see "men, MEN, walking together. . . . when men went together to concerts, celebrations, athletic games and theaters. . . . when men engaged in spirited conversation among themselves as they walked to and from classes." He judged that "the Illini race is becoming soft. Our men are losing their vitality and their virility: they are becoming nothing but pampered daters."[8]

What changed was both actual behavior as perceived from the outside and inner meaning. College men reworked their code to incorporate into it sexual play and conquest. In part, they were responding to new signals from college women who no longer had to pretend that females were non-sexual beings. As they cut their hair, shortened their skirts, and lit cigarettes, coeds and their sisters in the women's colleges announced that they were ready for fun. The coeducational campus became the scene of heterosexual play—at the soda fountain, the movies, and college dances. Those confined to single-sex institutions began to focus on the weekend, to which the automobile now brought access and privacy. While dating had its own rules that kept most college women technically virgins until engagement, it allowed large doses of foreplay and enough ambiguity to keep college men trying.[9]

A world that had once balanced manly striving with pleasure-seeking shifted its center to make more room for fun, including sexy fun. The University of Indiana in the 1920s that Hoagy Carmichael, the jazz musician and songwriter, remembered would have been inconceivable even a decade earlier. A Bloomington youth, he knew the university well, for he had spent his high school years playing for fraternity dances. He immediately moved into the Kappa Sigma house, one of the centers of his college universe. A good college man, he remembered his crowd as "smart aleck and eager, popular with the upperclassmen, happy except when the grades came through . . . we tried to uphold the daffy social prestige of our house on the campus. Music was not the dominating factor among our crowd. Fun was." In his evocative memoir, he recalled the smells of the fraternity house: "flat beer and acrid ashy air drifting toward you as you cling to a last few moments' sleep after a bull session that kept you all awake the night before. The odor of wet basketball shoes and old catchers' mitts. The smell of that particular hair lotion Louie doused on his head and which came from the steaming bathroom."[10]

The Kappa Sigma house might have existed in 1905, but not the other center of his world, the Book Nook, a restaurant and college hangout. Carmichael invited his readers back to that scene: "that little gink over there flogging the piano—that's me. The one with the long nose and exerted red face. . . . Observe the natives in poses of bored indifference—a fashionable state of mind: the males in greased hair, long sideburns, tight jackets, bell-bottomed pants. The flappers in knee skirts above large open overshoes, no girdles, often no underwear." At the Book Nook college life merged indiscriminately with the modern worlds of jazz and the new poetry. William E. "Monk" Moenkhaus, a professor's son, poet, and jazz aficionado, formed the Bent Eagles, a parody of a college extracurricular organization, which took the Book Nook as its headquarters. When the music and the poetry died down, Carmichael and his crowd would gather to talk "of things we were puzzled about. We confessed bewilderment and doubts and should a girl neck first date out? Are raccoon coats permitted on non-college males? Does gin taste better when doctored with home-brewed beer? . . . We also wondered where we were going."[11]

Carmichael led a double life. His commitment to the new music took him into black neighborhoods, into churches and bars. He traveled with his band, especially in the summers, met jazz greats, began to compose, and even left college for a musical stint in Florida. While his passion was jazz, in college he could never see it as his future and he kept planning to be a lawyer so that, unlike his peripatetic father, he might settle down and support a family. Thus, except for one crazed moment after an early recording session when he threatened the crowd at the Book Nook with an imaginary gun, he stayed a college man. All this was possible in the 1920s.

As the world of college men reached out to incorporate jazz and sex, the fraternity and club house took on a new meaning. College dating created and confirmed the system of prestige on the campus. Students did not simply choose the most physically desirable members of the opposite sex for parties and fun; they chose in ways that established and strengthened their social position. Where students were organized, the Greek system established the ranking order. Fraternities and sororities gave students access to members of the opposite sex. Not only did they provide the settings and the occasions for socializing; the group prestige they lent made the individual a worthy candidate for a potential date. Men from top-ranked fraternities therefore could pick from among the coeds.[12] Lynn and Lois Seyster Montross captured the crosscurrents of the campus in *Town and Gown,* a set of interconnected short stories. One of their characters, the fictional freshman Andrews, walked past fraternity row "taut with hope. Far back in his high school days of the year before, he had seen fraternity life in the picture offered by a score of university catalogues and descriptive booklets; the comradeship, the dancing and dates, the prestige."[13] In the 1920s the ability to date—and date

Jazz came to college in high style: Glee Club Jazz Orchestra, Berkeley. *University Archives, The Bancroft Library.*

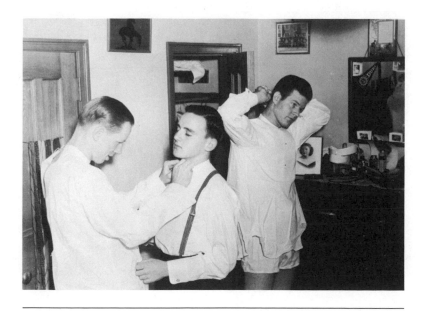

Dressing up, 1938–39. *Duke University Archives.*

The Four Horsemen of Notre Dame, 1924. *Courtesy of the Library of Congress.*

"The Kappa Sigs are voting the straight Blue Devil ticket" (second sign from the right): election rally, Duke, 1936. *Duke University Archives.*

well—had now joined male friendship and status as the critical attractions of the collegiate way.

Another important change in college life in the twentieth century involved the relative position of athletics and athletes. In the nineteenth century college men had organized teams and leagues and fought to have them recognized. At the turn of the century, as colleges and universities hired coaches and brought athletics into the curriculum, sports continued to attract collegians. This remained true after 1920 at the smaller private colleges. But at larger universities, public and private, undergraduate teams, especially in football and basketball, became the training ground for professional sports. Coaches recruited high school students who had made outstanding records and paid their way.

Some of the university athletes used their scholarships to get a higher education. Others came to make it into the pros. Joe Kapp, for example, came to the University of California at Berkeley in the 1950s because his athletic promise got him a scholarship and access to "a school with a great academic tradition." But, as he admitted, "this tradition, although important to me, was not as vital as the fact that its football team played in a major college league and that I might have a chance to play in the Rose Bowl. . . . I enrolled at Cal to play football and basketball and to get a degree. I was going to college specifically to prepare myself vocationally" for a career in sports. At Berkeley, Kapp received "training, by competent instructors, in the fundamentals and skills of a precise profession."[14]

The presence of athletes in a fraternity lent prestige to the house, and athletes remained welcome. But a special consciousness began to develop among university athletes. Long hours of practice, the pressures of the game, the limited purposes for which they had come to college, and their obligations as scholarship recipients gave them the sense that they were the guardians of college life. When conflicts among students erupted, athletes could be counted on to support college life and the administration.

One element remained constant: from the 1920s through the 1950s the fraternity dominated American colleges. With their prestige confirmed by official undergraduate organizations, recognized by the administration, and broadcast in the student newspaper, fraternity men had powerful instruments for ruling the campus. It was they who had defined and continued to control the major social events of the college year: the proms, student plays and musicals, elections, freshman hazing. Their activities had strong appeal, especially the football games. As the expanding universities built larger stadiums, the Saturday-afternoon game became the symbolic event that bound together all students, past and present.

Yet the power of the organized did not go unquestioned. Especially in the large public universities where the majority of students were outside the system, widespread disinterest and some clear opposition threatened the hold of college life. In such places, the prevailing clique went beyond existing institutions to enforce conformity to its vision of the college. At the Universities of Oregon and Kansas and at Oklahoma A&M, for example, vigilante committees—much of whose strength came from the muscles of athletes—policed student loyalty. They dragged into a student "court," paddled, beat up, or threw into a pond students who failed to attend rallies and sports events or sing college songs.[15]

Nationwide, roughly one-quarter to one-third of all college students in the United States belonged to a Greek-letter society. The proportion of organized students varied from campus to campus. Numerically the system was strongest at the smaller Eastern men's colleges, such as Williams or Amherst. A few schools effectively barred secret societies. Where fraternities existed, the power of the system exceeded any numbers. In 1926 at Syracuse, 57 percent of the student body belonged to Greek-letter societies, but many more students believed in the rightness of the fraternity system. Few independents wanted to abolish fraternities: all but 7 percent of the outsiders accepted their existence. Twelve percent of the Barbs wanted to limit Greek power, but 10 percent of them took the opposite position—that fraternities should be "encouraged and given some precedence in campus activities." These independents clearly identified with the organized and wished that they could be among the elect.[16]

In this period independents (on some campuses called neutrals) came from two different groups: those who refused and those who were never asked. At the University of Michigan those who remained outside by choice criticized the system. The sociologist Robert C. Angell, a close observer of students in the 1920s, found that they either looked down upon or pitied fraternity men and sorority women "as people who are leading a narrow, conventional, and rather undemocratic existence." By contrast, those independents who had not been chosen expressed a range of feelings: "some admire fraternity men and sorority women; others resent the advantages house groups give and the power their members enjoy; still others feel themselves simply of a different sort and keep aloof."[17]

Part of the strength of the Greek system was that it drew the richest and most worldly collegians. In the 1920s students in general at the University of Michigan came from the urban, relatively affluent sector of society. Their fathers were employers, not employees, and the family in 1926 normally owned both their house and a car. (Michigan students did not, however,

Stanford men between the wars living it up. *Stanford University Archives.*

come from the topmost stratum, for few had servants and five out of every six male students worked during the summer.) Fraternity members composed the elite of this elite, for they had more money and came from the larger cities. Members of their families had more often attended college before them, in part because selection favored the relatives of members.[18]

Advertising in college publications helped fix the image of the college man: Northwestern University, *Purple Parrot,* Feb. 1927. *Courtesy Northwestern University Archives.*

Enlivened by student parties, bonfires, proms, and football, their life in college was undeniably fun. It was pervaded by "a joyous . . . holiday spirit." In the 1920s the pursuit of pleasure characterized the four years of the college man.[19]

The undergraduate type we remember as Joe College took distinct form after World War I. He escaped from Main Street to come onto campus. In the community of the young, he could broaden his horizons, indulge his taste for pleasure, and win the acclaim of peers; or so he wanted the world and himself to believe. But as Henry Seidel Canby had realized about his college life at Yale three decades earlier, with emancipation came intense conformity. The college man did not merely step outside the rules of home, he stepped inside the rules of campus.

The new rules were as strict as any that he had known. College men did not spontaneously decide that one year pants had bell bottoms, the next year pants were straight. They did not simply take up alcohol because it was both there and illegal. They came into a community in which, if they were to succeed, they had to pay attention to style and join in the common pastimes.

Lois and Lynn Montross captured the process of becoming a twentieth-century college man in recounting the career of Peter Warshaw. The son of the pillars of Marbury, somewhere in the Midwest, Peter was the first in his community to venture to the State University. He tried to quell his panic that he could never learn the new system of talk and style and "be properly flippant and have that indefinable something in his grooming." He feared "he would be the only unknown—the only person looking through the fence at the breath-taking game inside." He had the break of rooming with Jimmy Tradinick, an upperclassman who had quarreled with his fraternity and moved outside the house. Peter learned fast. When he returned home for the summer he "was a Peter of well-pressed clothes, unfamiliar cosmetics and a strange, new, lounging gait. Under Jimmy Tradinick's tutelage he had acquired no small nonchalance and a modicum of social presence." His father could not understand his son's transformation, and they quarreled. When Peter returned to State, he immediately confided to Jimmy, "They don't want you to act like you really are down in a hick town like that, Tradinick. Ever notice? If you mention Khayyam or Kipling to'm they think you're throwing on the dog. By gosh, they think old Omar was some kind of a stew hound. They think the Wine in his verse is—" Wine was the signal for Jimmy to take out his "bottles of port and sherry and a flask of whisky from his suitcase" and to ply Peter with them. "Peter felt his stomach burning gorgeously and the room was a haze. . . . He beat a clashing tom-tom with two tin tobacco cans while Jimmy did an Egyptian dance clad in a sheet. It was delicious to be back."[20]

That fall Jimmy returned to the fraternity house and brought Peter with him. On his first visit to AOG house, Peter felt insecure: "The picture of himself at home, eating pancakes, recurred to him. . . . His grapefruit was spiked. . . . He used his silver carefully, correctly, but noted with alarm that the others kept their napkins folded in half." But the rewards loomed: "when the men sang between courses he leaned back and gazed into the fire, feeling warm, well-fed, luxurious. He realized how starved he'd been for it all. This was real—the real thing at last!"[21]

Once he was inside the house, new lessons came. "Peter was initiated into the society of women, the slipperiness of dance floors. He learned to speak with a sly innuendo of a 'mean woman' and a 'wicked party.' "[22] Such was the education of a college man in the 1920s, as imagined by two satirical observers. College humor written by undergraduates of the period confirms this fictional portrayal, focusing as it does on the fascination with style and sexual play of college men and women.

Reminiscences of such well-publicized college men as the flamboyant lawyer Melvin Belli concur. Belli's Berkeley years in the late 1920s began with a free-for-all fight, continued with fraternity house antics (eating moths and running naked around the block) and a good deal of alcohol, and ended with his greatest scrape—sending for truckloads of free samples in the name of a fraternity brother. Belli summarized, "I didn't take my undergraduate days too seriously. I led a carefree, floating-in-the-stream existence. I got B's and C's, cut a lot of classes, read a lot of astronomy, helped the local girls, mostly nurses and waitresses, in the exercise of their new womanly freedoms. . . . I became a manager on the track team and a sometime rooter for the Golden Bears' glory on the gridion."[23]

The attention to dress and pleasure-seeking of college men was measured by a researcher at the University of Indiana who studied student budgets in 1940–41. From this we know what students spent in the course of a year in college. Unquestionably the fraternity brother had more money than the independent. With the exception of rent, textbooks, university fees, and general reading, the unorganized student spent far less on every item than the organized. The greatest difference was inherent: the Greek men paid a considerable fee for fraternity membership. But the two budgets also showed striking disparities in clothing, refreshments, and recreation. The fraternity man spent almost two times more than the independent for his clothes and a quarter more for refreshments. Most significantly, the organized student spent more than twice as much as the unorganized for entertainment.[24]

Although this distinction between the entertainment patterns of Greek and Barb clearly could be traced back into the nineteenth century, an important change had taken place. College men had always had their fun, but now they took it with college women. They made "dates" both for the organized dances on the weekend and for informal gatherings during the week. By 1940, at Indiana University, students enjoyed as their primary form of entertainment the casual date during normal study hours: "a joeing date" in the local lingo, going for a Coke or a hot chocolate. Each date cost

Sigma Alpha Epsilon party, ca. 1939–40, Northwestern University. *Courtesy Northwestern University Archives and James L. Bixby, photographer.*

relatively little, but their frequency added up to a hefty bill for the college man at the end of the quarter, one that neither the coed nor the unorganized student, who had fewer such dates, had to foot.[25]

When researchers studied Cornell in 1950 they again found that fraternity members were richer. Not only did it take a certain minimum to pay dues; it cost money to keep up with the expected style of life. As one respondent put it, "It's not only the initial cost, it's the upkeep."[26] That upkeep meant money for clothes, dates, and alcohol.

One might argue that money made for the difference between college men and independents, that because the fraternity man had more to spend he could turn his college days into pleasure. However, money alone does not explain the difference in the way organized students lived. When researchers compared fraternity members with independents whose fathers made the same income, they found critical differences between their ways of life. Even holding wealth constant, the Greeks dated more and drank more, and they stated more frequently that in college they were having a "very good" time.[27]

Relative wealth did affect undergraduate attitudes toward careers. Students polled between 1950 and 1952 hoped for a creative job, but one that offered high economic rewards—far higher in fact than the actual national median income for college graduates. Freshmen entered with strong vocational concerns, but these weakened during college, to be replaced by an emphasis on general education, if the undergraduates came from the higher socioeconomic strata. Working- and lower-class students and those in state universities and at Fisk, a Negro college, retained their strong commitment to vocational training throughout their four years.[28]

Those wealthier students who joined a fraternity found themselves pressured into a certain college style. At the University of Michigan in the 1920s, only 34 percent of the student body belonged to Greek-letter societies, but they ran the key organizations on campus. Between 42 and 43 percent of fraternity members participated in extracurricular activities, in contrast to 12 to 13 percent of the independents.[29] The organized student had both the pressure of the fraternity on him and the pressure of the fraternity behind him, giving him an unfair advantage in campus politics. Because the independents lacked an organized base, they had no voice on campus. College organizations as a result reflected the opinions of only a small minority, the male fraternity members.

The fraternity pushed its pledges and members into extracurricular activities. At Michigan in the 1920s Angell observed that "a man is looked upon as a slacker in many quarters if he does not devote himself to what the

For some newcomers to college, the fraternity offered the hope of brotherhood: Alpha Epsilon Phi pledge party, 1959–60. *Courtesy Northwestern University Archives.*

To the successful college man came the rewards: the Red Friars at Duke tap the anointed, 1956. *Duke University Archives.*

undergraduates call the service of his university—that is, athletics and activities." Leadership brought honors and esteem. "The editor of the college paper, he who plays the 'leading lady' in the college opera, and the president of the Student Council have, in the opinion of most students, made a success of their university careers second only to that of the football star."[30] These were the disinterested heroes who had proved their mettle and their loyalty.

The fraternity, this witness judged, offered its members ready companionship, a homelike atmosphere, and lessons in good manners, at the price of a rigid conformity. Angell felt that the individual who joined lost the ability to choose how he wanted to live in college. The fraternities pushed their members into extracurricular activities, even against the better judgment of those with intellectual aspirations. As a result, the organized students on campus tended "to be more or less alike." Drawn from similar backgrounds and pushed into similar molds, the men of a fraternity ran "to a type."[31]

This type put small stock in academic work. College culture perceived the scholar as selfish. It thought of the big man "as denying his selfish interest in unselfish devotion to the common good," but it regarded the deep scholar "as working wholly for himself." "Getting by" characterized the ambition of most undergraduates. At the University of Chicago in the 1920s students spent an average of twenty hours a week on their studies outside of class. But this hardly measured the depth of their apathy. Even when studying, they were not engaged. In addition, the college men positively devalued academic life.[32] Study after study reported that fraternity members made the lowest grades of any group on campus.[33] As Angell put it, "There has been for a number of years a certain element among the male students at least which considers it bad form to receive high marks, unless they are undeserved; in the latter case, the individual has 'put one over' on his professor and is to be congratulated."[34] Our Yale correspondent of the 1870s could not have expressed it better.

In such a system faculty and students formed two streams that ran parallel but seldom mingled. As in the nineteenth century, cheating provided a key measure of the seriousness of the divide. Students, honest in their other relationships, submitted work not their own, brought "cribs" to exams, and gave each other information during tests. According to Angell, many believed "that a state of war exists between faculty members and students —no mere game, where the canons of sportsmanship prevail, but a downright, ruthless struggle in which any method of overcoming the foe is justifiable."[35]

In 1926, when Daniel Katz asked undergraduates at Syracuse why a student might seek to get to know his professor, fraternity members tended to check ulterior motives. A student sought out a professor outside class "to raise his grade" or "to show assumed interest." The neutrals tended to suggest a sincere reason, checking "for further knowledge" above the other possibilities.[36]

When queried about cheating, the litmus test for the strength of a collegiate mentality, fraternity members condoned cheating in far greater numbers than independents, and removed it from moral categories. This corresponded to the most shocking finding: 72 percent of fraternity members at Syracuse admitted to having "cribbed" (the polite undergraduate term for cheating) at least once in their college course. Neutrals could hardly be held up as paragons—slightly over a majority had themselves cribbed—but both their behavior and their code suggested that they perceived the moral dimensions of cheating.[37]

When asked what two kinds of students they most admired, both Greeks and neutrals favored the industrious, at least on paper. The fraternity members chose as second and third the active student and the popular student and put the brilliant student far down on the list. The independents, who also respected the active students, though less enthusiastically, voiced their approval for the brilliant far more strongly than did the organized.[38]

Syracuse in 1926, as Katz saw it, attracted essentially two different classes of students. On the one hand were those of the "scholarly type whose greatest interest lies in college studies." They "value contacts with their instructors, . . . admire most the brilliant and capable student, and . . . find that their studies give them real satisfaction." On the other were the fraternity members. "These individuals are more inclined than the others to show cynicism toward students who cultivate their professors." They also admire "active and influential" students above brilliant ones and find their college studies to be less satisfying.[39]

Thirty years later fraternity members still went out for extracurricular activities far more than independents. The Greek system retained its commitment to achievement in college life. One fraternity man at Cornell stated unequivocally, "Our house is BMOH (Big Man on the Hill). That is, we try to get the wheels. We pledge the ones who look as if they could make it." Some chose athletes; others, the fellows out for a good time. Cornell fraternity shape-up sessions of the 1950s sound remarkably like Yale of the 1890s: "You're not going out for enough activities. Better get on it."[40]

Students at some colleges put the greatest emphasis on style. In the late 1950s, in discussing the relative merits of Jews and the graduates of preparatory schools, the chairman of a Princeton eating club's "Bicker" or rush put it this way: "The 'name' of one's club depends in large measure upon the number of prep-school graduates and tweed-clad extroverts that are among its members. The Princeton club is primarily for the social side of life. There is no room for the nondrinker, the silent introvert, or the man who spends so much time on studies that he neglects the social life which is so much a part of college."[41]

When it came to grades, however, fraternity members of the 1950s scored significantly lower than independents. Earlier studies at the University of Minnesota and at Yale had shown that employment and extracurricular activity, other than athletics, could be positively correlated to grades, but these studies had not distinguished between fraternity members and independents.[42] The first study to correlate grades and fraternity membership came in the 1950s and examined eleven major colleges and universities. What it revealed confirmed every critic's suspicion: 63 percent of the Greeks reported a cumulative average in the 70s range, in contrast to 50 percent of the Barbs; 30 percent of the fraternity members scored above 80, compared with 40 percent of the independents.[43]

Even in the 1950s, when students sought professional school or high-paying jobs after graduation, the old pressure not to be a "grind" remained a part of the canon of the college man. As one brother put it, "We don't pride ourselves on having 'greasy grinds' in our house. There are three things we try to teach our men to handle moderately: liquor, women, and courses. Our motto is no excesses in any of them."[44] A Princeton club man, despite his aspiration to become a college professor, believed that "the club system . . . has a greater place at Princeton than the brilliant but colorless and socially ill-at-ease individual who spends his four college years closeted in a library or laboratory."[45]

At the private Eastern colleges and universities, fraternities and clubs favored the graduates of preparatory schools. Because of their discriminatory policies and high fees, prep schools served to establish social credentials. But repeatedly researchers learned that, despite their academic emphasis, the private schools did not graduate students of high scholastic attainment. In a study of Princeton students, even when investigators took into account the higher admissions standards required of public school students, undergraduates from the high schools achieved significantly better grade point averages than their prep school classmates.[46] In a wide range of studies from the 1920s through the 1950s in many different settings, discounting for aptitude differences and previous grades, public school graduates did better academically than those from private schools.[47]

Repeatedly researchers at Harvard rediscovered that knowing whether a student had come from a private or a public school predicted best his undergraduate career. "Time and time again, apparently chaotic data falls apart into two clean but opposite findings when the experiment is done within the public school group and within the private school group. . . . One certainly begins to feel the real force that subcultures exert upon personality during the college years." Not only did they have different grade point averages; they responded differentially to a battery of mental and psychological tests. The cognitive styles of high school and prep school men differed as "between equally able writers who contribute to the *Journal of Consulting Psychology* and to the *Atlantic Monthly*."[48]

This summary of studies did not point out that the two groups had different positions within the college world, but it might have. At Harvard, despite Lowell's efforts, the great divide between clubmen and the other Harvard remained, and the right prep school gave the key to club doors. Thus we can use the data on private school graduates to construct a portrait of the Harvard clubman. He was, first of all, an underachiever. Given an inkblot, he tended not to describe it in much detail, but to elaborate on a single facet; though unusual in that he mentioned color, he frequently got the color wrong, demonstrating impulsiveness. Vocational testing did him no good, for it predicted little; simply asking him determined best what he would become. Even if he had considerable aptitude, he would not choose science. In selecting items, his tastes ran to the "social, aesthetic, statusful, and romantic outdoor activity items." Emotionally he was more constricted than the public school man, but he smoked, a symbol of abjuring the work ethic.[49] All in all, though drawn by a social scientist a half century later, a portrait not unlike that of Owen Wister's Bertie and Billy.

Cheating remained widespread in the early 1950s, engaged in by nearly two-fifths of all students surveyed. Nothing like Syracuse's figure of 72 percent of fraternity men admitted to cheating, but cheating and membership in a Greek-letter society were clearly correlated.[50] Even when researchers compared different schools within a university and contrasted those students who saw themselves as intellectuals with non-intellectuals, fraternity members in each category cheated more than independents.[51]

Did a certain type of student with a propensity to cheat join a fraternity? No; freshmen, whether they were headed for the Greek world or had decided to stay Barbarians, demonstrated no difference in attitude toward cheating. "The differences appeared only in the sophomore year and were maintained throughout the subsequent years of college life." Among seniors, 32 percent of the fraternity members admitted to having cheated more than once, but only 23 percent of the independents repeated the act.[52] Cheating thus emerges as a behavior learned especially well in the fraternity house.

An earlier generation of college men had abjured politics, but in the twentieth century they could not avoid it. The rebels on campus insisted on keeping it in the foreground. In addition, survey takers constantly measured student opinion on a wide range of issues. Unfortunately, most social scientists tended to see the campus as a single bloc, rather than as a complex that included sharp differences between student groups. Thus when they took the political temperature on campus, they asked questions of a class or a student body to learn its collective attitudes and how those attitudes had changed over time. During the 1930s and 1940s they generally learned that students became more tolerant and liberal in college. In more conservative eras, such as the 1950s, going to college had no such effect.[53]

A few studies did separate out students by gender or religion, and this offers some clues into the differing political attitudes on campus. A University of Chicago study in the 1930s found that Jews were consistently more liberal on social questions than Protestants or Catholics; since the Christians tended to be the organized students in those years, a differently worded study would have found the Barbs more liberal than the Greeks.[54] A 1950s study to determine the support for civil liberties among college students reported a similar finding for religious groups. In addition, it determined that members of fraternities and sororities formed the most conservative group on campus.[55]

In the 1950s a more comprehensive study measured the intensity as well as the direction of student politics. In general, undergraduates in the McCarthy era abjured strong political commitments: only a small minority confessed to getting "worked up" over politics. Although Republicans led Democrats 29 to 26 percent, 42 percent of college students sampled declared themselves to be aloof from either political party. As freshmen, these college and university students accepted their parents' politics, but became more conservative as they went through college.[56]

An important conservative force in these years turned out to be the fraternity. Upon entering college, both future fraternity members and future independents included liberals and conservatives. The liberal neutral persisted in his liberalism, but the fraternity member who came to college as a liberal was likely to turn conservative in the next four years. Something happened to the organized student that pressured him to conform to the dominant conservative culture. By contrast, independents could resist the pressure. On college campuses dominated by fraternities and conservatism, the liberal neutrals formed a distinct, deviant subculture.[57]

The public debate about the mentality of the college man in the twentieth century has principally been concerned with the nature of his prejudice. At Syracuse in 1926, researchers found that students of all kinds were bigoted. For example, although Jews composed roughly 15 percent of the student body, only 20.7 percent of the students in the university were willing to admit them to their fraternity or rooming house—i.e., only 5.7 percent after subtracting the Jewish students. Even this figure stood slightly above the 5.4 percent of all students who expressed a willingness to admit Negroes, who along with Bolshevists and Anarchists composed the most despised group.[58]

Prejudice among college students found its institutional form on campus in the Greek system. In the course of the first half of the twentieth century, despite their quotas, colleges and universities became increasingly open to talent. Jews and blacks entered in growing numbers. Not all felt content with being outsiders or satisfied with becoming rebels; some wanted to join in an open, unambiguous way. But the existing fraternities barred both Jews and blacks.

The pain this caused some Jewish undergraduates is documented in Gilbert W. Gabriel's novel *The Seven-Branched Candlestick,* written in the first person. Pushed by a socially ambitious, assimilated aunt and guardian, the unnamed narrator enters a fictional Columbia prepared to be "its most loyal son." From his first hazing he encounters anti-Semitism, but its full force comes when, after he seizes the flag at the freshman-sophomore rush, a nearsighted junior from a wealthy, aristocratic New York family invites him to lunch at his fraternity house. Out of the awkward encounter between innocent Jew and half-blind college man, the narrator learns the rules: "Because I was a Jew—that was their one and only reason for showing me the door in so polite and gentlemanly a fashion."[59] Over the course of four years, the Jewish undergraduate meets personal friendship among individual college men, but institutional exclusion.

Success that often proved elusive in life could be imagined in fiction. Barred from the track team and the newspaper, the narrator does end runs on the humor and literary magazines, in the manner of the real Robert Moses. Unlike Moses, who had to be satisfied with the Kit Cat Club, our fictional hero becomes the first Jew chosen by a senior honor society. In a melodramatic finale, he scales for others the barriers that had barred him. When the student newspaper excludes the son of immigrant Jews whom he has championed, the narrator goes to the football captain and YMCA president for help. The good Fred calls a class meeting. Two members of the senior society turn out to be undergraduate toughs. To block the narrator from the meeting, they wound him on the head and lock him in his closet. He breaks free and at the critical moment speaks out openly and successfully for full inclusion for Jews in all undergraduate activities. With his Judaism reclaimed and his conscience clear, he receives the ultimate mark of acceptance, a bid to the nearsighted friend's fraternity that had once snubbed him. Four years wiser, and aware that membership could mean little in the last months of college, he politely declines.

The fictional undergraduate earlier rejected a second option, membership in the newly forming Jewish fraternity, for he thought it better to insist that all such groups be open. However, real Jewish students who sought to be college men were joining. In 1898 Jewish men in New York created Zeta Beta Tau, which shifted in six years from a college Zionist youth organization to a fraternity. Although perhaps more attentive to the brothers' collective grade point average than other fraternities, ZBT and its successors effectively mimicked fraternity style and politics. Negroes founded their parallel Alpha Phi Alpha. On some campuses, the administration discouraged the creation of Jewish and Negro fraternities; on others, they refused them official recognition, leaving Jews and blacks completely outside the system of power.

In 1937, out of a total of 105,000 Jewish students in colleges in the United States and Canada, only 18,000 belonged to a Greek-type organization, a proportion far smaller than the 25 percent of U.S. college students who were members of fraternities and sororities in the period.[60] Even the joiners found, moreover, that their fraternities lacked the prestige and power of their Gentile or white precedents. As Heywood Broun and George Britt put it in 1931, "In many universities . . . the stronger fraternities are political organizations with almost vested interests in certain student offices and appointments. Exclusion from a fraternity automatically bars the student from some of the more important honors. In some colleges the Jewish fraternities have sufficient standing to compete on rather even terms, but not in many." These critics felt that the poisonous effect of anti-Semitism on the non-Jewish student constituted one of its worst elements. Often from a background "with no Jews and no prejudices, he is taught that custom excludes Jews from the best and most sacred circles that he is to know."[61] In the Syracuse study of 1926, members of Greek-letter societies were far less willing than independents to admit Jews and blacks: 19 percent versus 37.7 percent for Jews; 4.3 versus 12.5 percent for Negroes. Those fraternity members identified as institutionally minded had the lowest proportion of acceptance of all: 13.9 percent for Jews; 3.5 percent for Negroes.[62] The fraternity turned out to be an all too effective school for prejudice.

So, too, it seemed to many, did the fraternity teach discrimination. The issue came to a head in the late 1940s and 1950s. Beginning after World War

II, both Negroes and Jews increasingly sought membership in the established restricted fraternities. Some veterans returned from the war against fascism committed to the cause of ending bigotry. The exclusionary clauses in fraternity charters barring blacks and Jews cut against the grain. College newspaper editors began campaigns against fraternity discrimination, gathering wide support on campus.[63]

As social scientists repeated earlier surveys of college students' racial and ethnic stereotypes, they learned that undergraduates of the post–World War II period were far more tolerant than the generations preceding them. When

Phi Alpha Psi (formerly Phi Kappa Psi) of Amherst College: *Olio, 1949. Amherst College Archives.*

researchers asked Princeton students to attach attributes to Negroes and Jews, the number of students suggesting negative qualities dropped by half, and far more innocuous traits—such as musical talent or intelligence—took their place. Many students expressed an uneasiness about attributing any traits at all, especially where they had no direct knowledge of a group; some even regarded the question as an insult to their intelligence.[64] In the 1950s at the University of Michigan fraternity members demonstrated both individual tolerance and a herd mentality. The brothers rated their housemates as far less tolerant than they proved to be and assumed that they opposed admitting Jews. Those who did not know about discriminatory house policy expressed greater tolerance before they learned of it than after.[65]

Efforts to change the fraternities moved within, and some fraternities accepted a black or a Jew. They found that the national organization, dominated by alumni, controlled basic policy and that the fraternity men of the past wanted to keep their organizations restrictive. In 1948 at Amherst, Phi Kappa Psi decided to pledge a Negro. The Amherst alumni accepted this departure from tradition, but the national convention threatened to throw the local chapter out of the fraternity if it initiated the black collegian. After a difficult period of turmoil marked by pressures and threats, the Amherst chapter, as the independent club Phi Alpha Psi, initiated its first Negro member.[66]

Some colleges and universities, such as the University of Washington and the University of Chicago, proceeded cautiously to require their fraternities to bring their constitutions into line with official anti-discrimination policies. Roughly 20 percent of the institutions of higher education took such a course; another 10 percent issued statements of pious hope. Although most administrators personally did not like fraternity discrimination, they feared the consequences to endowments of moving against it. Students at the University of Michigan fought for legislation that gave fraternities a maximum of six years to remove restrictive clauses; the university's president vetoed it.

Faced with a minority of administrators and the majority of students opposed to "group rejection," the national organizations gradually dropped their discriminatory clauses. However, discrimination did not end; it just went underground.[67] Some Gentile fraternities accepted a black or a Jewish token member, but until the changing climate of the 1960s they largely kept the white Protestant brotherhood intact.

College life as institutionalized in the fraternity can be looked at in a variety of settings; the degree to which it set the tone for any campus, however, depended on its relative weight. At the University of Minnesota it fought evenly for campus power. The City College of New York in the 1930s barely felt its effects. At the prestigious Ivy League institutions, a definite shift took place toward meritocracy in the years after World War II, lowering the proportion of preparatory school students to high school students, increasing the numbers on financial aid, raising the test scores and grades of its entering classes, intensifying Jewish presence on campus, and sharply diminishing the influence of the college men.[68] But in some settings, college life still dominated. Students at a small, upper-class men's college, such as Williams in the 1950s, knew little else. Thus an inquiry into New England campus culture gives us a glimpse into college life as it stood in the mid-twentieth century.

When two researchers closely studied undergraduates at such a school (which they renamed Ivy), they found that almost all of them joined a fraternity at the end of sophomore year. No definable subcultures existed as alternatives. They called college canons at Ivy "button-down collar culture." To them this captured the conformist essence of undergraduates' insistence that the individual be "well-rounded." Students did not value achievement in any one area but "versatility of behavior and interests."[69]

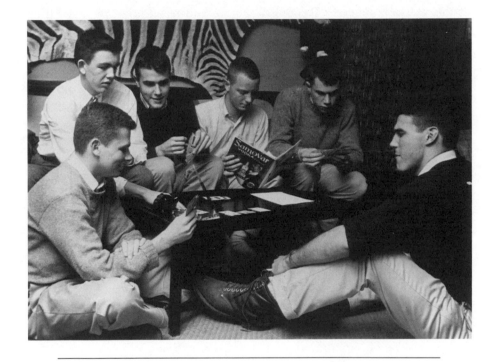

Button-down-collar culture: Williams students, 1957. *Williamsiana Collection.*

Although students believed that academic success bore some relation to their future, each person interviewed insisted that other facets of college were more important: getting along with others, becoming independent, or extracurricular leadership.

When asked to describe an intellectual, they variously described him "as 'a creep,' 'a skinny little guy with glasses,' and a 'mental snob.' " Being smart did not disqualify a student in the eyes of his fellows, but intellectual achievement in and of itself held little value. As one student put it, "You can't be just a junior Phi Bete and nothing else to be a good guy. You should participate in sports, be in one extracurricular activity or more, be able to get along easily with others, drink, etc." Students regarded grades in the B and C range as acceptable. Nothing in the college culture encouraged students to work more than the minimum. A student who ignored these standards risked being called a "grind" or an "individualist."[70]

Thus despite immense changes in the nature of knowledge and its relation to society, the life that college men created in the early nineteenth century remained intact in the mid-twentieth century. America stood on the verge of entering the space age, but college men were still caught in the conflicts of the years of the early Republic. Science and technology were splitting the atom, with its immense dangers and promises, but college men knew better than to take study too seriously. To them the real triumphs of college continued to be style, fun, prestige, and winning the races of the extracurriculum. In their eyes students remained at war with their faculty, and only traitors went over to the other side.

# 7

# Jacobins and Other Rebels

Unlike college men of the nineteenth century, who had the stage all to themselves, those in the twentieth century had to jockey for the limelight with their rebellious classmates. Outsiders had always existed aplenty, but they generally did not take on the opposition, or at least not on its own ground. What was new in the twentieth century was that college rebels confronted college life openly and collectively and fought for dominance in the hallowed realms of the college man—the college newspaper and student government.

The rebels of the 1910s flouted two critical canons of college life. They demanded that college not be a place of withdrawal from politics, but a platform from which to confront the hard issues of the day. They brought onto campus questions of war and peace, capitalism and socialism, and insisted that undergraduates debate them. Perceiving the faculty neither as enemies in battle nor as steppingstones to a career, they dropped the characteristic stances of college students toward their teachers. They regarded professors, like books, as there to be used—when they were helpful. When not, they should be treated with contempt and flung aside.

During the 1920s, one of the heydays of college life, the rebels persisted in their fight for the hearts and minds of college students. Yet in the aftermath of World War I, the search for alternative possibilities became dual. In the 1910s social critics—inside and outside college gates—had blended political and cultural radicalism. The sense of the new that pervaded artistic innovation often took the political form of a cheerful, conflict-free socialism. While some 1920s undergraduates were able to sustain the integration of politics and culture that had enlivened the prewar years, others found themselves caught in the countercurrents of the broader society. The war and the Russian Revolution challenged both the optimistic and the peaceful assumptions that had underlain the earlier radicalism. In addition, the conservative resurgence of the 1920s, following wartime repression of civil liberties and the Red Scare, came on campus. While college men often joined to their free and easy approach to morals a political conservatism in keeping with national politics, campus rebels followed a less predictable path. Some sustained political commitments on the Left; others moved away from politics to search for aesthetic or personal solutions.

Supporting undergraduate rebellion in the 1920s—both political and aesthetic—were social critics hostile to the connection between college and big business and to the social conformity this interrelation fostered. Though important to intellectual history, Thorstein Veblen's indictment of American colleges and universities, *The Higher Learning,* published in 1918, went virtually unread by collegians. Though a far weaker book, Upton Sinclair's *The Goose-step,* published five years later, had an undergraduate audience. His sprawling catalogue of educational sins—especially those of alliance with American corporate life—served as a reference point for the disaffected.[1] J. E. Kirkpatrick's *The American College and Its Rulers,* published by New Republic, Inc., in 1926, offered a more judicious critique coupled with a call to return college authority to its appropriate masters, the resident members of the community—its faculty and students. As a hopeful sign, he saw "students in revolt."

Kirkpatrick chronicled the rise of dissent among undergraduates. On many campuses, college rebels had created new publications, such as the *Saturday Evening Pest* at Yale and the *Tempest* at the University of Michigan, to bypass the censorship imposed on established campus papers. At a number of colleges, undergraduates were staging protests against required military training. At more conservative colleges, especially black institutions, collegians actively revolted against the discipline of an earlier century. Students at Oberlin set themselves in opposition to compulsory chapel. At Harvard and Dartmouth, they demonstrated a growing interest in the nature and form of their courses, and Dartmouth undergraduates participated in a report to reshape the college curriculum. Although the majorities on American campuses still remained "complacent," Kirkpatrick concluded that one could look "with more of hope than of fear to the rising of militant minorities on the campus."[2]

Rebellious students graduated. Before taking up their adult careers, several of them gave a few years to fostering dissent on campus. A few, such as Henry Hurwitz (Harvard '08), the founder of the undergraduate Menorah

Society, gave their entire professional lives. Others, such as Horace Kallen (Harvard '03) in his *College Prolongs Infancy,* wrote stinging critiques of the canons of college life.[3] *The New Republic,* founded by Walter Lippmann, among others, used its pages and its book-publishing subsidiary to provoke collegiate rebellion. Its 1929 collection *The Students Speak Out!* sampled rebellious student opinion from campuses across the nation.[4]

Rebellious alumni were crucial in sustaining key organizations and publications. In 1921 two liberal student organizations merged to form the National Student Forum. Graduates served on its executive committee, along with faculty and undergraduates. The National Student Forum sponsored several conferences in its early years. Between 1922 and 1929 it published the first national college newspaper, *The New Student,* edited until 1927 by Douglas Haskell.[5]

Although its political emphasis fluctuated during its seven-year life, *The New Student* consistently fought to liberalize rules on campus, to offer an alternative to fraternities, and to oppose militarism. It stimulated rebellion: its monthly "magazine" supplement published sections of *The Goose-step.* Most importantly, *The New Student* gave college rebels a critical forum in which they could air their dissent. It printed their iconoclastic poems and quips. As it published news from many institutions, it gave rebels the sense that their local battles formed part of a nationwide struggle. It reported student efforts, such as that at Miami University in 1924, to take power from the fraternities.[6] It publicized individual fights, such as Beatrice Anthony's battle in the courts for reinstatement after she was expelled from Syracuse because she was not the "Syracuse type."[7]

Its pages gave language to student conflict, both lofty and low. In 1923 the dramatic refusal of twelve Amherst undergraduates, including the senior class president, to take their degrees from a college that had fired President Alexander Meiklejohn became a symbol of courage "to stand up and talk, work, and fight for . . . living knowledge."[8] On a different plane were quotes from undergraduate publications, such as the one from the University of Indiana's *Vagabond* that criticized conformity and intellectual sterility. The *Vagabond* writer found to be a "pitiful spectacle" the "wretched degradation of human nature . . . the putrescent mess of flesh and bone, be he Babbitt or be he Dean, who, never having experienced the right-about-face in his opinions, goes through life accepting his beliefs on authority and mouthing them with an air of sageness."[9] An eclectic collection of undergraduate and alumni writing, *The New Student* persistently encouraged college rebels of the 1920s.

Although the initial rebels of the 1910s generally had shared a middle-

or upper-class background with their club or Greek opponents, they were distinctive in that they came from nurturant backgrounds that nonetheless barred them from college life. Their adolescent rebellion took the form of opposition to the conformity that excluded them. After World War I, well-educated, child-conscious families continued to breed rebels, and in some cases the forces of exclusion continued their catalytic effect. When Earl Miers went to Rutgers in the fall of 1929, he entered with a special handicap —cerebral palsy. It marked him as clearly as if he were Jewish or black. During freshman "Pledge Week" no fraternity knocked on his door: "In that age, no fraternity would have considered pledging an athetoid . . . any more than a fraternity would have selected a Negro." Miers determined to fight back. "Rebellion—that streak of impudence without which, no handicapped person can rise above the ignorance and superstition surrounding him —stirred deeply. A variety of four-letter words expressed neatly what I thought of the entire fraternity system. Nor would I accept the belief that fraternities had to run the whole campus. There were on the campus more neutrals than fraternity men, who needed only organization to become the dominant political force in the college. . . . I intended, by God, to break the system."[10]

Although he ran for freshman president, he knew he had no chance. His eye was on the long haul, ultimately the editorship of the *Targum,* Rutgers' campus newspaper. As he gradually built support, he came to rely on Earl Reed Silvers, professor, mentor, and confidant. But others on the faculty and administration opposed him, those "old fraternity boys" who "now revered the system as though it were as sacred and as indispensable to a stable society as membership in a church and a good country club (to say nothing of a discreet association with a reliable bootlegger)."[11] Miers won his war and emerged as a crusading *Targum* editor-in-chief.

Miers' iconoclasm was not reserved for deans. While he learned a great deal from Reed Silvers, it was the rebel's way to be selective. Once when a young psychology lecturer tried to elicit from the class responses to inkblots, Miers spoke up: " 'There, sir,' I said, 'are two girls chasing a frightened senior across the campus and his pants are falling down. On the steps of Kirkpatrick Chapel a drunken night watchman is laying the housemother of one of the dorms. The dean, hiding in the bushes, is splitting his sides with laughter.' "[12] Fortunately for Miers, the onset of the Depression meant that his tuition was valued above the dignity of the academy, and he was not kicked out.

Handicapped though he was, Miers enjoyed his Rutgers years. "College was not a place where we went to learn how to live; here we lived." Each night ended in a bull session. On the other side of the great sexual divide, "a dozen of us, crowded in someone's room, talked and talked: about books, music, girls, masturbation, bootleg whiskey, parents, the future, what was wrong with the college, profs, and sex, sex, sex." In his senior year he met Starling Wyckoff, a student at Rutgers College for Women (later renamed Douglas). They became "inseparable." Yet although Miers and his buddies could talk about sex, without a fraternity house or a car, finding places for lovemaking was not easy for young couples. Miers' former housemother understood his need for privacy with Starling. She invited both over and then announced that she would have to be away for an hour and a half. But at Rutgers in the 1930s, not all were so accommodating, and, in Miers' case, one even indicted the innocent. Starling's vindictive housemother learned that the two had been in an unsupervised building (while Miers wrote an editorial for the *Targum*) and tried to make an issue of their breaking of the rules. Miers wisely turned to his faculty mentor, who moved to his defense and prevented any proceedings against the two.[13] In the years after World War I, college authority spoke about sexuality and rules in many different tongues.

In some cases no apparent disability set off the college rebel. He was simply an outsider who wanted to be inside. To become a rebel required ambition, in some cases blind ambition. It meant both bucking the dominant college clique and fighting to win. In 1927 Lyndon Johnson at San Marcos College had just such ambition. He found it relatively easy to ingratiate himself with the college administration, but power over other students was more difficult to achieve. In that Texas setting athletics provided the single route to collegiate prestige. The athletes confirmed their power in a local social fraternity, the Black Stars. Because he was not an athlete, Johnson did not make the fraternity and found himself cut out of the ruling elite. To a young man of his energy and drive for power, this was clearly unacceptable.

Johnson quickly figured out a strategy. He joined the White Stars, a secret club, and helped turn it into an instrument for gaining power at San Marcos. Convinced that secrecy was essential, club members never congregated in public. In an interview with Doris Kearns, Johnson recalled the rule "that no more than two of us could be seen together on the campus. If a third member came along, we had special code signals as to which one was expected to leave."[14] Each club member took responsibility for learning about a different group on campus and pooled his information with that of the others at club meetings. San Marcos' non-athletes, who formed 90 percent of the student body, were its outsiders. They clearly felt aggrieved over the athletes' privileges and their inequitable share of the student activities fund. Initial success came when a number of White Stars, who had grown to twenty, beat Black Star candidates in elections to the student council and the student newspaper.

From his position on the college paper, Johnson covered news of non-athletes. His closeness to the college administration helped him get student jobs for his supporters. The White Stars' ascendancy in the student council led to a reallocation of student funds to the cultural and intellectual activities

Even the most ambitious rebel could take time off: Lyndon Baines Johnson, right, with his college roommate, Alfred "Boody" Johnson. *Lyndon Baines Johnson Library.*

of the non-athletes. Johnson's final goal was symbolic, to win for his group the presidency of the senior class. Unwilling to accept the judgment of informal White Star poll-taking that the Black Star candidate had the lead, Johnson spent a long night traveling through the student boardinghouses to argue for his man. The next day his best friend won by eight votes.[15] Although Johnson's later career suggested an extraordinary lust for power, his college days read like those of other successful rebels. It took Johnsonian drive to win against the odds.

Although Earl Miers became a campus rebel because his disability excluded him from college life, and Lyndon Johnson because he could not play football, by the 1920s other undergraduates required no such catalyst. Collegiate rebellion was an available alternative to students, in some cases a compelling one. It was supported by alumni and by *The New Student.* The groove had been made. Some of those who later became rebels had joined fraternities or sororities, but became converted later in college. A fair number were Jewish, but by the 1920s many Jews had the option of becoming college men and women in their own branch of the Greek system. The distinction that emerged in the 1920s between rebels and college men and women was of temperament and style. Collegiate rebellion attracted those who were nonconforming, ambitious, and restless. In the world of Main Street, such undergraduates thought of themselves as Sinclair Lewis.[16]

In 1923 at Harvard, for example, two wealthy clubmen turned against their own kind. Corliss Lamont began his long career as a maverick by publishing in the *Harvard Advocate* an article exposing and attacking the divisions that sustained the "Two Harvards." *The New York Times* reported that he demonstrated that the "sons of well-to-do families" who came to Harvard from preparatory schools dominated "sport, club and editorial activities, while the students recruited from public schools almost monopolized scholastic honors." His classmate Charlton MacVeagh, son of a United States Steel executive, publicly attacked the low academic standards that allowed the well-prepared clubmen to loaf their way through college. Both joined together to create the Harvard Debating Union, modeled after that of Oxford, to interest their more privileged classmates in public questions.[17]

Columbia's Reed Harris, later to be a government official and deputy head of the Voice of America, was a rebel in this mold. The son of wealthy New Yorkers, he had prepped at Staunton Military Academy. Historically Columbia College had offered students a talented faculty and significant diversity.[18] But Reed Harris initially made the conventional choice. On entering Columbia, he joined a prestigious fraternity, went out for freshman football, and began writing for the student daily, the *Spectator.* Once he became editor-in-chief, however, Harris turned to attack. He wrote exposés of Columbia football practices, its honor society, and the administration of its dining halls. On April 1, 1932, Dean Herbert Hawkes expelled him. Although Reed Harris' family represented the establishment, his father supported him against the Columbia administration. Tudor Harris announced that he "would regard a diploma received at the hands of a college president who could sanction, let alone direct, such an action for such a cause as a stigma." The elder Harris' permissive understanding of youth is clear from his statement that he respected his son for having "brought new vigor and life" to the student paper. In contrast, President Nicholas Murray Butler and Dean Hawkes "seek to hold growing and active minds within the limits of prescriptive thinking."

Outraged undergraduates, organized by radical groups, staged a one-day strike protesting Harris' expulsion. As they demonstrated in front of Low Library, they were pelted with eggs by fraternity members and athletes. To many in his class, however, Reed Harris was a campus hero: in May he garnered enough votes to be elected the senior "most likely to succeed."[19]

While rebels such as Lyndon Johnson and Reed Harris operated in a political fashion, the 1920s saw the birth of a more elusive form of collegiate rebellion, one that vied less for the votes than for the inner assent of classmates. This aesthetic or intellectual iconoclasm questioned values, institutions, and mores, but stayed aloof from political engagement. As college students with an independent cast of mind confronted a changed world, some of them chose to remain outside the political fray and turn inward to struggle for psychic freedom. As a result, the cultural and political strands of rebellion split apart.

By the 1920s at Harvard some experimental-minded undergraduates, uncomfortable with both the conformity of college life and the assumptions of the more politicized forms of college rebellion, found their voice as independents. David Riesman and his roommate entered Dunster House as seniors. As editor of the *Crimson,* Riesman had taken a position—opposed by the clubmen—to support the new House system. As he later recalled, "the new Houses made a difference for those of us who needed adults who would support our intellectual and academic concerns, since we could not always find enough support for these among our peers."[20] In the company of young faculty—Carl J. Friedrich, Crane Brinton, and Seymour Harris—Riesman and his friends created a world in which they could discuss music, art, and literature. Although of Jewish descent, Riesman was no outsider. The son of a distinguished professor of medicine at the University of Pennsylvania and an alumna of Bryn Mawr, he became a managing editor of the *Crimson.* Nor was he a political rebel: "I was one of those who mocked Roger Baldwin and Corliss Lamont, civil libertarians and Harvard alumni, when they protested the wages of Harvard scrubwomen." Feeling "little class guilt," Riesman stood aloof from political protest, but kept his inquiring mind.[21]

Riesman's independence of established modes suggests a shift that began as early as the late 1920s at Harvard. Already by Riesman's undergraduate years the sharp boundaries between college men, outsiders, and rebels at

Harvard were beginning to dissolve. What in the nineteenth century had been clear social divisions maintained by the Greek and club system gradually began to fade to become more elusive mental constructions against which individuals struggled for self-definition.

Several forces intersected to corrode the old categories. Reform effectively altered the atmosphere to break the power of college life and allow worldly students entry into the life of the mind. Anti-Semitism, which had maintained a *cordon sanitaire* between Gentiles and Jews, began to lose its potency among sophisticated college students, opening the way to friendships and spirited interchange. And finally modern consciousness penetrated to question established traditions, even the tradition of questioning. As a result, beginning in the late 1920s a small number of undergraduates were able to distance themselves from existing modalities.

Published in 1933, George Weller's novel of Harvard, *Not to Eat, Not for Love,* captures this new possibility. The multiple voices of the work sound unlike any previous traditions of college fiction. Modeled after Dos Passos' *U.S.A.,* the novel suggests a musical composition, whose melodies, taken by different students, play against a counterpoint of deans, professors, and alumni. Authority as represented by these elders is complex and contradictory. It speaks the many languages of official administration, college men, rebels, and outsiders.[22]

As an upholder of the old moral order, Dean Carron demands that a student who has spent the night with his girlfriend resign from the college. The Dean's justice is abstract: "If I make an exception in your case I have to make it in all cases." The iconoclastic composition professor pushes the freshmen to consider a Harvard of individuals, where "no one cares what you do," where each graduate is not "much like any other young man that ever went there," and where only the uninteresting strive for college life. The collegiate alumnus returning to his annual club banquet can think of nothing about which to converse with an undergraduate other than alcohol and football. The outsider alumnus bitterly condemns the Harvard that valued the "mummery" of clubs and cliques.[23]

What is intriguing is that these are the background figures, not the foreground. By the Harvard of the early 1930s a mentality existed that perceived these stock types as the props of the drama, not its substance. The book centers on the inner consciousness of Epes Todd, a Harvard junior. Todd plays football because he loves it, but he is Second Varsity. He eats at the Varsity Club during the season but is outside final club life. At the opening of the novel, Todd's grades have slipped. He does not care, for his passion of the moment is football. Through the course of the narrative Todd comes to shift his intensity from football to art history. As he strives to gain insight and mastery, he concentrates on the subject itself, not the grade. At the center of Todd's Harvard life are emerging commitments to work and to love.

In his struggle for a creative adulthood, Todd makes a critical alliance with his tutor in art history, Warren Brant. Brant is not a professorial type but an individual of quiet kindness and clear intellect. Brant opens his apartment, library, mind, and personal life to Todd. The two engage in true intellectual discourse that redirects Todd and helps him find his calling. As Todd reads in Brant's study in the afternoon the "crevices in his knowledge began to fill in. It became probable that the neoclassic French had not blindly scourged themselves into order, but that they had honestly raised up a code of laws and voluntarily made it governor of their creativeness."[24]

Once Todd meets Ellen Thwyte, his growing intellectual power becomes entwined with the opening of his emotional and erotic life. He leaves his first examination with the satisfaction that "he had written freely and fluently. . . . Ellen's coming had taken away a filter through which all his thoughts had once been forced to pass."[25] With full knowledge of Todd's need of Ellen, Brant offers Todd use of his apartment when he and his wife take a vacation, and thereby gives Todd a place to gain sexual fulfillment.

Nothing about Todd's growing love for Ellen Thwyte echoes college fiction. It is passionate and serious, not comic or melodramatic. The two speak the language of sensitive youth emerging into adulthood. As they leave the chapel after hearing Christmas carols, Ellen Thwyte reflects, "My trouble, after evenings like this, is to find out which music I heard and which was my own." The consummation of their love in the Brants' apartment, suggested in an intense and dramatic dream sequence, does not end the narrative, but merely moves Todd to another plane of development. Todd remains at Harvard. Despite their deep feeling, he and Ellen are forced by their ignorance of birth control to withdraw temporarily from sex. More importantly, Todd must work through a second relationship, that with his mentor, Warren Brant, and with Brant's wife, Ina, a couple to whom he felt he owed everything. His knowledge that, after years of infertility, Ina is bearing Warren's child frees Todd from the sense of indebtedness that had clouded their relationship and opens the way to his imagining a full life with Ellen. He leaves the Brants to telephone Ellen: "As he drew near the lightbathed Square he understood that he was now educated. It could not be given back, no, nor taken. He tightened himself, not to tremble."[26]

Except for a minor character desperate to get a job after graduation, the novel gives scant attention to the Depression. The personal and developmental issues that Weller addresses through Epes Todd suggest their roots in the consciousness of certain undergraduates of the 1920s. However, in the decade in which it was published—the 1930s—the independent mentality that Weller evoked was overwhelmed by undergraduates' response to the Great Depression.

The 1930s saw a marked change in the fortunes of the political college rebels. During the hard times, many students who might have joined a Greek-letter society had to economize, shrinking the ranks of the organized. Rebels were able to mobilize the independents to win power on some campuses, gaining control over some undergraduate government associations and campus newspapers. In numbers the political rebels were few. They led with little following among their own kind. Some gained power by playing it safe within the Greek orbit until elected. Others openly mobilized outsiders from the beginning. Rebels gave to outsiders candidates and a battle plan. What the rebels received in return was votes. Through this route the rebels broke through the oligopolistic control of the Greek system, which, where it was a minority on campus, required the apathy and the disorganization of the outsiders to win college-wide elections.

In the intensely political atmosphere of the 1930s organizational victories became substantive ones. For example, at the University of Oregon, Richard L. Neuberger spearheaded a campaign in the *Oregon Emerald* against the university's compulsory athletic fee. Many college papers and student councils came out for the Oxford pledge, originating in England, that committed its takers to oppose their government in any future war. At some institutions campus organizations supported the April student strikes against war, initiated by radical groups. These became annual events in the late 1930s.[27]

Eric Sevareid attended the University of Minnesota during years of political ferment. The grandson of Norwegian immigrants, he came from the small town of Velva, North Dakota, where his father was the local banker. At Minnesota in the early 1930s he encountered struggle, not of the gridiron, but "the battle, in deadly earnest, with other students of different persuasion or of no persuasion, with the university authorities, with the American society of that time." His college days had their intense moments of exhilaration and bitterness, but of a different sort from media portrayals. Emotional exhaustion for him came "not from singing about the 'dear old college' but from public debate." Whenever he read a college novel or saw a Hollywood depiction of college life, he was "astonished and unbelieving" or had "a faint twinge of nostalgia for a beautiful something I never knew."[28] For in college Sevareid became a rebel.

With like-minded friends, a small intense group of ten or twelve high academic achievers with radical convictions, he formed a tight circle. The group took the name Jacobin Club. It first gained university attention when it appeared on a fraternity ranking list where it received the highest academic average of any organization on campus in thirty years.

The Jacobins turned to campus politics. They took on the Greek system, which at Minnesota was led by a few seniors in the law school. Heretofore, this clique had controlled nominations, parceling out the elective offices among the fraternity brothers and the social honors, such as positions in the line of march at the class dances, among the sorority sisters. "The Greek houses suddenly discovered that while they had been immersed in such matters as the class proms, other students by some diabolical and mysterious means had overreached them and were controlling the really vital instruments—the daily newspaper, the literary review, the law review, the board of publications, the student council, and so on."[29]

As they gained control of campus organizations, the Jacobins turned them to new purposes. They tried to make student government into a real policy-making body, rather than the puppet of the university administration. They turned the newspaper into a radical forum. And they used their support of the Minnesota Farmer-Labor Party and Governor Frank B. Olson to change the composition of the board of regents in order to abolish military training, which had been compulsory for all University of Minnesota students for the preceding sixty years.

Although successful, this band of rebels had one notable failure. For several years the Jacobins controlled the campus newspaper. By "right of seniority," Sevareid assumed that he would serve as editor his senior year. Because of Sevareid's open leadership in the fight against military training, the ROTC and the administration opposed him. The incumbent editor, one of the rebel group, went over to the enemy. He allowed himself to be persuaded by the university administration to stand for re-election. In the bitter fight that followed, the ROTC, the administration, and the Greek system mobilized against Sevareid. In the publication board election, he lost by one vote.[30]

Sevareid and his cronies took politics seriously, but they had a playful side. As part of its campaign to end compulsory military training the newspaper joined in support of "Jingo Day," a counter-celebration to the annual ROTC reviews. At a mock political convention in 1936, to ridicule the preparedness movement, Sevareid nominated Bernarr Macfadden, the elderly health proponent, as a "Strong Man in the White House" and to parade the convention floor hired a bugler, a well-endowed female acrobatic dancer, and a muscular football player. To mock the American Legion and the Gold Star Mothers, he and his friends joined the "Veterans of Future Wars."[31]

Like Walter Lippmann in 1910, the Jacobins connected campus politics to the larger world. Philosophically they were socialists, but on the state level they fervently backed Governor Olson. In 1934 they sympathized with striking truckers, led by Trotskyists. Sevareid covered the strike for the Minneapolis *Star* and was shocked to see fraternity men with baseball bats supporting the police and the Citizen's Alliance against the strikers. When the strikers, running away from a police ambush, were shot with buckshot, Sevareid felt he had seen fascism in the American Midwest.

But not all the lessons were out of school. Sevareid entered intensely into some of his courses. He felt that before college he had learned nothing. He "strayed one day into a class on political first principles" taught by a radical exponent of the Socratic method. Bombarded by questions he could not answer, Sevareid became, like many others, "not only confused, but angry and resentful. Some did not come back to his classes. For those of us who stayed it was not an easy time, but it was wonderful. We were just discovering the exciting world of Ideas, the world of Theory and of Principle." Sevareid began a serious study of philosophy, working his way from the Greeks to Trotsky. "It was a long trip." But through it he learned how to find his way in the political universe. The experience of his first encounter with the life of the mind "was like learning a foreign language after one is grown. For a long time the words and phrases beat without effect upon the brain—then suddenly one day they all drop into place; one can understand, and he can speak."[32]

For Sevareid collegiate rebellion merged into political radicalism. This link went back to early-twentieth-century beginnings. Some initial college rebels had joined the Intercollegiate Socialist Society, created in 1905 by adult socialists to educate students to the cause. In the period from the early 1930s until the entry of the United States into World War II, radicalism appealed strongly to rebellious college youth. Thus a study of the 134 known members of student socialist and communist groups between 1932 and 1942 at the conservative University of Illinois is instructive. Their numbers were extremely small: on a burgeoning state university campus, the average annual membership in all radical organizations was 34. (The activities that they sponsored attracted between 100 and 450.) Compared to their classmates, a far higher proportion of the known radicals were urban, children of professional parents, Jewish, and enrolled in the College of Liberal Arts and Sciences. Not only was their participation in all campus activities lower; only 15 percent of the radicals belonged to fraternities and sororities on a campus where 30 percent of the student body was Greek and where the system dominated campus organizations.[33] University of Illinois radicals of the 1930s thus fit neatly the profile of the undergraduate rebel.

It would be a mistake, however, to identify radicalism in any total way with undergraduate rebellion. Until the 1960s adults initiated and largely directed radical activity on campus through the youth and college branches of socialist and communist organizations. Radicals focused on national politics and foreign policy. By contrast, what defined college rebellion was its stance within the college setting. Rebels were not so much radicals as iconoclasts. They sought to break the hold of campus idols. They took on fraternities, rather than capitalists; the dominance of football, rather than war. Yet, given the temper of the times, many rebels justified what they did in the name of higher causes: they argued that they fought the games of undergraduates because college life served as a distraction in a world marked by cupidity and violence. Despite the rhetoric, the central power struggle in which the rebels were engaged was the one on campus.

Such a distinction was difficult to maintain in the 1930s, especially on the larger urban campuses. Two phenomena blended collegiate radicalism and rebellion. First of all, the presence on campus of older students and young faculty who were committed radicals, especially members of the Communist Party, led to active efforts to recruit undergraduates. Pauline Kael remembered Berkeley in 1936 as "a cauldron": "You no sooner enrolled than you got an invitation from the Trotskyites and the Stalinists. Both were wooing you. I enrolled at sixteen, so it was a little overpowering at the time."[34] College students drawn into the conflict against football became potential candidates for party membership. Secondly, some colleges attracted freshmen who had already been radicalized, a few of whom turned their attention to the politics of college life.

James A. Wechsler, later the controversial liberal editor of the New York *Post,* found himself the object of communist persuasion in his college course. He had always wanted to be a newspaperman and, on his second day at Columbia, headed for the *Spectator* office. To Wechsler at fifteen, Reed Harris and his associate editors seemed "incredibly old and wise." Wechsler next joined the Jewish fraternity Zeta Beta Tau, a decision he later regretted. The house "was the last refuge of an earlier, carefree student time, when young men were expected to devote themselves to love and liquor." Its "infantilism" quickly became "embarrassing."[35]

In his editorials and reporting Reed Harris offered to Wechsler a short course in collegiate rebellion, as, one by one, Harris attacked campus gods. His expulsion by the dean offered another lesson. With a touch of irony,

# EXTRA!

# The Minnesota Daily

*The World's Largest College Newspaper*

MONDAY, JUNE 18, 1934.  Al Kosek, Arne Sevareid, Editors

# COMPULSORY DRILL KILLED BY REGENTS

### By Arnold Sevareid

Compulsory military drill at the University of Minnesota is dead.

It died this morning.

The board of regents killed it with a vote of 6 to 5.

The resolution to abolish compulsory drill and to continue it as an optional feature of the school's curricula was made by Anna Determan, the only woman member of the board.

Mrs. Determan was appointed to the board by Governor Floyd Olson last winter.

The resolution came as a surprise move. There apparently had been no knowledge of it among the many outsiders interested in the highly controversial question.

The resolution, it is taken for granted, becomes effective next October when school convenes again full time.

No reporters from city papers were at today's meeting to hear the vote. Gradually, however, the news leaked out. It got into the hands of the many students and faculty members interested in the problem of drill and rapidly went around the city by telephone.

Since the news go around so late, editors of THE DAILY could not get in touch with President Coffman, nor board members, all of whom were attending the commencement exercises tonight when the news broke.

No afternoon papers carried the story, but it will appear tomorrow.

Apparently there are two reasons for the outcome of today's vote.

One is that Regent Butler from Mankato, staunch opponent of the optional forces, was in Washington today, working on the newspaper code.

The other reason is that somebody switched his vote. Who it was could not be ascertained for certain, but the rumor is that the man was Mr. Hagen.

Last fall a similar vote was taken on the question and the board voted to retain the compulsory feature by seven to five.

So that matter stood during the school year. A new commandant at the armory came in, Colonel Fredendall and the school's military forces continue their work as in former years. But the agitation went on—by faculty members, by church and peace organizations, by individual students, and by the Minnesota Daily, which has waged a fight against drill for the last decade.

Today's line-up on the vote could not be determined, but on the action last fall, the sides were as follows:

In favor of compulsory drill:
Butler
Coller
Hagen
Mayo
Rand
Snyder
Williams

In favor of optional drill:
Determan
Lawson
Murphy
A. E. Olson
A. J. Olson

A group of deans, named by the board, has been giving the drill question study this year and for many weeks word has been expected from them as to their decision. None came and apparently there was no report from them at the meeting today. It was a simple resolution, uninfluenced by any outside group, apparently.

Today's action represents the most significant change in the policy of the college since its history began, as far as thousands of students are concerned.

Compulsory drill is 65 years old—as old as the University itself—and until today there has never been a crack in its hoary armor.

That is—except for one or two minor cracks which had occurred this year, which may have had something to do with today's decision. Last fall, a young freshman, Ray Ohlson of Minneapolis, was excused from compulsory drill by President Coffman because he was a conscientious objector. The president, however, insisted that that move did not represent a "precedent" in his policy on drill.

Several other cases of conscientious objection have been hanging fire this year but none of them have received action by the administration who ostensibly were waiting for the deans' report.

Another young man won a moral victory in a controversy in which he was charged with being absent from drill on two days after signing an agreement to attend. He fought the decision of the administration to suspend him from school and although a "military court" gave a decision against him, he was reinstated by the president, who has since refused to discuss that particular case. The boys' name is Sheldon Kaplan. He is one of the highest ranking scholars in the Arts college.

In the many years of its existence, the military department at the school has turned out thousands upon thousands of cadets. That the number of graduates from the two-year basic course will drop next year very drastically is a foregone conclusion. About 2,500 are now enrolled in the basic corps.

The advanced course will continue, of course, and should remain about the same size since it has been only those interested in drill who have gone on into the advanced course.

However, if the number of basic students drops too much, some of the officers on the present staff no doubt will be transferred to active duty by the war department or to some other schools.

Minnesota is the second "land grant" college to abolish compulsory drill. Wisconsin did several years ago and the basic enrollment there has dropped very much.

De Pauw University made their course optional about five years ago and since that time the basic enrollment fell so low that the regents of the school this year asked the War department to completely remove the military unit from the campus.

And such a possibility for Minnesota is likel yto become the next objective of the group of students and others who have fought against drill for so many years. However, nothing can be predicted now.

The fight against drill this year resulted in a flaring up of sentiment on both sides to new heights, a big rally against drill on the day of the annual military review and a temporary censorship over the Minnesota Daily.

Petitions were circulated among students by cadet officers, asking that the Daily be made an optional paper. With that and the pressure backing the petition from the administration the Daily was forced to say nothing about drill for some time.

---

*Minnesota Daily*, June 18, 1934. *Minnesota Daily.*

Wechsler later recalled his undergraduate sense that the event was "a shattering episode in what we came to describe rather grandly as our 'disillusionment' with the professed liberalism of Columbia."[36]

The third lesson came during the protests that followed, as Wechsler observed the communists mounting effective demonstrations. In college Wechsler became convinced that the world was on the verge of "breakdown," that he was living "on the edge of catastrophe." To him the efficient, self-assured Marxists offered both a convincing explanation and a means of action—"certitude and salvation." By his sophomore year he had left his fraternity and had become a socialist. In the spring of 1933 when Columbia failed to renew the appointment of Donald Henderson, an economics instructor and open radical, the protests of 1932 resumed. Wechsler covered the torchlight parade for the *Spectator*. On impulse he rose to speak in Henderson's behalf. The paper reprimanded him for his breach of reportorial neutrality, but his stock rose among radicals.[37]

By Wechsler's junior year, he had repaired the damage to his newspaper reputation and felt confident of becoming the *Spectator* editor. He came increasingly to feel that his "failure to join the communists was simply proof of my own timidities and prejudices rather than the product of any reasonable objection," that he was bound by his middle-class prejudices. A few days before his election as editor, a young instructor in zoology approached him: "Wasn't it time, he asked, for me to become a communist in fact as well as in spirit?" Wechsler's fears about losing his editorial freedom to write his own opinions were quieted by the verbal reassurance, of dubious logic, that because he would have participated in any decision of the Columbia chapter of the Young Communist League, he would agree with that decision. And thus, he signed the card.[38] In the three years that followed, he edited the *Spectator,* participated in the American Youth Congress, rallied in the spring strike for peace, spent several months on the executive committee of the Young Communist League, worked for the National Student League, and wrote the persuasive and still useful *Revolt on the Campus.* Disillusioned with communist intellectual rigidity and sobered by a trip to Russia, in 1937 he resigned formally from the party.

While Wechsler moved from rebel to radical at Columbia, some freshmen at the City College of New York moved from radicals to rebels. This free, non-resident college attracted the ambitious children of immigrants, and by the 1920s over 80 percent of the student body was Jewish. Some, such as Irving Howe, a student between 1936 and 1940, entered with an advanced political education that had begun in high school.

At City College the "real center" of Howe's life was the lunchroom. His turf was Alcove 1, the hangout of the anti–Stalinist Left, a loose coalition of perhaps fifty Trotskyists, Socialists, and Lovestonites. Next to them was Alcove 2, the territory of the Stalinists, the four hundred members of the Young Communist League. Throughout the day and evening they argued in Alcove 1 about the various issues that divided the Left: the New Deal, the war in Spain, the theory of permanent revolution. "I can remember getting into an argument at ten in the morning, going off to some classes, and then returning at two in the afternoon to find the argument still going on, but with an entirely fresh cast of characters."[39]

Only the peculiar conditions at City College allow us to consider Howe a college rebel as well as a radical. Undergraduate rebellion at CCNY did not mean a confrontation with its tiny, ineffectual fraternity system, but rather the struggle for power with the stronger and better-organized communists of Alcove 2. Just like those other rebels who were creating alternative campus publications, Alcove 1 waged its warfare in leaflets. Howe got journeyman experience as a writer as he waged college political warfare, writing and printing socialist leaflets to be distributed every two weeks or so.

Unlike that of other campus rebels, Howe's education at CCNY had little to do with the classroom. Faculty provided a formal education that was "all right," but "not enough for the time or for us." With a few exceptions, such as the brilliant sessions with Morris Raphael Cohen, Howe learned outside of class. He had a mediocre record because he spent "little time in class and less doing homework." "I'd go to class, sit impatiently for a few minutes until the roll was called, slip out, head for the lunchroom where a political argument was waiting, and at the hour's end race back to get the books I had left in the classroom." Howe did admire Cohen, who retired in the late 1930s, but he failed to make contact with most of his professors. The gap between professors and students seemed "beyond bridging." The students demanded an intellectual intensity that their professors could not meet. "Intellectual to a fault, entranced by abstraction and deficient in the graces of life," undergraduates "educated and miseducated" themselves.[40]

City College was a unique case, an intense concentration of Jewish immigrants' sons learning to speak the language of socialism, taught by a decent but conventional faculty from an earlier era. Columbia, too, in the heart of New York, was a special world. And the 1930s was an unusual decade. In the most unexpected places, political college rebels flourished and created a style that mixed seriousness and gaiety. The Vassar College that writer Richard Rovere remembered from his college days at Bard was the Vassar of 1934 whose students and faculty staged a peace parade. A traveling circus in Poughkeepsie for a day joined the parade: "debutantes and profes-

sors mingled with bearded ladies, weight lifters, and peep-show performers."
Rovere had come to Bard an unquestioning conservative. He "became a
radical almost overnight . . . I am sure that the fact that the Vassar girls I
knew . . . were members of the Young Communist League had a lot to do
with my speedy conversion."[41]

World War II ended an era. Undergraduates who had opposed all wars
their government might undertake rallied to the flag to defend the United
States against fascism and Japanese aggression. Many postponed or interrupted college to join the troops, enter intelligence, or perform war service.
To go to college during the conflict meant preparing oneself to be a better
worker in the national cause. In the war's immediate aftermath, the campus
became the place of opportunity for returning veterans, whose no-nonsense
approach to higher education gave little room for nonconformity.

In the postwar years, radical ideology found few followers. Knowledge
of totalitarianism in Russia and the rise of the Cold War disillusioned many
on the Left. The McCarthy hearings reverberated to make many students
and professors cautious. Wealth and conservatism returned to campus. Upon
the nation settled a sober mood that some students interpreted as a license
to return the campus to college life. Most took the routes of the college man
and woman or the outsider.

As the campus was swept first by war and then by its wake, the nonconforming undergraduate felt isolated, without mentors or allies on campus.
Intense individualists, caught in the drama of their psyches, played out their
conflicts in their personal relationships and in poetry. At Columbia and
Barnard the beginnings of a literary underground emerged, its ties more
with the streets and bars of New York than with the colleges.

One cannot read undergraduate rebellion into the college careers of those
who later were called the Beats. Some of them never went to college. The
painful metamorphosis of those who did cannot be encompassed by college
rebellion because it was too removed from campus and only began in their
college years. Two of the Beats went to Columbia. Jack Kerouac entered
in 1940 as a football hero with literary ambitions. A leg injury ruined his
athletic hopes, but freed him for writing. The war made college seem
meaningless. He left to wander and ultimately joined the Navy. Discharged
as psychologically unfit after months of observation, he continued to flail.
After a stint in the Merchant Marines, Kerouac returned to Columbia in
1944. He took up with Edie Parker, a Barnard student. Through her he met
Lucien Carr, a willful but captivating freshman, and, through Carr's homosexual admirer David Kammerer, the writer William Burroughs.

Allen Ginsberg entered Columbia in 1943 to begin years of pain and search. In crisis over his identity as a homosexual, the effects of his mother's mental illness, and the demands of his poet father, he found allies in Carr, Kerouac, and Burroughs. Encouragement by Lionel Trilling and Mark Van Doren paled beside the pull of his new friends. Despite some praise of his undergraduate poems and recognition of him as a literary figure by college publications, Ginsberg began to live a life more off campus than on. Ultimately it led to his suspension. When Carr killed Kammerer, Kerouac was arrested as a witness and expelled from Columbia. After a brief stint as a married workingman in Michigan, Kerouac returned to Columbia and hung around, living in Ginsberg's room. Ginsberg was suspended for writing obscene slogans on his windows and for harboring Kerouac against college rules. Outside of Columbia, Kerouac and Ginsberg entered into the underground into which Burroughs' drug addiction was leading him. Although Ginsberg eventually returned to Columbia and received his degree in 1948, his college experience had less importance than his life outside, an increasingly disordered life of tedium, anxiety, ecstasy, and danger.[42]

Although the emergence of the Beats into writers and poets had little to do with patterns of undergraduate rebellion, their impact on later generations of college rebels was profound. As the Beats took to the streets and the road, they created a romantic image of the genius, inspired by drugs, sex, and opposition to bourgeois America. By the late 1950s undergraduates uncomfortable with conformist pressures began to gather on campus to listen to Beat poetry and to sing folk music. Struggling to find their authentic selves, they questioned their parents' compromises about sex and drugs and began to experiment. Although the media still focused on either the conformity of American college students or their academic striving, apparent to a few were the increasing numbers of undergraduates who felt alienated from the society and its central values.[43]

One observer of Princeton undergraduates in the 1950s departed from the usual questions asked about students to study the possibilities of their personal and intellectual growth in college. As an alumnus and adviser, psychologist Roy Heath may have been too sympathetic to his subjects and, therefore, may have exaggerated small signs of change. Yet he set forth a possibility with resonance in the past and implications for the future. As he studied his all-male advisees during their four years, he divided them into psychological types, which he labeled Non-committers, Hustlers, and Plungers. He had no interest in collegiate cultures, ignored class and ethnic variables, and dealt with students' self-presentations during interviews and social hours, not their behavior on campus, but his composite profiles bear significant relation to the three male categories of college men, outsiders, and rebels. His Non-committers were conformists and joiners who followed safe paths and held themselves back from intense involvement. His Hustlers were competitive high achievers who worked hard, monopolized class discussion, and saw life as a battle. His Plungers, few in number, were impulsive, moody, inconsistent, nonconformist, and concerned with intellectual integrity.

In addition, Heath isolated a fourth type of student, as both a separate category and a goal toward which his other three might strive: the Reasonable Adventurer. These young men stood out because, unlike the others, they were satisfied with both their work and their friendships. They were connected to the world and had the capacity for change. Heath found that they shared "intellectuality, close friendships, independence in value judgments, tolerance of ambiguity, breadth of interests, and sense of humor." Although able to find personal satisfaction, these young men were hardly bucolic. Their knowledge of the world led to "sobriety and, at times, anguish." Out of his group of thirty-six Princeton men, Heath found seven Reasonable Adventurers among his freshmen. Overenthusiastic, he advanced roughly half into that category by graduation.[44]

Heath told us far too little about his Reasonable Adventurers, giving us no data about them beyond their psychological profiles. Despite this limitation, what makes his study tantalizing is that it raises the possibility that George Weller's Epes Todd may not have been merely fictional and that, largely unnoticed, the independence of mind that began at Harvard in the late 1920s may have been quietly growing and spreading to other places in the years after World War II.

Inner development may be invisible to most campus observers, but political rebellion is, by definition, public and dramatic, and in the 1950s political rebellion returned to campus. By then college life in its prewar forms seemed clearly in the ascendancy, shaping the expectations of entering freshmen. When Willie Morris came to the University of Texas from Yazoo City, Mississippi, he expected it to be like his hometown, "only bigger and better." A joiner, he expanded his field in college to include the fraternity, the student government, the Freshman Council, and the ROTC band. But something began to work inside him and gradually he grew "more lonely, more contemptuous of this organized anarchy, more despairing of the ritualized childishness and grasping narcissism of the fraternity life."[45]

His final moment of truth came when he was a junior. Left naked and tied to a tree out in the country in a campus service club initiation ritual, Morris freed himself and walked back to the university. "It was the last indignity: homesick, cold, alone, naked, and lost, off on some meaningless adolescent charade." From a hill overlooking Austin, he viewed the campus in all its beauty. "All of a sudden, I got mad, probably the maddest I had ever been in my whole life—at homesickness, at blond majorettes, at gat-toothed Dallas girls, at fraternities, at twangy accents, at my own helpless condition. *'I'm better than this sorry place,'* I said to myself, several times, and be damned if I didn't believe it." He did not turn openly against fraternity

Rebels in the 1950s might come with quite conventional exteri-ors: Willie Morris, chosen by the *Cactus 1956* staff as one of its "Outstanding Students." *Eugene C. Barker Texas History Center, The University of Texas at Austin.*

life. Campaigning for the editorship of the *Daily Texan,* "with cynicism in my heart and the tally of the fraternity and sorority vote in my secret ledger, I sought their support."[46]

Like Reed Harris and other rebel editors, Morris used his position to investigate and question critical areas of university life. At Columbia in 1932, these had been football and the administration of the dining halls. At the University of Texas in the late 1950s, Morris turned to the university's relation to Texas economic interests and racial segregation.

Morris' transformation did not happen by magic. As a freshman on the

*Daily Texan* his first job was to read the other college newspapers. There he discovered, among the standard articles about football and homecoming, the minds of rebellious college journalists, bringing to the campus the critical issues of the day. He met contemporaries whom he admired. He had dinner at the apartment of two young married graduate students. Their walls were lined with books, and they talked about ideas. Morris left stirred by what he had seen and heard and embarrassed by his ignorance and naïveté. He went to the library determined to read "every important book that had ever been written." He read tall stacks "in a great undigested fury." He had some fine professors. The university was teaching him that "books and literature . . . were not for getting a grade, not for the utilitarian purpose of being considered a nice and versatile boy, not just for casual pleasure, but subversive as Socrates and expressions of man's soul." As he later reflected on the meaning of his education, he knew it had changed his life. His coming into intellectual consciousness had not involved refinement or ideological change, "but something more basic and simple. This was the acceptance of ideas themselves as something worth living by. It was a matter . . . not of discovering *certain* books, but the simple *presence* of books, not the nuances of idea or feeling, but idea and feeling on their own terms."[47]

For political college rebels, such as Morris, the 1950s were not "silent," but as filled with controversy as the 1930s. Morris' story is similar to that of Sevareid and Wechsler and countless others. Future iconoclasts entered college with freshman enthusiasm, joined a fraternity or sorority, or found themselves excluded, and then opened their eyes to the foolishness of college life. They were often outgoing and ambitious, and their independence of mind pushed them to nonconformity. Once outside traditional college life, they discovered ideas and books and faculty mentors ready to guide them. They linked up with others who shared their vision and set out to edit the college newspaper or gain control of student government. In power, they pledged themselves to treat the real issues confronting college students. This brought them into conflict with the college administration, which, out of conservatism or fear, tried to censor statements or bring the rebels down.

Cultural rebels, less easy to describe because their struggles were more inward and more diverse, withheld their assent throughout the 1940s and 1950s. Nonconformity began to take a common shape on campus in the late 1950s as alienated youth responded to new artistic currents and to the promise of psychic release from conformist America. Less visibly, independent-minded undergraduates quietly pursued their own ends.

Despite the commonalities, each rebel—in 1955 as in 1910—experienced his or her conversion and struggle as if it were a unique experience. Even though surrounded by others dealing with the same issues, the rebels felt intensely alone. Perhaps the personal urges that drew them into questioning made them unaware of others like themselves. Perhaps the bohemian tradition of radical individualism lent an aura to the loner. Or perhaps the intense inner changes that intellectual and personal growth demanded made the experience feel isolating even when one was in a crowd. Despite this remembered feeling, in the years after World War II, collegiate rebellion returned as an alternative for students, as clearly delineated as the path of the college man and woman or the route of the outsider.

# Meatballs and Other Outsiders

In the years between World War I and the 1960s outsiders played a curious role on campus that affects our ability to understand them. At most schools they composed the bulk of the students, but they were often invisible to observers. Few investigators between the wars paid attention to them. Thus, in contrast to what we know of college men, we have little knowledge of outsiders collectively. One way, of course, to learn about outsiders is to see them as the flip side of the insiders: if the organized students had more money, then the independents had less; if the former made lower grades, then the latter made higher. What we miss in this approach is the ability to get inside their consciousness to understand what made them tick. Fortunately the later prominent careers of a good number of outsiders have called forth memoirs that give sharp portraits of college years.

One study that allows some collective understanding of outsiders involved Yale students in 1926. Albert B. Crawford, with the cooperation of student leaders, administered a lengthy questionnaire to undergraduates. Students answered questions about their motivation, the hours that they studied, extracurricular activities, and their families' wealth and educational background. Crawford correlated their responses with their grades and aptitudes as measured by the College Board examination. He learned what others had suspected: Yale students, even in the 1920s, tended to come from the two extremes of the economic spectrum—the rich and the poor—rather than from the middle class. Of the two groups of students, the poor made significantly higher grades, even when they had to work to support themselves. In part, they came with greater ability. But even when Crawford took this into account, the economically disadvantaged fared better academ-

When they arrived on campus, not all undergraduate men looked alike: *Yale Record*, vol. 52, no. 1, Oct. 10, 1923, cover. *Manuscripts and Archives, Yale University Library.*

ically. Crawford concluded that the difference between the two represented, in addition to possible "superior academic potentialities . . . the greater motivation and seriousness of purpose which, naturally no doubt, distinguish the student who is making a very real personal effort to acquire his college training."[1]

As the director of Yale's Bureau of Appointments, Crawford had a particular interest in the career interests of undergraduates and asked a number of questions about family expectations and future goals. To his surprise, he learned that neither the occupation of the father nor parental college background affected grades. However, the specific direction a student planned to take did influence academic achievement. Students hoping to enter a profession made higher grades than those planning to become businessmen.[2]

Some Yale undergraduates, caught in the century-old war between students and faculty, mistrusted the survey. One student commented on the questionnaire that he opposed it "for the simple reason that many of the questions are *too personal,* and also because we, the students, do not know whether or not the remarks within this sheet will be held against us in any way."[3] This hostility may have limited Crawford in his queries, for he failed to asked the obvious Yale question: what relation did fraternity and society membership have to grades? The answer is implicit in his data, however, because wealthy students became clubmen and poor boys did not.

One of the few studies ever done on the unorganized student in the state universities came as the result of rebel agitation at the University of Minnesota in Eric Sevareid's years. As champions of the independents, student leaders petitioned the president to establish a committee to study the social needs of undergraduates and to make suggestions. As a way of learning about undergraduates, the student and faculty committee surveyed the student body. Only about 27 percent returned the questionnaires, demonstrating that most students were either too busy or too uninterested even to respond. A greater proportion of members of the Greek system answered than did the independents, thus skewing the findings in favor of the organized.[4]

Of the respondents, one half of the men and 40 percent of the women students engaged in no campus activity at all. They simply went to class, worked, and went home. Only 2 percent stated that they had no interest in clubs or athletics. Their non-engagement outside the classroom came from lack of time, money, and suitable clothing. Some did not feel informed enough about organizations or activities. Others felt "so aware of their ignorance of social customs and were so uncomfortable at social functions that they preferred to stay away."[5] And so they did, even when the campus affair cost nothing.

A major element limiting extracurricular participation at Minnesota and elsewhere was that many students commuted to campus. In addition, many students, both commuters and residential, worked. At Minnesota 50 percent of the men and 25 percent of the women earned money during college. One fifth of all students—women as well as men—supported themselves completely, working as many as forty hours a week in addition to a full-time class schedule. A University of Michigan student criticized higher education for casting on the working student "a certain stigma . . . a shadow," making it impossible for him to enter into the extracurricular life on campus.

ABOVE

One place where outsiders and college men and women might meet was at library circulation, although they may have been at opposite sides of the desk: Walters Library circulation desk, 1937. *University of Minnesota.*

LEFT

The declaration of war brought together student waiters and those waited on: Duke Union, Dec. 8, 1941. *Duke University Archives.*

Gatherings over bag lunches led to friendships among undergraduate commuters: coffee shop, University of Chicago. *Special Collections, Regenstein Library, University of Chicago.*

Examinations gave no advantage to those with style. *Special Collections, Regenstein Library, University of Chicago.*

"Fraternities, social committees, publications and organizations, all oppose a blank wall to the man who works."[6] The same might have been said for the commuters, although they and the working students were frequently one and the same. Outer barriers, however, may have reinforced inner motivation. At Yale, working students had higher scholastic averages than those whose parents paid all the bills. At the University of Chicago, commuting students—who tended to work for pay more and to participate less in extracurricular activities—had higher marks than those living on campus.[7]

Did outsiders choose their path in college? Some clearly did. They saw college only in terms of getting an education to move on in the world. When I recently asked a prominent historian, who had commuted each day to Case Western Reserve, what college life was like in the late 1930s, he merely shrugged his shoulders: "I had no time for that." His choice, as he remembered it, was only to study and to work.

Others have delineated a more complicated, interactive process between failure to be chosen and choosing. Thomas Bergin, later Yale's Sterling Professor of Romance Languages, entered Yale in the early 1920s with an ambition whetted by Yale football games and college books. *"Stover at Yale* I not only read but practically memorized. . . . I could not fail to be like Dink Stover." But fail he did. As a high school graduate and a townie on scholarship living at home, he remained an outsider. "I never felt that I was truly a member of my class. I played no games; I never sang in the Glee Club, nor heeled the *News* or the *Record."* Although he took part in the freshman-sophomore rush, he had no one to talk it over with afterwards, for he took the trolley home. He went to the organizational meeting for the soccer team, but boots cost more than he could afford. "Up to graduation time, most of my classmates and practically all of the prominent citizens passed me on campus with no sign of recognition."[8]

Yet, with all his poignant sense of loss, Bergin recognized that his was a fortunate failing. "The only success I had in freshman year was in the classroom. I worked very hard and in the course of my labors found that study was the one field in which I could hope to excel." Bergin began to compete in the classroom. What started as compensation became love of learning for its own sake. "By senior year, if I was still a 'grind,' it was no longer for consolation, nor even for competition—for me it was unadulterated rapture."[9]

Some have recalled only the sense of defeat because they could not become college men and women. In 1921 George Kennan, the future diplomat and foreign policy adviser, arrived at Princeton. Coming as he did from the modest middle class of Milwaukee, Wisconsin, his choice of Princeton was unorthodox: he "owed it" partly to the advice of his dean at St. John's Military Academy, and "partly to the excitement and sense of revelation derived from reading Scott Fitzgerald's *This Side of Paradise.*" But Fitzgerald's Princeton was not to be his. A year younger than most of his class, and because he was the last admitted, relegated to a rooming house far from the campus, Kennan was "hopeless and crudely Midwestern." Awkward and slow to learn the system, Kennan "went through Princeton as an innocent, always at the end of every line, always uninitiated, knowing few, known by few." Scarlet fever kept him home during the critical winter months of his freshman year. He returned in the spring to find his class sorted out in cliques. "To these tight and secure little communities there were now few paths of access, particularly to one who was younger than most of the others, behind in his studies, forbidden participation in sport, and too poor to share in the most common avocations." Neither ridiculed nor disliked, he was simply "imperfectly visible to the naked eye."[10]

During Bicker Week in his sophomore year, Kennan zigzagged. First he avoided the process, by absenting himself from campus. Then he rather unthinkingly joined a club that needed members for its quota. Ultimately he resigned and had to eat in the upper-class commons "among the non–club pariahs." As had Margaret Mead in her year at DePauw, Kennan suffered for a time in stoic silence, accepting the clubman's standards that had excluded him: "So deep was the bitterness that one seldom spoke to a stranger at table; everyone feared that to open a conversation would lead the others to suppose that he couldn't take it." Kennan gradually came to feel that the standards applied to him may have been wrong, but he remained under the sway of Princeton's glamour. When, as a student, he read *The Great Gatsby,* its "hauntingly beautiful epilogue . . . of the Midwesterner's reaction to the fashionable East" resonated, and he "went away and wept unmanly tears."[11]

Even more alienating than Kennan's experience at Princeton was that in the same years at Columbia of Langston Hughes, the future novelist and poet. He had a Chinese friend who assumed that Columbia would be open to him, but life in white America had already taught the black freshman that no girl would dance with him and no fraternity would ask him to join. But he expected more from the Columbia *Spectator;* instead he got an assignment impossible, given the racial divide on campus, to fulfill, "to gather frat house and society news." Closed out of Columbia's extracurricular world, Hughes found little to interest him in his courses. "What an unpleasant winter! I didn't like Columbia, nor the students, nor anything I was studying! So I didn't study." Hughes left Columbia after the one year, ultimately to find among Lincoln University's all-black students a life compatible with his ambitions as a writer.[12]

For some, lucky enough to find professors and administrators to encourage them, the experience of being an outsider was liberating rather than crippling. In 1934 Theodore H. White, later the keen observer of China and of American presidential elections, took the subway from his impoverished home in Boston's Jewish ghetto to Harvard. Like that of many before and after him, his was a long journey. White's father had died, leaving the family destitute. For two years after his graduation from the Boston Latin School, White had worked to support his family. Two scholarships whose sum exactly equaled Harvard's tuition opened the way to college.

At Harvard his group sorted out undergraduates into three neat categories: white men, gray men, and meatballs. Theodore White was a meatball. Unlike the men of distinguished pedigree—the white men—who belonged to clubs and went to Boston deb parties, or the high school Harrys—the gray men—who dominated athletics and publications, the meatballs were the day and scholarship students at Harvard. "We were at Harvard not to enjoy the games, the girls, the burlesque shows of the Old Howard, the companionship, the elms, the turning leaves of fall, the grassy banks of the Charles. We had come to get the Harvard badge, which says 'Veritas,' but really means a job somewhere in the future, in some bureaucracy, in some institution, in some school, laboratory, university or law firm."[13]

White's life as a meatball did not mean withdrawal, but intense engagement of his own choosing. Not in politics, not in associations, but in the intellectual offerings of the university. In his own words, he was a "looter." "Harvard had the keys to the gates; what lay behind the gates I could not guess, but all that lay there was to be looted." That meant that he not only worked hard on required subjects; he sought out the courses of famous men; went to lectures, museums, and libraries; and read. Harvard "was a place to grab at ideas and facts, and I grabbed at history."[14]

He was particularly fortunate in coming to Harvard when he did. James Bryant Conant, who had just succeeded A. Lawrence Lowell as president, sought to turn Harvard College into a national institution committed to excellence. Conant had an unusual perspective, for as an undergraduate in the 1910s he had lived in both of the Two Harvards. As a writer for the *Crimson* and a member of the Signet he had consorted with the more literary of the college men. He regarded the luncheon discussions at the Signet tables as "probably far more significant in broadening my interests" than, with one exception, all the non-scientific courses he had taken for distribution requirements. As a chemistry student at Harvard he had worked alongside future scientists who had no time for or interest in college life, and he had admired them.[15] Thus Conant valued college life and believed that "meatballs were Harvard men, too." He set aside space in Dudley Hall for commuters to eat their brown-bag lunches, gave them a house master, the historian Charles Duhig, and thus created the beginnings of a real campus life at Harvard for outsiders.[16]

PHI BETA KAPPA
*Back Row:* Trenerry, Dow, Pratiner, Shahan, Trueblood, Vogt
*Second Row:* Weiner, Wernick, Johnson, Cleveland, Selz, Griswold, Damon
*Front Row:* Moore, Geismer, Dampeer, Schlesinger, *First Marshal;* Davis, Blake, White

Phi Beta Kappa provided a symbolic place where Harvard's meatballs might enjoy the pleasures of fellowship: Phi Beta Kappa group portrait, 1938 (Theodore White seated at extreme right). *Harvard University Archives.*

And then there was what, in the 1930s, Harvard's historians taught—what White could only call "a wonder." "Quite simply, history was not yet considered a science but was still thought more noble than a craft. The professors were a colony of storytellers, held together by the belief that in their many stories they might find a truth. They still cared about students and lingered after class for conversations." White recalled the roster of his great teachers: Roger Bigelow Merriman, Arthur Schlesinger, Sr., Paul Buck, Crane Brinton, Abbott Payson Usher. But most influential and challenging of all was a young man new to Harvard, John King Fairbank, who taught him to think, forced him to read far afield, honed his writing, and polished his manners. "Fairbank approached me as if he were an apprentice Pygmalion, assigned a raw piece of ghetto stone to carve, sculpt, shape and polish. He yearned that I do well." White did, and upon graduation received the Frederick Sheldon Traveling Fellowship, which gave him a year to travel abroad. In the fall of 1938, White left for China, armed with two graduation gifts—a secondhand typewriter, from Fairbank, and from Duhig, the "custodian of the meatballs at Dudley Hall, . . . his father-in-law's worn-out tuxedo."[17]

"Harvard's intellectual upper-class Communists" tried to educate White and his Dudley Hall companions, but they remained aloof from radicalism, on and off campus.[18] Were they typical? Yes and no. Outsiders were divided. In the 1920s, most remained uninvolved in politics, concentrating on their studies, although what support there was for the small rebellious minority on campus came from students excluded from college life.

In the 1930s, despite the Depression, the numbers of sons and daughters in college from working-class and immigrant backgrounds increased, as a generation trained in the public schools matured. The frightening economic situation at home and the rise of fascism abroad lent credence to radical ideology. Socialist student organizations attracted a significant following among college outsiders and were particularly effective in getting them to demonstrate against future wars. Beginning in 1935 radical groups sponsored an annual April student strike, where for an hour students abstained from normal campus activities. It is difficult to get an accurate count of participants, because the only figures we have derive from college reporters, who, sympathetic to the strikes, may have inflated the numbers participating. In 1937 the reporters collectively estimated that one-half million students took the Oxford pledge during the April student strike. When Murray Kempton, a radical student newspaper editor in the 1930s, reflected back on those figures from the perspective of 1955, he deflated the number of actual student radicals to fifteen thousand.[19] Why such a disparity?

As Hal Draper has pointed out, the difference was between leaders and followers. At Brooklyn College, where he was chairman of SLID, the Student League for Industrial Democracy, "the large majority of students devoted themselves to studying and getting their sheepskins and pursuing their personal lives just as if there were no student movement, but even while doing so they could not help absorbing the climate of ideas which pervaded the *political* life of the campus. . . . The tone was set by the small vanguard of student activists."[20] The number of committed radicals on each campus was small, but they had the ability to bring to their demonstrations a significant segment of disaffected students normally outside college activities. This gave them strength well beyond any tally of the membership of radical student organizations. For example, reporters covering the City College of New York April strike in 1935 estimated, perhaps with exaggeration, that 3,500 students, out of a total registration of 22,702 (8,286 full-time), had participated;[21] but Irving Howe counted only 450 radical students in the late 1930s. He disparaged the rest of the CCNY student body. They were either undergraduates "utterly indifferent to radical or any other

William Randolph Hearst hanged in effigy at the University of Chicago Peace Strike, 1933–34. *Special Collections, Regenstein Library, University of Chicago.*

politics, [who] kept faithful to their studies, perhaps hoping for a better future than seemed probable at the time" or were "hopeless careerists (especially, we thought, the engineers), determined at any cost to 'make it.' "[22] Nonetheless, when led by radicals, a significant proportion of them demonstrated against future wars.

College outsiders added to protest numbers in the 1930s, but with few exceptions they did not set the tone on campus. For a brief moment after World War II, however, the outsiders came into their own. Under the GI Bill of Rights, the federal government paid the tuition of veterans. GIs came in great numbers, some 2,232,000 in all, swelling college enrollments, especially at the institutions with highest prestige. In 1948 at the University of Michigan, the undergraduate student body reached 20,000, of whom 11,000 were veterans. In the three peak years from 1946 to 1948 veterans comprised the majority of all males in college.[23]

The GIs brought the consciousness of the outsider to the fore. Their vision of college tells us much about the mind of the outsider in the twentieth century. The veterans came to college eager for the vocational and academic rewards that it offered, but completely uninterested in college life. They were older, many were married, and they were serious. In 1948 at Lehigh University in Pennsylvania, they constituted a majority of the student body: 940 out of 1,336. They injected a new spirit into the classroom, as they listened intently and asked questions. "Even the gentlest of pre-war classroom diversions, such as passing notes, sharing an idle joke, whispering to a neighbor, have ceased. The veterans, it seems, won't tolerate any 'messing around.' " The younger college men mourned the change in the atmosphere. One of them sighed, "Here it is spring. . . . And all we do is go to classes, and study. . . . Those guys don't even know it's spring. They're vets." A comment by one undergraduate suggests that to college men the veterans of 1948 were perceived as had been Jews at Harvard in 1922: "All they care about is their school work. They're grinds, every one of them. It's books, books all the time."[24]

A comprehensive study of veterans' academic achievement concurred with the impressions of students and faculty: veterans did make higher grades than civilians. Again the issue was not native intelligence, but motivation, for the veterans did not score higher on aptitude tests than the civilians. Nor did it turn out to be family background or previous educational preparation. One measure is particularly intriguing: when they compared the postwar grades of veterans (who had interrupted their college course to fight) with their prewar grades, researchers found considerable improvement. After careful examination, they could not attribute this difference to age or war experience. They concluded, "Those veterans who decided to go to college included a larger *proportion* of strongly motivated and academically-minded men than would otherwise have gone to college." Like the impoverished Yale students of the 1920s, the veterans had a reason to study.[25]

Not all veterans, however, appreciated the academic environment of the classroom. Some found themselves impatient with the imprecision of professors who had seldom been challenged by students before. Others wanted a clearer vocational direction to their course of studies.[26]

Not only did the veterans raise the curve; they threatened, in the language of college men, to wreck the school because they had no interest in extracur-

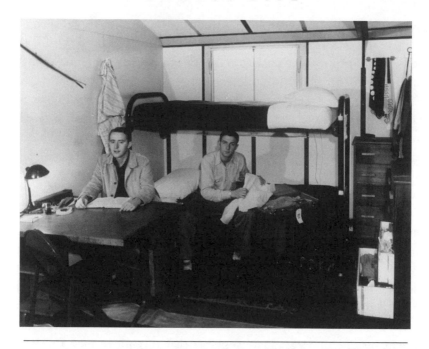

The veterans gave seriousness a good name. *Courtesy Northwestern University Archives.*

Makeshift housing added to the legend of the post–World War II veterans. *Courtesy Northwestern University Archives.*

ricular activities. They did not go out for sports or for the newspaper or dramatic club. They balked at college traditions. At Lehigh they refused to wear the brown cap required of freshmen or light the cigarettes of upper-classmen. When the college newspaper appealed to them to show school spirit, the few veterans who bothered to respond condescendingly asserted that "amusements for 17-year-olds could not be imposed on veterans."[27] Most veterans simply ignored college customs, but a few went further to attack the upper-class vigilante committees that tried to enforce freshman subordination. Their feistiness forced college administrations for the first time to prohibit even mild freshman hazing.

Unlike the ministers of the nineteenth century, the veterans were not moral paragons. Although they worked hard, when they took time off they played hard, drinking and womanizing like soldiers on leave.[28]

The veterans remained on campus only a few years, but they left institutions substantially different from the ones they had found. By the 1950s observers perceived a divided, rather than a unified, college environment. Especially at the larger universities, a significant proportion of students were openly responding to higher education's insistence that it had a critical connection to future success.

This insistence was strengthened by an important and popular study of college graduates. In 1947, as a way of investigating its readers, *Time* magazine gathered data on graduates, which it then turned over to Columbia's Bureau of Applied Social Research. *They Went to College,* the resulting study by Ernest Havemann and Patricia Salter West, effectively demonstrated the monetary value of a college education. College graduates earned more than non-graduates: they held more remunerative jobs and advanced higher in them. This held true even when geography and place were taken into account: "the college man makes more money not only job for job, not only age for age, but also town for town." Moreover, annual income followed the prestige of the institution: those from Harvard, Yale, and Princeton outdistanced graduates from the other Ivy League schools, followed by the prestigious technical institutions, the well-established Eastern colleges, the Big Ten, other Midwestern colleges, and other Eastern colleges.[29]

The study examined the relation between occupation and income. It found that, by one measure at least, in the mid-twentieth century, professional men had outdistanced businessmen: 59 percent of the male graduates over forty who had entered a profession earned $7,500 or over, in contrast to 57 percent of the business executives, 28 percent of the business professionals, and 16 percent of the rank and file. If clergymen and educators—whose median income of $3,584 lowered the total for professional men—were eliminated, then the proportion of older professionals who were financially successful was significantly enlarged.[30] These aggregates did not take account of the potential for great wealth among businessmen, but they did demonstrate how important the professional route to success had become. Although the business of America remained business, in addition the country also rewarded professional training. Those who achieved in college and entered professions assumed the remunerative jobs of a technocratic and bureaucratic social order.

When the authors explored the relation of grades to income and careers, they learned that grades only mattered to some. For those in business, high marks did not affect income. "For all practical purposes, and thinking only of income, the man who plans to enter the business world can well argue that grades mean nothing at all." However, grades did make a significant difference in income in the professions. "Their advantage is most pronounced in the learned (and low-paid) professions," where A students had two times the chance of C and D students to earn $5,000 or more. "In the high-paid professions, mostly law, medicine, and dentistry, they also have a clear advantage. Even in government jobs, they reach the top more frequently."[31]

Campus activities bore a relation to future income—but in the opposite direction: "For the most prominent men on the campus, those who participated in four or more extra-curricular activities, the median income is $4,345. For those who never participated in any extra-curricular activities at all, the median is $5,248! Try to find any justification for the winning-friends-and-influencing-people theory in those figures!" The authors admitted that their evidence may have been skewed because the sample was weighted toward younger college men who had not reached their income potential and included professionals who had little time in college for anything but study. They were nonetheless struck by the fact that even businessmen had not benefited by college life: "It may be that business is more a matter of whom you know than what you know—but obviously you do not meet them through campus activities. Nor does leadership or lack of it in college necessarily imply leadership in the business world."[32] *Time*'s aggregate data confirmed what John Tunis had found about his Harvard class of 1911 in 1936: the "unknowns" or outsiders did better than the college men.

One could argue that the income advantage that college yielded—greatest in the most prestigious schools—really demonstrated the effect of parental wealth on graduates' futures. In fact, those supported by their parents as undergraduates did better financially as graduates: although always better off than the non-graduate, the self-supporting began behind and stayed behind throughout their subsequent careers. But here we see a clear distinction between business and the professions. It was the businessmen who profited most from family backing: "If the self-help student went into a profession . . . he is now doing almost as well as the man who was sent through school by his parents." Moreover, Jewish graduates—the prototypical outsiders—who slightly more frequently than Protestants or Catholics helped support themselves in college, were more likely to hold jobs of higher status and to garner higher incomes.[33] Though family wealth never hurt, its absence proved not to be a bar to those college graduates who entered the professions.

Havemann and West always retained a multifaceted understanding of the American occupational structure, but within a decade theorists drawing on their work were suggesting that higher education had become *the* principal route to position and influence in American society. The most persuasive of these, Burton Clark (sometimes in collaboration with Marvin Trow), set out to examine the new mission of the college and university. He argued that whereas once colleges had served to stabilize class relationships across generations, barring social mobility (a dubious proposition for nineteenth-century America), in the twentieth century colleges and universities had become the principal means of social mobility, opening the way to higher occupations and income. Institutions of higher education had responded to the demands of technology and bureaucracy. They had opened their doors to all students and altered their curricula to offer the critical training for professional schools. The function of higher education, once the production of cultivated men, had become the "training of employees, as colleges and universities become the pre-employment training arm of industry and government— and of education itself."[34]

The new tasks made institutions of higher education the chief gatekeepers of the social order. They had once barred entrance; now they controlled the means of exit. Although the higher a family's socio-educational status, the greater were the odds that its children would attend college, nonetheless, an increasing number of American families from all classes expected their children to go to college. The proportion of eighteen-to-twenty-one-year-olds in college had risen remarkably: in 1870, only 2 percent of the age group attended college; in 1930, 12 percent; but by 1950, 30 percent were in college.

When all could potentially enter college, the way to improve one's chances for future success shifted from mere attendance to the kind of institution and grades. Ambitious youth began to aspire to certain colleges and universities. As these schools put a ceiling on numbers and established admissions procedures, applicants had to compete for places. As the economy increasingly rewarded those with professional training, more college students sought entry. Engineering firms asked not merely for those with degrees, but those who had done well in their courses. Professional schools, once open to all comers, began to set higher standards for admission, requiring not only college graduation but evidence in college of academic ability and character.

By the 1950s the impact of these major changes on the economy and its relation to higher education was clear. Clark saw the college population divided into several different subcultures: collegiate, bohemian, vocational, and academic. Once organizations hiring graduates and professional schools became seriously concerned with transcripts, students were less likely to join the collegiate subculture and more likely to identify with the vocational or academic. "The number of students who can afford to ignore the record is diminishing. As a result of this and other tendencies, the collegiate subculture, whose panoply of big-time sports and fraternity weekends has provided the dominant image of college life since the end of the nineteenth century, is now in decline."[35]

Clark's typology met severe criticism, especially among those uncomfortable with the use of the concept of subculture for student groups. Both he and his critics were right and wrong. College men and women and rebels (the students whom Clark calls "collegiate" and "bohemian") have formed distinct subcultures; the outsiders (Clark's "academic" and "vocational") have not, but have remained within their cultures of origin.

Others criticized Clark for assuming that the meritocracy created an open system and that education actually prepared students for work. One scathing attack, directed less at Clark than at the system, charged education with offering false credentials to preserve existing class relations.[36] Criticism justly deflated the exaggerated claims Clark had made: meritocratic premises may have undergirt a significant portion of positions offering high income and prestige; but in 1960 there still remained an elite white Gentile enclave where academic achievement counted for little and a strong, though shrinking, sector of business opportunity indifferent to credentials. While the years since World War II had seen an expansion of the meritocracy, opportunities outside it remained.

What Clark correctly perceived was that many undergraduates in the 1950s came to college to rise in the world or to sustain, by entering the professions, the class position that parents had gained through business. Their ambitions required them to work hard in college and to try to do well academically. The result was that, especially at large state universities that did not have competitive admissions, an intense grade consciousness was emerging. To certain observers it appeared to be all-pervasive.

In a series of studies published in the 1960s, but based on close observational research between 1959 and 1961 at the University of Kansas, Howard Becker and his associates uncovered the "GPA perspective" of the student body.[37] Students in college experienced different living situations, but they all confronted the same merit system controlled by the faculty and administration. Faced with a threatening situation in which they lacked essential power, undergraduates created a protective subculture that turned learning into "making the grade."

Becker skillfully delineated the transactions by which students altered the exchange in the classroom: for the undergraduate, classes become the "places in which he can get the grades he wants by performing as the teacher wants him to." As the professor instructs, students "search for cues" to learn what he wants, supplementing this information with old examinations, advice from those who have taken the course before, and mutual help. They figure out the professor's idiosyncrasies and his personal style and opinions. During the semester students work to perform as they think the professor wants. They reflect back what they understand as the professor's perspectives in the belief that this will help their grades. If a professor likes controversy, they adapt and take him on, developing not a questioning mind, but their powers of accommodation. They read what they believe the professor requires, organizing their study around the cues they have picked up, adopting "strategies designed to counter the testing strategy adopted by the instructor."[38]

The converse is that they pay no attention to that part of the course that they will not be tested on. As one student put it, "I've got one class where the fellow lectured about one set of things and then gave us an exam on a completely different set of things out of the book. I really don't think I'm going to that class any more. I mean, what's the sense of sitting there and taking notes if he's going to ask questions straight out of the book?"[39]

Students also seek to better their marks by getting "brownie points." They not only curry favor by their classroom behavior; they attempt to get to know their professors out of class. One fraternity man described his systematic "apple-polishing," the form of which depended on the teacher: "Mainly, I just get to know them. I go up to their offices and talk with them. . . . Now my English teacher last year, he was a tough one to figure out. . . . It took me almost a whole semester to figure out what to do about him. Finally, I figured it out. I praised him, that's what he liked. It paid off, too. I got my mark raised a whole grade."[40]

In this striving world, students measured their success by grades. Grades were the currency of education. Students stored them in a "bank," their transcript. Their cumulative account was their GPA, or grade point average, which students at every level knew to the decimal point.

Becker focused on the classroom transaction between all students and faculty in an effort to delineate the common elements of undergraduate culture that crossed all lines. Many of his specific observations still resonate, even after twenty-five years. The nature of his research, however, did limit what he saw. His team of adult observers could not penetrate to the inside of hostile camps; thus he learned little about those for whom grades mattered little or who cheated to beat the system. We find no partisans of "button-down collar culture" at Kansas, though they were there. Nor do we find a Willie Morris.

Becker and his associates did see, however, an important and growing element of undergraduate experience: grinding. Hardly new in the 1950s, it became more visible in an era in which grades increasingly shaped future career prospects. Whatever the genuine intellectual interests of undergraduates—which Becker found to be almost nonexistent at the University of Kansas—they had to protect their grade point averages. To do this, they sought to find out and accommodate their professors' expectations, expressed most decisively on examinations. They calculated all academic behavior, including contact with professors out of class, to achieve the final result, a good grade. At Kansas in the late 1950s, the need to "make the grade" became so pervasive that even the fraternity man bowed to the inevitable, imitating the behavior of the grind whom he had once despised.

The important studies of Burton Clark and Howard Becker had the misfortune of being published in the heat of the 1960s, when educators and the broader public had little interest in students who worked to make good grades or who positioned themselves for places in the technocratic order. Undergraduate radicalism seized center stage and, for a decade, investigation centered on student discontent and protest. The demands of the social order for high performance in college, which Clark emphasized, did not disappear. Nor did the undergraduate response observed by Becker. Both just lay in wait for campus turbulence to cease.

# 9

## College Women and Coeds

Up to now, we have looked at the women who went to college in the nineteenth century and the first half of the twentieth only through the refracted lens of male college life, or as they intersected with male outsiders and rebels. It is time now to focus on female undergraduates. Their experience in college partook of many of the elements of their male counterparts, but it also varied in significant ways.

The first women who went to college were outsiders. Those who entered Oberlin in 1837 differed little from the men. All shared in the life of pauper scholars. When women entered the University of Michigan in 1870 and Cornell in 1872, the college men on campus put them into the outsiders' mold, and to a large extent that is where they fit.

In the first years when higher education was open to women it took a certain courage to attend one of the women's colleges or the coeducational institutions. Alice Freeman exemplifies the pioneer woman scholar. Like the ministers-in-training at Yale, the young Freeman delayed her education until she could earn enough to pay for it. She arrived at the University of Michigan with scant resources. She studied hard. She took interim jobs during vacations. She was working her way out of the family farm by going to college to become a teacher. Like other outsiders before her, she identified with her professors. They, in turn, played a critical role in her career. President James Angell recommended her to Henry Fowle Durant as he gathered the first faculty of Wellesley College. Freeman traveled far quickly and in 1882 became Wellesley's second president.[1]

Few early female collegians had Alice Freeman's remarkable career, but many shared her origins, ambitions, and independent spirit. Olive Anderson, who graduated from the University of Michigan in 1875, captured the life of the first coeds in her autobiographical novel *An American Girl and Her Four Years in a Boys College.* The title expressed Anderson's sense that in coming to the university she and her women classmates were treading on male turf. At the freshman rush her spunky heroine, Will (short for Wilhelmine) Elliott, was pushed against the banisters, giving her a nosebleed: "Would you believe it," she wrote to her sister, "not one of those two

In the early years of coeducation at the state universities, women enjoyed an easy social life, unburdened by rules: Cromwell's mixed boardinghouse, University of Michigan, 1902. *Michigan Historical Collections, Bentley Historical Library, University of Michigan (na 1229).*

hundred and fifty boys offered any help or sympathy, simply because they feel that we are trespassing upon their domains!"[2] Ultimately Will wins her male classmates' affection, and even love. But on the way, she must ward off a passionate Greek tutor, turn away with her revolver a medical student who accosts her on the road at night, rescue an enemy who has fallen through the ice, and slip a translation to an unprepared fellow during recitation. The university feeds both her growing feminism—she cuts off her hair, takes the affirmative in a debate on woman suffrage, and resolves to become a doctor—and her desire for male acceptance on conventional terms. At the end she is unresolved about her future: she goes off to teach in Wisconsin without a clear decision as to whether she will become a doctor or marry.

What makes Anderson's account so intriguing is not only her own ambivalence (never resolved due to her early death in a boating accident) but also her portrait of the independent women coexisting at the university with largely conventional men. In these early experimental years no formal codes or rules separated the sexes. In actual fact, some of them shared the same rooming houses and eating clubs. At Cornell, where male life had not yet coalesced into the fraternity system, the pioneer women enjoyed a rather comfortable, informal social life that included faculty families and undergraduate men.[3]

The first generation of women to attend college held the serious purpose of becoming someone in the world. Characteristically they came from modest backgrounds, but a few affluent young women defied convention to attend college in the early years. Florence Kelley, the daughter of Pennsylvania's robber baron senator, had found in the wastebasket of her father's study the news that Cornell had opened its doors to women. For the next two years, she "lived for it." "Entering college" thus became "an almost sacramental experience." She gloried in the chance for study, her friendships, and the beautiful landscape. College was indeed serious business. "Our current gossip was Froude's life of Carlyle. We read only bound volumes."[4] The wealthier pioneers lived in greater comfort, but their sense of their purpose differed little from that of their poorer classmates. Out of fear of violating propriety, some of them insisted, however, on protecting themselves from social contacts with male undergraduates. M. Carey Thomas, at Cornell in the mid-1870s, worked hard, lived intensely with her female friends, and self-consciously associated very little with the young men around her. Professors and their families provided her chief social life, inviting her to tea and skating. Except for these familial diversions, Thomas kept herself within a world of Cornell undergraduate women, forming at the outset of her two years a passionate female friendship.[5]

Women at Vassar differed from women at Cornell, not in their backgrounds or interests, but in the scale and opportunities the women's college offered. In the large Main building at Vassar College, which opened in 1865, over 400 young women of varying ages gathered. At Vassar and at the other Northern women's colleges, female undergraduates had a chance to define themselves on their own terms. They quickly developed a collective culture that they, too, called college life. It shared the independence and the exuber-

The women's colleges helped to nurture the New Woman: Radcliffe College student, ca. 1900. *Radcliffe College Archives.*

Constance Applebee teaching women's basketball, ca. 1910. *Bryn Mawr Archives.*

ance of male college culture, but it lacked the hostile edge of its masculine counterpart. Women had not participated in the conflicts of the late eighteenth and early nineteenth centuries. They did not see themselves at war with their professors. Thus, though their self-assertion and hedonism conflicted with institutional goals, students in the women's colleges generally took their studies seriously, and they did not cheat.[6]

By the turn of the century, into the expanding women's colleges came greater numbers of affluent young women. Although hardly common among daughters of the upper middle class before 1920, college-going was becoming socially acceptable. Greater wealth changed the college atmosphere, introducing more expensive pleasures—teas, suppers, flower giving —and lightening the tone.

Undergraduates sorted themselves out into different types: swells and all-round girls, corresponding to college men; and grinds and freaks, to outsiders. The swells came from the wealthier strata, oriented to society. Increasingly they built a conventional life for themselves, one that prepared them to become gracious hostesses and guests. The grinds in their commitment to study either resisted this world or were barred from it by humble origins. Freaks, whose derogatory label underscored their class or racial difference, suffered from ostracism as great as any male outsider.[7]

The "all-round girls" formed the distinctive element in the women's colleges. Unlike college men, they did not sacrifice grades for extracurricular leadership. And they learned unusual skills for American women. In the extracurricular world of the women's colleges, undergraduates played aggressive team sports, organized meetings, politicked among classmates, handled budgets, solicited advertisements. For men, such elements of college life confirmed patterns of socialization that led to the world of business; for women, learning the routes of power contrasted with feminine upbringing and led to no known future. Thus, because they broke the canons of feminine behavior of American culture outside college gates, the female campus leaders in the women's colleges emerged as unconventional women. Some entered public life and took up social causes. Their career paths led to the settlement house, social work, and reform politics, rather than to the institutions of American capitalism.

A high proportion of these women remained single, as did their contemporaries in coeducational colleges and universities. In the last two decades of the nineteenth century, almost half of female college graduates did not marry, in contrast to roughly 10 percent among American women in their age cohorts. Why? College women were concentrated in the East, where marriage rates were lower (but never lower than 84 percent), but colleges

drawing significantly from the Midwest and South had no greater proportion of their graduates marrying. Expanding employment opportunities for
educated women made marriage, or at least early marriage, less desirable.
College graduates entered into secondary school teaching, garnering a salary
greater than that of a male unskilled worker. They became settlement house
workers and doctors. In pursuing careers, they postponed marriage. Because,
over time, the pool of eligible men shrank as they grew older, for some the
decision to postpone marriage inadvertently led to single lives.[8] In addition,
for women at the turn of the century there was an accepted alternative to
marriage. They could enter into the female community of reformers and
professional women, a subculture that provided them with companionship
and love and respected their choices and achievements.

Beginning with the new century, a change took place, and the proportion
of women college graduates who married began its gradual climb. By the
1940s this accounted for over three-quarters of women college graduates.
A close study of Mount Holyoke College alumnae during the early decades
of the twentieth century reveals that it became more possible for women
to continue to hold jobs after marriage, especially in education.[9]

But the ability to blend job and marriage is not the only source of change.
The intentions of women on entering college need be taken into account.
A modest study of single and married women graduates of Florida State
University found the primary difference between those who married and
those who remained single was that the single women came from a lower
socioeconomic class than the married.[10] One of the team who studied Vassar
alumnae in the 1950s found just that same difference between the serious and
the social students. The serious ones from modest backgrounds planned
careers; the social ones came from wealthier families and hoped to become
wives and mothers with their college degrees.[11] Observation and research
on women in college in the first half of the twentieth century suggest that,
like male students, they were not all alike. Some came to college to advance
in the world through their own efforts; others, through the efforts or the
patrimony of future husbands.

This distinction points to a critical change by the early twentieth century
in the composition of female undergraduates, a change that reshaped their
college worlds. By the end of the nineteenth century more affluent women
were entering college. We have seen the effect of this on the women's
colleges. Now it is time to turn to coeducational institutions. Once it was
no longer unthinkable, although still unusual, for women to go to college,
they formed essentially two types, complementing their male colleagues.
The lineal descendant of the first coed, corresponding to the male outsider,

In the women's colleges, female students could learn to wield power directly: Student Government, Barnard College, 1916. *Barnard College Archives.*

Even after the first wave of feminism had passed, women's colleges continued to offer female students direct lessons in leadership: Student Council, Sarah Lawrence, ca. 1936. *Archives of Sarah Lawrence College.*

was the strong-minded woman. She sustained the serious purposes of the preceding generation. Generally from a modest background, she entered college to prepare herself for paid work: teaching and medicine in the late nineteenth century; psychology, social work, scientific research, and teaching in the early twentieth. Such coeds fit the profile of the male outsider, and they followed his path. They took their studies in dead earnest, identified

Brilliant future scientists often looked liked ordinary coeds: Barbara McClintock, *Cornellian,* 1923. *Department of Manuscripts and University Archives, Cornell University Libraries.*

with their professors, and looked to the future as the time when their personal dreams would be fulfilled. At the smaller coeducational colleges, such as Alfred University or Oberlin, specializing in moral fervor rather than in college life, these women students were little different from the men. Extracurricular life retained the literary societies, and females participated in them almost as actively as males.[12] On campuses with a well-developed male college life, such women took the brunt of the college man's hostility. Yet it would be a mistake to see women as isolated from male companionship. Though seldom welcome at fraternity gatherings, they might find friends and even spouses among male outsiders.[13]

In coeducational institutions the female version of the outsider existed from the beginning, but the female equivalent of the college man began to emerge only in the 1890s. By the late nineteenth century a new group of young women were entering the coeducational institutions. Colleges and universities successfully convinced middle-class families that their daughters could remain safely feminine even when exposed to higher education away from the protection of home. In part the schools did this by building dormitories on campus and by regulating boardinghouses.

Initially many of the coeducational institutions did not supervise the living arrangements of their students, male or female. They let them board in town, making private arrangements with local landladies. For the venturesome early generation, some of whom had been on their own as schoolteachers, this freedom fit their expectations. But to attract a broader constituency of women students, colleges and universities started to reassure parents by overseeing their daughters' living arrangements. At Cornell, the endowment of Henry W. Sage enabled the university to build Sage College, a comfortable residence hall for women. The need to fill it led the university to set up strict rules to convince skeptical parents of their daughters' future welfare and to require women students to live in Sage.[14] At the University of Michigan, the faculty wives who formed the Michigan League established a list of approved boardinghouses, the landladies of which had to rent only to women and to set aside a public parlor for them to receive male guests. At the turn of the century the League began its campaign for women's dormitories.[15] In these years the smaller coeducational colleges, such as Grinnell and Carleton, moved away from reliance on boardinghouses and built on the campus separate living areas for men and women that located their respective residence halls at some distance from each other.[16]

The coeducational colleges and universities calculated correctly: the middle class began to send its daughters to them. Unlike their pioneering predecessors, these daughters of the middle class brought more conventional notions of womanhood into the college world and the belief that they, like college men, had come for fun. They did not see college as a steppingstone to a career, but as a way station to a proper marriage. Neither they nor their families had sacrificed to send these relatively affluent women to college. Good grades were pleasant to get, but they had no intrinsic relation to future life. Such women wanted to enjoy their college years and saw them as an extension of the round of parties appropriate to their courting age. As they sought to create a college life of their own, they quickly moved to establish

female fraternities that gradually and intermittently took the name sororities. Some women students stayed within the liberal arts departments, and
others went to the normal or education schools or to the new schools of
home economics within the university.

At many places, an obstacle emerged to the creation of college life among
women. On some coeducational campuses a faction of male students were
seeking to create traditional male college life. As they organized their
fraternities and societies, sports, and campus activities, they pretended that

College men pushed college women to the margins of organized college life: *Texan*
force at work (Girls' Edition), Jan. 13, 1925. *Eugene C. Barker Texas History Center,
The University of Texas at Austin.*

only men attended the university. They pushed the women students aside,
barring them from any place where they might serve as troubling reminders
that Cornell was not Yale. What this meant was that women were kept out
of key activities on campus: student government, the newspaper, honor
societies, athletics. In response, the women created female equivalents, but
these lacked the status of the dominant male groups. In time, coeds would
find a new source of prestige, but this awaited changing sexual codes and
the discovery by college men that college women could be amusing.

What were the conventional coeds like? Essentially, they were not very interesting. Unlike college men or the female collegians of the women's colleges, they did not inspire a literature: until the flapper era, they seemed simply too much like the world from which they had come. Vincent Sheean remembered their clubs at the University of Chicago. (The university had encouraged fraternities to provide housing for the men, but had banned Greek-letter sororities at the outset.) It was a coed who had informed him of the anti-Semitic codes at the University of Chicago. She was one of the conventional ones, a member of one of the "better" clubs. "Four or five of these clubs were 'good' and the rest 'bad.' Their goodness and badness were absolute, past, present and future, and could not be called into question." Though at Chicago these clubs had no houses, they nonetheless set the social standard and imposed "upon the undergraduate society a tone of intricate, overweening snobbery."[17]

Women at Grinnell came to college as a continuation of the self-improvement regimens of Chautauqua circles and women's clubs designed to help them become better wives and mothers. They typically chose to concentrate in areas of the curriculum compatible with their femininity: modern languages and English proved the most popular. Only 6 percent in the years between 1896 and 1914 chose one of the sciences. Male Grinnell students resisted the building of dormitories and compulsory dining on campus, but these conventional coeds accepted the changes, for they fit the female students' notions of appropriate accommodations and encouraged the life of female friendship that the young women valued. After college, the Grinnell alumnae moved back home or to another small town, perhaps taught for a brief period, then married. As Joan Zimmerman has concluded, "Going to college . . . did not introduce change into their lives." It was "an act of conformity and not an act of independence."[18] Not a very exciting story.

What is interesting, especially in light of the contemporary gender gap, is the evidence that women students held more conservative attitudes than did men. In 1926, in his investigation into the attitudes of Syracuse University students, Daniel Katz did not separate men and women for the purpose of study. He did, however, look at the differences between schools. The business school, with the largest percentage of fraternity members, housed the college men, largely because athletes registered there; the conventional college women studied in the school of home economics. As well as being identifiable as female, the students in home economics joined sororities in greater numbers than the women in the other schools.

The attitude of the home economics students fit that of the fraternity men on most measures: after the industrious, they, too, valued the active students on campus; in determining the worth of their college activities, they, too, ranked their college studies and contact with their professors very low. They did differ significantly on one measure: the conventional women students were far more prejudiced than any other group on campus.

On his questionnaire Katz asked students whether they were willing to admit individuals from thirty listed groups to their fraternities or rooming houses. The list is an intriguing one, for it included conservatives, grinds, queer-looking students, students with relatives who had jail records, socialists, reactionaries, students of unconventional morals, and members of various racial and ethnic groups. Across the board, compared to students in the other schools in the university, home economics students had the lowest degree of tolerance. Katz contrasted them to the students in the school of liberal arts, who included both males and females. Only 1 percent of the home economics students were willing to admit Negroes, Hindus, or Slavs; only 0.5 percent would admit anarchists, bolshevists, or students of unconventional morals. Twenty-eight percent of the liberal arts students might accept Jews (who comprised roughly 15 percent of the student body), but only 10 percent of the home economics students felt so willing. Although 31 percent of the liberal arts students would not discriminate against shabbily dressed students, only 19 percent of the home economics students felt so inclined. Only 8 percent of the home economics students said that they would not bar another because a relative had a jail record, far less than the 26 percent of liberal arts students who would tolerate such a person.[19] This collective portrait of the attitudes of the conventional woman student at Syracuse in 1926 shows her to be exceedingly narrow, fearful of any associations that might reflect badly on her own social standing.

The Syracuse study is particularly intriguing because it suggests a somewhat different interpretation of women's attitudes and behavior than did others at the time. In the vast number of inquiries into student values and politics at a range of coeducational colleges and universities across the country in the interwar years, not all researchers took gender into account. When they did, they generally found little difference between men and women in moral judgments and political preferences. Taken as a whole, women students were slightly more likely than men to retain their religious beliefs in college, to hold to certain traditional moral standards, to oppose communism, and to support prohibition.[20] They tended more than men to follow their parents' views and that of public opinion.[21] These studies, however, looked at aggregates and did not break down the categories in a way that allows us to see the critical divisions between students. Nor did they pose the questions about values or beliefs in a personal form that forced the students to make decisions that reflected on their individual reputations. At the level of abstraction women differed little from men; when confronted with a situation where the perception of them by others was at stake, sorority women proved to be the most conservative group on campus.

It is important to understand that with women, as with men, the experience of college differed widely among different groups. Female collegians,

The pleasures of female friendship were not limited to women's colleges: Duke women students in dormitory room. *Duke University Archives.*

like males, did not respond to the ethos of the campus as a whole or even of their dormitory so much as to the values of the subgroup with which they identified. As a sociologist discovered in the 1940s, "loyalty to clique codes is of supreme importance to the members, and frequently status in the clique was enhanced by disloyalty to or ridicule of some of the formal campus codes." Although he studied small friendship groups composed of only a very small number of students, these cliques formed pieces of the larger patterns that divided women students into several types. One

Fraternity men made life more interesting for sorority women: University of Texas, ca. 1950. *Eugene C. Barker Texas History Center, The University of Texas at Austin.*

Glowing in reflected light: Celia Buchan chosen University of Texas Sweetheart, 1955–56. *Eugene C. Barker Texas History Center, The University of Texas at Austin.*

group with high literary ambitions dominated the literary associations, but the others specialized in varieties of sociability that devalued academic distinction.[22]

On any coeducational campus, the women students divided themselves into the organized and the outsiders. They further sorted their sororities into a sharply calibrated pecking order. When asked by researchers, University of Minnesota coeds ranked the twenty sororities on campus according to their relative prestige. The women students ordered the groups identically, even if they belonged to sororities on the bottom of the list. Prestige within related to prestige without: all sororities drew from the more affluent college population, but the higher-ranked sororities had the wealthiest members. Those coeds belonging to the more prestigious groups valued most the position the sorority held on campus and the ability it provided them to get dates.[23]

As dating entered the college scene, it fundamentally reshaped the college lives of coeds. Not only did it promise romance and excitement; it established the key way that women gained status. College men vied for positions on the field or in the newsroom; college women gained their positions indirectly by being asked out by the right man. Their primary contests became those of beauty and popularity, won not because of what they did, but because of how and to whom they appealed. By the 1920s the conventional college woman was becoming the consort of the college man. Coeds glowed in reflected light.

Yet in one area they were active. In the 1920s conventional coeds domesticated sex, creating campus codes congruent with future marriage. According to their canons they could enjoy sexual activity—to a point—along with certain symbols of the new freedom: bobbed hair, short skirts, cigarettes, jazz, and automobiles. As Paula Fass has demonstrated, in the 1920s female college students, at least those who joined sororities, did not take up the jazz age simply as liberation. They created around its new elements a code that, however much it relaxed the old rules, still regulated behavior and shaped perspectives. Its new rules allowed a young woman to spend the evening with a young man, alone or in the company of others. She could date a sequence of eligible youths. She might experiment with and enjoy the erotic pleasures of "petting," a new term that included the range of kissing and fondling short of sexual intercourse. To adult critics, such young women seemed to flaunt sexual freedom, but in conventional coeds' eyes, dating enabled them to get to know and choose a future husband. They drew a line that separated them from the promiscuous, a line that required acceptable women to reserve full sexual expression until they were engaged.

One of the more public rituals of college life: the good-night kiss at Stanford. *Stanford University Archives.*

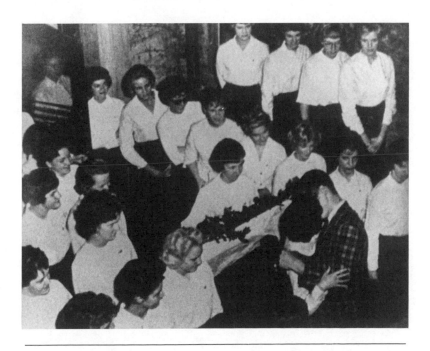

A pinning ceremony sealed the future of a midcentury coed. *Courtesy Northwestern University Archives.*

LEFT

Getting in solid with the women first: sorority rush at the University of Texas. *Eugene C. Barker Texas History Center, The University of Texas at Austin.*

BELOW

Even during the Depression undergraduates carried on in style: coeds at the University of Wisconsin, 1939. *The State Historical Society of Wisconsin.*

And although dancing and cigarette smoking among women increasingly found approval, relatively few coeds joined college men in drinking, and both men and women college students generally disapproved of their doing so.[24]

For conventional coeds college dating created and confirmed the system of prestige on the campus. Though men had numerous ways of attaining status, the number of dates a woman had and her dates' relative social prestige provided the key determinants in establishing a traditional coed's position on campus. On campuses where the women had sororities, fraternity men normally chose dates from those in the top-ranked ones.[25]

The sorority's job became ensuring that all its members were properly eligible and safe. This put considerable pressure on its members to choose conservatively and to conform. Sororities carefully screened out those who might not obey the codes. When Betty, the fictional coed in Lynn and Lois Montross' *Town and Gown,* was pursued by Kuldaroff, a Russian student, her friend Dot from Pi Omega suggested that Betty write him a note to stop his attentions: "I think if you could manage never to be seen speaking to him—maybe I could—fix things." Betty's future social life in college, Dot explained, hinged on this: "To get by with the men you have to be in solid with the women first."[26]

The critical importance of dating underlay the greater conservatism of the conventional college woman compared to the college man. It also explains the difference between the budgets of male and female students. Significant class disparities divided college students. But among the wealthier, whose parents could foot not only the basic costs of tuition and room and board but also the premium for the Greek-letter societies, the socially inclined college men and the conventional coeds spent their money in different ways. He spent his money on cars, movies, and liquor. She spent hers on clothes. In the balance of trade, she exchanged her carefully studied appearance for his evening's entertainment.[27]

Appearance proved to be a tricky element in the college environment. Not content merely to conform to the changing fashions of the larger society, students adopted college fads in rapid succession. This took money and constant attention. Conformity was the badge of belonging. A student who waited too long risked being lumped with the outsiders. At a women's college researchers closely observed the initiation and adoption of fads in dress. They learned that although only a special kind of avant-garde college woman became a trendsetter, her observant, but more timid, classmates conformed quickly, within several weeks. Fad initiators outside of college cliques found themselves leaders with no followers, but those already in the ranks of the reigning groups had a willing audience. Only the most obtuse loners, who participated in no extracurricular activities, ignored campus fads.[28]

Again, such attention to fashion cost money. Sorority sisters spent more than any other group on clothes. The unorganized women, however, spent less than fraternity men. In a study of student budgets at a major university in 1940–41, the expenditures of the independent women on clothes averaged roughly a third that of members of sororities.[29] Looking at the Greeks on campus, a reporter observed that "at coeducational colleges the girls generally dress to the teeth," wearing "all the bait they can, for the omnipresent male."[30]

The canons of college life held by conventional coeds established standards against which women students measured themselves, but such codes did not necessarily determine the actual behavior or attitudes of college women. This becomes clear when one turns to questions of sexuality. Unfortunately, until the late 1930s, there is little collective knowledge. College authorities, fearful of contributing to license, generally prevented researchers from asking questions about sex on campus.[31] Earlier studies had surveyed mature women, long out of college, or had lumped college women with working women. Although limited in what they can tell about college women, these studies revealed growing acknowledgment by women of their sexual selves, considerable concern about the possibility of combining careers and marriage, and the loosening hold of traditional moral standards that inhibited sexual intercourse before marriage.[32] In 1938 Dorothy Dunbar Bromley and Florence Haxton Britten published a study of the sexual attitudes and practices of undergraduate men and women based on a survey administered to undergraduates in five coeducational, five female, and five male colleges. They learned that 75 percent of the women were virgins and 25 percent were sexually experienced. But within these gross divisions, there was wide variation in practice and attitude. Only 38 percent of all women surveyed insisted on marriage before intercourse: the rest who remained virgins were so out of lack of opportunity. Four percent admitted to homosexuality.[33]

A series of group portraits emerges. Of the 38 percent who disapproved of sexual relations before marriage, Bromley and Britten labeled roughly a third of the women "Virginal," unawakened and prudish. Two-thirds belonged in the category of "Wait-for-Marriage" girls, whose sexual feelings were aroused, but who through idealism, religious scruples, or fear of pregnancy determined to hold out. When they turned to the minority of college women who had actually had sexual relations, the largest group was "The Loving," who insisted that love was more important than rules. If to their numbers were added the roughly 40 percent of women students accepting of sexual relations but lacking sexual opportunity, this category would contain about half of all undergraduate women. These numbers from the 1930s suggest considerable deviation from the codes of conventional college women, codes that themselves had changed little from those of the 1920s.[34]

Two groups, moreover, stood farther to the sexual left. Those who garnered the most attention were "The Sowers of Wild Oats," the 4 percent of women undergraduates who were genuinely promiscuous. They reported casual attitudes about sex, frequently tinged with anger against men or self-hatred. In Bromley and Britten's eyes, more interesting were "The Experimenters," out for physical and psychological experience. They wanted sexual intercourse, not to express love to another, but to feel its sensations and probe its meanings. They "have nothing in common with the giddy type of girl who comes to college for gayety and little else. They are interested in psychology, sociology, biology, anthropology, and economics. A certain number are likely to be identified with the student radical movement." They tended to come from middle-class, liberal, accepting homes. Virginity was for them not a virtue, but a handicap to be overcome. In contrast to those who simply sought pleasure, "the young women iconoclasts ... [were] intellectual and conscientious objectors to the time-honored belief that a woman's virtue is priceless."[35]

Thus, the campus of the 1930s was as divided about sexual practices and attitudes as about other issues. During the 1920s and 1930s the iconoclastic student subculture persisted. It included women as well as men. Female rebels were likely to reject traditional sexual morality with its insistence on virginity at the altar and proclaim their right to sexual intercourse not only without engagement to marry but also without entangling commitments.

Moreover, as part of their rebellion against the conventions of both the university and American society, these students self-consciously tried to break down gender divisions. Thus at a time when most extracurricular activities were segregated by sex on campus, one finds some college women knocking down sexual barriers, especially on undergraduate newspapers. During the heady years of the late 1930s, Laura Bergquist, later a senior editor of *Look* magazine, became the first woman editor-in-chief of the University of Chicago's *Daily Maroon*. She recalled her classmate Kay Meyer, the daughter of wealthy publisher Eugene Meyer, who as Kay Graham of the Washington *Post* has had her own distinguished career. Although the society world would have welcomed her, young Meyer chose to study hard, join the American Student Union, and take part in the vigil

# EDITORIAL STAFF

### BOARD OF CONTROL

LAURA BERGQUIST
*Chairman*

MAXINE BIESENTHAL

SEYMOUR MILLER

ADELE ROSE

EMMETT DEADMAN

### JUNIOR EDITORIAL ASSOCIATES

Robert Sedlak, David Martin, Charles O'Donnell, William Grody, Ruth Brody, Harry Cornelius, Alice Meyer, Marion Gerson, Barbara Phelps, Virginia Brown.

### SOPHOMORE EDITORIAL ASSOCIATES

John Stevens, Ernest Leiser, William Hankla, Marion Castleman, David Gottlich, Richard Massell, P. C. Rubins, Judy Forrester.

### FRESHMAN EDITORIAL ASSOCIATES

Lester Dean, Leonard Turovlin, Walter Angrist, Elvira Vegh, Robert Reynolds, Chester Hand, Richard Himmell, Hart Wurzburg, George Beebe, Dorothy Fantl, Leo Shapiro, Phylis Hansen, Ernest Schultz, Dan Mezlay, Jim Burtle.

MAROON EDITORIAL STAFF

*Grody, Himmel, Bertel, Mezlay, Martin, Massel, Angrist, Leiser, Reynolds, Schultz, Dreyfuss.*
*O'Donnel, Miller, Biesenthal, Bergquist, Rose, Sedlack, Cornelius.*
*Meyer, Wolfhope, Kessner, Stevens, Vegh, Brown, Boeger.*

— 98 —

---

The *Maroon* editorial staff surrounded chairman Laura Bergquist in the yearbook: *Cap and Gown*, 1939, p. 98. *Special Collections, Regenstein Library, University of Chicago.*

outside Republic Steel in support of the striking union. Her group of friends were "close, tight, ran to the very bright, audacious, drunk with ideas, short on cash—children of the Depression." On Saturday nights, "like most of us low-budget undergrads," Meyer hung out at Hanley's Bar, "*the* campus *boîte* for professors and students, stretching a glass of beer (dutch treat). There was a lot of raucous singing, amid heady talk of F.D.R., Hitler, Truth, Beauty, Aristotle."[36] The rebellious mode knew no gender.

At certain of the women's colleges during the 1930s, undergraduate rebellion moved into the ascendancy. This may explain why, at a time when many measures indicated that women in coeducational institutions tended to be more conservative than the men on campus, students at the non-denominational women's colleges outside the South were known for their liberalism and occasional radicalism. In 1935, 900 of Vassar's student body of 1,200 signed a protest against the Nunan Bill making a student loyalty oath compulsory in New York State.[37]

At Vassar a strong radical contingent that included a communist cell achieved a certain notoriety, but the best-documented left-wing student body was at Bennington. Daughters from quite conventional backgrounds entered Bennington in the early 1930s with only the vaguest expectations about the new women's college. There they encountered a young faculty, unusually progressive in its politics and open to the spirit of liberation of avant-garde culture. One of these professors decided to study them, not intentionally as participants in a college culture, but as individuals with different personality characteristics forced in a new situation to adapt to change. What he learned turned out to be as much an intriguing document about Bennington life as a contribution to social psychology.[38]

Between 1935 and 1939 Theodore Newcomb gave to Bennington students from all four classes questionnaires that focused particularly on the issue of the Spanish Civil War. He correlated the students' responses with knowledge gained about them from official college records, from other students, and from his own close observation. He learned that the students who wanted to belong and to lead—the conformists—became, the longer they stayed at Bennington, better informed, more political, and more radical. Bennington students were "impelled, with varying degrees of awareness, toward varying degrees of leadership and prestige. The more they are so impelled, the more it is necessary for them to fit in to what they believe to be the college pattern."[39] Only those with no campus ambitions or particularly rigid personalities remained impervious to the radical political claims of the Bennington community.

Because of the growth of the radical student movement in the 1930s and the methodological sophistication of the study, Newcomb's book encouraged a vast industry of researchers looking at political change among college students. But no research disciples took into full account the distinctive quality of the Bennington environment. Bennington was not only a women's school; it was a new college, without campus traditions. It attempted to organize itself democratically along the lines of a New England town meeting. Its professors included young, attractive, single men. They worked both in the classroom and outside to break down the barriers that separated students from faculty. In this setting, the initial college culture that the women created included the faculty as its most prestigious members. As freshmen came to Bennington they faced a highly articulated status system that had faculty on top, bright seniors who associated with them next, and then down the imitating classes. Bennington students would later divide, in ways similar to other women's colleges, into good-time Charlies (who lived largely in a suitcase waiting for weekends at men's colleges), academically oriented students, and bohemians; but this awaited the future. In the 1930s Bennington was *sui generis*. Few other colleges had faculty as consistently liberal. No other college had students, even female students, so vulnerable to professorial influence. The college culture of Bennington combined academic orientation with the spirit of rebellion.

In the years immediately following World War II, political rebellion weakened at the women's colleges but not the tradition of nonconformity. One unsympathetic observer found that during the week undergraduates at the women's colleges enjoyed the various costumes of the "Beast" (reserving "Beauty" for the weekends). The simple explanation of the absence of men did not suffice. For dressing as an Eskimo, an Iowa farm girl, or a member of the Ballet Russe involved a conformity to campus mores. Along with the ease and comfort of most of the getups were their associations with bohemianism. As the observer ruefully explained, "It's fun to look like an intellectual, like an artist, or like a pauper—particularly when you're none of these things."[40] Moreover, sloppy dress served as a uniform to mark the Vassar or Wellesley student, setting her apart from other college women.

As veterans arrived on campus following World War II, women students found their interests ignored. Some veterans brought wives with them to college, and this heightened coeds' interest in marriage.[41] Ideological pressures mounted on women to return to the home after college. In this atmosphere, it took a certain independence of mind for a college woman to envision a future career. At coeducational colleges and universities, such career-minded women identified with collegiate rebellion or remained outsiders. In 1950, when she studied Cornell students, Rose Goldsen found two

The Beast: mock primaries, April 1952, Wellesley College. *Wellesley College Archives.*

Beauties: Tree Day, 1960, Wellesley College. *Wellesley College Archives.*

quite distinct groups of college women, the traditional and the career-bound. The questionnaire that she administered to women dealt with only a narrow range of issues, but she did determine certain important differences among female students. The career women had a higher proportion of academic achievers—double the proportion of those with top marks—in contrast to the traditional women. Their career expectations paralleled those of male students, emphasizing creativity and achievement in work. They were less interested in the status and monetary gains of life than the conventional coeds, who hoped to attain position through their husbands. In addition, in contrast to the traditional women, who generally accepted the rules and held conservative positions on sexual questions, many of the career women were "nonconformists." Their numbers included "a greater proportion of women who indicate a certain irreverence for rules and conventions." Career women were more likely, for example, to regard college rules, more strict for women than for men, as useless. And they held far more permissive views about premarital sex for men and for women.[42]

Female collegians at coeducational institutions in 1890 consisted of strong-minded women and conventional coeds. Sixty years later career women and traditional women followed in their paths. Women seeking careers rejected the canons of college women about work and play. Such women were prime candidates for collegiate rebellion. Activities of unconventional women at Cornell suggest that after World War II certain female college students were preparing the ground for the women's liberation movement to come.

The situation of alumnae of the twentieth century offered one of the clearest arguments for the need for change in the status of women. Ernest Havemann and Patricia Salter West, the authors of the 1952 study *They Went to College,* were most startled by the degree to which women graduates still failed to marry—31 percent in contrast to 13 percent of all U.S. women in 1947. They learned, however, that the single life was most likely among women who went to college before World War I. Thirty-five percent of alumnae over fifty had never married, in contrast with 8 percent of the female population. Though recent women graduates tended to delay marriage until their thirties, they were marrying in greater proportion than their older sisters: only 22 percent of alumnae age thirty to thirty-nine had not married (in contrast to 11 percent of those of their age in the population at large). Nonetheless, although male graduates "were actually more prone to marry than the average . . . the college woman was avoiding marriage —or being cheated out of it—in almost alarming numbers."[43]

For the contemporary reader the real shocker is not marriage rates, but the pay differentials between college-educated women and men that this study documented. The authors considered the alumnae in three categories. Housewives, married women without outside jobs, constituted 42 percent of their sample; unmarried career women, 31 percent; and working wives, 19 percent. Seventy percent of single alumnae with careers held professional titles, but their income profile contrasted markedly with their male counterparts. Eighty-six percent of male graduates in 1947 earned $3,000 or above, in contrast to 36 percent of female graduates; only 1 percent of the career women graduates earned $7,500 and over, while 23 percent of male graduates did. "Our typical working girl ex-coed was nothing so glamorous as a Portia, or a female Dr. Kildare, or a lady dentist. . . . [She] was a schoolteacher." But inequity existed even here: the median salary for female graduates who were teachers was $2,610, in contrast to $3,584 paid to male graduates for the same work.[44]

The college-trained women who worked tended to be single, but by 1947 there were many working wives among the college graduates. They, however, garnered incomes even lower than those of unmarried women, with a median of $2,466. And 31 percent of working wives who were college graduates earned under $2,000 a year. Most of the working wives had no children, including two-fifths of those over age forty. Because their income combined with that of their husbands was roughly equal to that of the housewives dependent upon their husband's paycheck, the authors believed that "many of the working wives hold jobs because of financial necessity." The authors felt forced to conclude that "the working wife occupies a rather ambiguous twilight zone. By and large she does not combine the advantages of marriage with the advantages of a career—rather, she seems to be in the unhappy position of being neither fish nor fowl."[45]

Although female graduates in the work force had advantages denied less well-trained women—the median income for all working women in 1947 was only $1,000—they nonetheless failed to gain the prosperity of their college-educated brothers. The authors had gloried in the income value of higher education for men, but for women a different picture emerged. Beyond sharing professional prestige, "all resemblance between the economic success of the career woman and her male colleague comes to an abrupt end." The authors were clear: "Our Former Coeds are much more successful than the average working woman. . . . But compared with the Old Grads, they were nowhere."[46] In mid-twentieth-century America college-educated men and women faced altogether different futures.

# The 1960s

No one surveying the campus scene in 1959 could have predicted the 1960s.[1] In most places college men and women seemed firmly in place, the student wing of the establishment. Acrimonious debates about fraternity discrimination had exposed a sensitive nerve, but there had been enough stirrings in the houses so that an observer could be optimistic that the fraternity might extend the brotherhood to those who were not white Christians. Less apparent was the softening of lines between insiders and outsiders and growing disaffection from college life. College men and women still proclaimed the value of the extracurriculum and distributed rewards based on service and style, but suspicion was growing that adherents of college life might be missing the real value of higher education.

Visible were the increasing numbers of those who valued academic success. The veterans on campus had gone, but their insistence that they were in college to study and do well had lingered. Their older, dominant voice had commanded respect. Shifts in the economy that continued to create more well-paying and prestigious jobs for professionals strengthened the resolve of serious students to focus on their academic work and leave the fun and games to others. Meritocracy, although hardly the only system, was gaining in power. The official college of curriculum and grades seemed inextricably bound into the system of jobs and careers. Relatively affluent students, who earlier might have joined the ranks of college men in preparation for entering business, felt new pressures to earn high marks to get into law school.

Not only were the outsiders' voices stronger; there were more of them. The democratization of higher education, intensifying after World War II, had greatly expanded old institutions and had created new ones. Especially after the Russians launched Sputnik, talk of growth and excellence pervaded public debate and led to federal and state appropriations for higher education. Expansion benefited most the middle class, but it also opened the way for more children of lower-income groups to enter college. The media image of the late 1950s paid less attention to the fads and frolics of college men and women than to the new seriousness of potential scientists. Scenes of students in laboratories and libraries were replacing those of goldfish swallowing.

Yet among a few observers, all was not well. The sociologist Howard Becker and his team at the University of Kansas found that the students they observed were less committed to learning than to making the grade. Strategies for wresting high marks from their professors determined how undergraduates acted in class and how they approached study.

Moreover, pockets of rebellious youth seemed to be growing. To a society unaware of the persistent tradition of collegiate rebellion, its public re-emergence appeared to challenge the known order. College rebels of the 1950s, as had those of the 1910s and 1930s, brought politics back on campus and again staged demonstrations. In some places, a small but visible minority of cultural rebels was adopting the style of alienation broadcast by the Beats. In the academy and outside, radical or iconoclastic elders such as C. Wright Mills or Paul Goodman greeted with hope visible signs of nonconformity and political engagement.

A decade later, these early signs of change appeared prophetic. In May 1969, from the vantage point of Cambridge, Massachusetts, or Berkeley, California, the social order seemed to be disintegrating. At 350 colleges and universities, students declared themselves on strike. Over half the campuses nationwide experienced some kind of demonstration.[2] Violence or the talk of violence filled the air: students seized university buildings; police, armed with tear gas and clubs, returned them to college administrations. Protesters set campus buildings on fire. To a sizable segment of the undergraduate community, a mass revolutionary party seemed an appropriate response to American foreign and domestic policy.

How did this happen? How had the relatively stable world of conflicting undergraduate cultures dissolved to turn college youth into raging demonstrators disaffected from American society?

First of all, we must be clear about what happened. Because they were so dramatic, appearances during the 1960s were deceiving. By the end of the decade, the majority of college students opposed the Vietnam War. At the height of the bombing of Cambodia, in the conflicts provoked by radicals,

By the end of the 1950s some undergraduate rebels publicly mocked the presumptions of college men: the 1959 Trumbull College Marble Team prepared for their banquet. *The Yale Banner, 1959.*

BELOW

For a time science students overtook college men as media favorites: Prof. Warren C. Vosburgh with two students in undergraduate chemistry lab, 1951. *Duke University Archives.*

a group of students on roughly one-half of American college and university campuses felt enough hostility to national war policy or anger at the response of the college administration to stage a demonstration. On 350 campuses, a majority or a vocal minority refused to attend class and called this refusal a "strike." But divisions still remained on campus. The Greek system, although battered, stayed intact. Many future engineers still went to class and worked for A's. In fact, in 1969, at the height of the protests, only 28 percent of the college population had taken part in a demonstration of any kind during their four years.[3] Media coverage greatly exaggerated both the degree of radicalism and the extent of engagement.

This said, the 1960s were different, undeniably different. And the cumulative effect of events in the decade altered the campus in ways known and unknown.

What happened essentially is that campus rebellion swelled, growing both in radicalism and in attractiveness to a broad segment of middle-class youth. Certain boundaries between competing undergraduate cultures diminished, enabling an even larger number of students to feel a kinship with college rebels, even if they disagreed with their politics. And the hegemony of college life eroded, making it one option, but hardly the most important. The 1960s did not sweep the campus decks clear, but when the decade was over, the pieces on the board took new shapes and fit together differently.

When sociologist and participant Richard Flacks studied the initiators of 1960s campus radicalism, he found that they were frequently the democratically bred, intelligent children of highly educated parents. As children they had grown up in professional households where the demands of success within the American economic and social system had compromised their parents' youthful idealism. As high school students, many future radicals had focused on academic achievement, holding themselves aloof from the group experiences of the popular crowd. They believed in the intrinsic value of education and came to college with the expectation that in it reposed value and virtue.[4]

Although Flacks did not fully realize it, this collective profile describes many college rebels throughout the twentieth century. Margaret Mead at Barnard in the 1920s fits the picture well. Moreover, no sharp line divides the concerns of the 1960s from those of earlier decades. Activist students took up the issues that Willie Morris exposed in the *Daily Texan* in the mid-1950s—radical discrimination and the collusion of the university with major economic interests.

Although the initiating dissenters of the 1960s formed part of a continuous campus tradition, they quickly grew more radical. They sharply increased in number. Unlike the dissenters of the 1930s, their supporters came not only from outsiders but from the ranks of college men and women. These developments changed the terms of undergraduate culture. The changes generated new commitments and attitudes in a broad segment of the college population.

To understand the growth of student radicalism we must look at the undergraduates turning to cultural and political rebellion in the late 1950s. In addition to the influence of Beat poetry and traditions of folk music, there were the arguments of adult mentors challenging the society. In 1960 in *Growing Up Absurd* Paul Goodman offered as a model for American society "an apparently closed room in which there is a large rat race as the dominant center of attention." The successful Organization Men run the race; but they do so, not because they believe in it, but only because "they are afraid to stop." Goodman sympathized with juvenile delinquents and the Beats, who chose in different ways to withdraw from running.[5] C. Wright Mills challenged assumptions about the diffusion of power within the society, asserting that the country was governed not by elected representatives or by local dignitaries, but by a unified "power elite" in positions at the head of key national economic, political, and military institutions. Linked by family, education, and social class, "a set of men who, by training and bent, are professional organizers of considerable force and who are unrestrained by democratic party training" moved interchangeably among top positions and acted in secrecy, unchecked by traditions, institutions, or public opinion.[6] In 1960, responding to the growth of radicalism in England, Mills called on the "young intelligentsia" to serve as the new vanguard to break through the smoke screen of consensus politics.[7]

Certain professors rankled at their duties as controllers of the gate and questioned the direction of change in American higher education. Inspired by modernism, they saw the humane tradition as questioning the culture, not confirming it. They introduced the new critical works to students, and they encouraged iconoclasm both within and outside the classroom. Graduate students, many of whom had themselves been rebellious undergraduates, felt in an anomalous position as teaching fellows, caught between teachers and taught. Identifying more with the oppressed than with the oppressors, some became provocateurs, determined to prick the conscience and awaken the political consciousness of their undergraduate charges.

Influenced by these critiques, college rebels began to challenge not just football and fraternities, but the curriculum. Responding to efforts, such as that of Clark Kerr, to define the university's task in a technological and bureaucratic society, outspoken students opposed the new ends of education. They fought against the notion that college was a factory in which the faculty turned out intelligent and efficient professional products for the society. They demanded intellectual challenge, flexibility, and the recognition of individuality. They asked to be consulted when tenure decisions were made. They began to request courses designed to meet their own agenda.

Political radicalism had remained alive in the 1950s, especially on the campuses of large state universities. Religious groups, such as the YMCA

The lecture system turned students into audience: Berkeley, ca. 1950. *University Archives, The Bancroft Library.*

and YWCA, sustained the tradition of social conscience and kept open questions of peace, socialism, and racial tolerance. Although numbers were small, at the University of Michigan radicals joined the Student League for Industrial Democracy (SLID); at Berkeley they formed SLATE, a student party that in 1957 successfully challenged Greek rivals for student government offices. As the 1960s began, veterans from these organizations were on the lookout for new strategies and new recruits on campus.[8]

The strengthening of political and cultural rebellion inside the campus, however significant, would not have led to broad-based political radicalism and the widespread feeling of cultural change that swept across American college youth in the 1960s. It took three additional elements. Campus rebels as a group had to become activists and then radicals. They had to grow in number. And their support on campus had to broaden.

Forces outside the college brought this about. Flacks calls them " 'triggering' experiences." These turned "previously privatized youth toward collective action and organization."[9] The sit-ins of the spring of 1960, initiated by four black students who attempted to sit down for coffee in a Woolworth's in Greensboro, North Carolina, provided the first catalyst. The moral legitimacy of the emerging civil rights movement was overwhelming, and sit-ins involved direct action by students themselves. In the spring and summer of 1960 between 5,000 and 10,000 Northern students picketed branches of those chain stores that refused to desegregate their Southern lunch counters in response to the sit-ins. The sit-ins drew large, sympathetic support from those outside college life. During the early 1960s white and black students worked together—sitting in, going on Freedom Rides in the South, and registering black voters in Mississippi.

The early battles over segregation and discrimination against blacks moved rebellious college students off the campus and into politics, taught them techniques of non-violent protest, and gave them a complicated, but exhilarating, education about American society. As they returned from summers in the South, some college students felt eager to move beyond the particular issues of their individual campuses to develop theoretical and collective approaches.

In the 1960s campus rebels not only became radical and oriented to action; they began to have a broader appeal. Cultural change was softening the boundaries that separated the worlds of college men and women, outsiders, and rebels. It also helped shape the content and the language of college rebellion.

Into colleges and universities came those born after World War II, the first of the expanding age cohort we now call the "baby-boomers." Followed by American manufacturers since their birth, they emerged fully into the consumer market when they entered college, and they brought their tastes and their style to the fore. A youth culture emerged which created new bonds between once-divided students. College men had always been hedonistic, but they had balanced their drive for pleasure with the claims of authority, if only to remain students. Spread and intensified by the new music, the youth culture disrupted this balance. Popular songs changed their message to the young: whereas before they had expressed inward rebellion

College men and women danced to the new music: Chi Phi party, 1966. *North Carolina Collection, UNC Library at Chapel Hill.*

By the early 1960s, some students were following a different drummer: Sam Hinton with Berkeley students and others in the Northern California woods, 1962. *University Archives, The Bancroft Library.*

against the pressures of conformity, they now insisted on authenticity. The sexual revolution destroyed the older dating codes that had persisted since the 1920s, codes that had insisted upon male courtship, focused upon petting as an end, not just as foreplay, and limited, at least theoretically, sexual intercourse to the committed. Many young people coming of age in the 1960s, with access to the Pill, demanded complete sexual freedom. Sex could be casual, divorced from commitment, out in the open, and initiated by women. Drugs began to edge out alcohol as the mind-altering substance of choice. Each of these moves flouted adult authority, driving a wedge between generations. Confronting a hostile world, young people lowered the barriers among themselves.

As many young people in college began to respond to new messages that encouraged them to reject the suppression of their impulses and desires, style became the symbolic code that identified changes in consciousness. Dress designed to reshape or disguise the body, distinguish between the sexes, and enhance status gave way to revealing, "natural," androgynized looks, demo-cratized by denim. Young men with long hair and beards confronted bewildered parents; young women shocked their hometown friends by neglecting to make up their faces or roll up their hair. In the highly charged generational conflicts of the 1960s, to take one step seemed like claiming the whole. Youths who tried the fashion of long hair found themselves on the other side of a great cultural divide. Many of them elected to stay.[10]

Tom Hayden both exemplified the new forces and captured them in *The Port Huron Statement.* In the spring of 1960 Tom Hayden was a junior at the University of Michigan, a campus rebel moving up at the *Michigan Daily.* Robert Allan Haber, a radical graduate student, got him to participate in a sit-in. Al Haber, the son of a college professor once active in the League for Industrial Democracy, had taken a leading role in SLID since his Michi-gan undergraduate days. He contributed to SLID's reorganization and be-come the first paid field secretary when it emerged under its new name, Students for a Democratic Society, or SDS. Hayden spent a summer in Berkeley among SLATE radicals and returned to Michigan to edit the *Daily* and to found VOICE, a new campus political party. When he graduated, he joined Haber as a paid worker for SDS. Hayden went South as an SDS field secretary. He worked with the Student Nonviolent Coordinating Committee (SNCC) voter registration drive, sending back dramatic reports from the field that SDS then circulated on college campuses.[11]

In 1962 Hayden helped draft *The Port Huron Statement,* which SDS accepted as one of its first position papers. Presuming to speak for all students, it caught the mood of the growing number of rebels: "We are people of this generation, bred in at least modest comfort, housed now in universities, looking uncomfortably to the world we inherit." In an America shaped more by racism and the threat of nuclear war than the slogans of democracy, American children, now grown, "sense that what we had originally seen as the American Golden Age was actually the decline of an era." The statement called on American students to break through their privatism and political apathy to imagine a better world and to articulate the political means to bring it into being.

The SDS creators of the statement envisioned a polity that focused on the full person, replacing "power rooted in possession, privileged, or circumstance by power and uniqueness rooted in love, reflectiveness, reason, and creativity." They called it "participatory democracy," a willed form of decision-making based on small scale and full equality, supported by an economy that allowed creative, independent work. Students had to help the university take a vital role in shaping political ideology and strategy. Given the current campus order, the job was not easy. Those active in demonstrations were "breaking the crust of apathy and overcoming the inner alienation that remain the defining characteristics of American college life." They faced a campus that was "a place of private people, engaged in their notorious 'inner emigration,'" apathetic, living in a "privately-constructed universe, a place of systematic study schedules, two nights each week for beer, a girl or two, and early marriage." But because the university was critical for change, students allied with faculty must "wrest control of the educational process from the administrative bureaucracy," build alliances with labor and civil rights activists, and restore public issues to the classroom in an atmosphere of "debate and controversy."[12]

In its early years the emerging ideology of SDS galvanized questioning college students. Led by former college radicals who had graduated to full-time activism or the pursuit of higher degrees, it assumed a youthful, articulate, challenging voice that appealed to a segment of its undergraduate audience. SDS's loosely controlled network of affiliated campus organizations served as an important base on many campuses.[13] With civil rights groups, especially SNCC, and a constellation of other student organizations, many of them short-lived, SDS helped create the New Left or, more familiarly, the Movement.

It changed political campus rebellion. College rebels in the 1950s felt themselves to be beleaguered, a small minority on a campus indifferent or hostile to the issues they were raising. The Movement provided their 1960s counterparts with a sense of momentum, increasingly radical explanations for their discontent, and linked plans of action. Unlike both rebels and

Mario Savio addressing Berkeley students surrounding the police car containing Jack Weinberg, Oct. 1, 1964. *University Archives, The Bancroft Library.*

radicals in the 1930s, members of the New Left did not intend to educate fellow students with words and pledges. They engaged in direct action to build a moral society.[14]

The first collective expression of the changing consciousness of some college students came at the University of California at Berkeley. For at least seven years, radicals at Berkeley had engaged students in off-campus public issues: the Caryl Chessman execution, the HUAC hearings, state political campaigns, and civil rights. In the fall of 1964 the Berkeley administration informed students—whose political rights were already restricted—that they could no longer use a strip of pavement for outside political activity. Civil rights groups, led by radical veterans returned from a summer's activism in the South, decided to fight the ban through direct action. When police arrested a non-student civil rights worker for setting up a table on the strip, several hundred students (over half of whom had participated in at least one prior demonstration) sat down around the police car, trapping the arresting officers.[15] Within a few hours two thousand students had rallied. As Allen Matusow describes it, "There was shared danger when the fraternities threatened violence, shared singing to bolster courage, shared discomfort during the long night—and the shared conviction that a new community, better than any they had known before, had sprung into being." Out of that conflict, a coalition of student groups created the Free Speech Movement, which drew its leadership from the Left and its language from *The Port Huron Statement.*[16]

Mario Savio, a junior philosophy major who emerged as student spokesman, linked the Berkeley struggle against bureaucracy to SNCC's battles in the South. He saw the careers for which Clark Kerr's multiversity prepared its graduates as "intellectual and moral wastelands," in an America that he called a "utopia of sterilized, automated contentment." In this boring world, movements for change were "the most exciting things going on in America today." They demonstrated that "an important minority of men and women coming to the front today . . . would rather die than be standardized, replaceable, and irrelevant."[17]

Over the next months the Free Speech Movement proved not only exciting but successful. It achieved its limited goal of opening up the Berkeley campus to political discourse. After a protracted series of moves and countermoves, involving student sit-ins and strikes, administrative directives, arrests, turbulent faculty meetings, and Regents' redeclarations of principles, a new chancellor relaxed the rules to allow politics to come legitimately onto the campus. Moreover, out of the Free Speech Movement came the Free University, organized by graduate students, a consumer-oriented collection of non-credit courses in radical politics and self-help. The institution was copied in other university settings. Some of its courses were brought into the curriculum of the University of California and of other colleges and universities.[18] Finally, the Free Speech Movement initiated a decade of debate about students' role in university governance. On campuses throughout the country, faculties and trustees agonized about change. Some rewrote their bylaws to bring students onto committees, faculty assemblies, and governing boards. Although initiated with rhetorical flourishes, such efforts have been more symbolic than real, not altering the basic structures of power that reside in academic departments and in trustee executive committees.

In the course of the 1960s radicals in the Movement turned from optimism to anger. The society's resistance to change gave them new insights. Many radicals turned to Marxism and some of them to violent action. The Vietnam War escalated and spread to Cambodia. During President Johnson's administration, butter became guns, eroding social programs that initially had promised to confront poverty and urban decay. Black riots in many cities left a heritage of bitterness and confusion, as well as vivid reminders of the deep despair and frustrated hopes that underlay the conflagrations. Black leaders of more radical organizations shifted their goals from integration to Black Power and kicked out their white supporters, leaving them with assuageless guilt. Radicals lost their early hope of reforming the system and committed themselves to its overthrow. In one of its critical redirections, SDS turned its attention away from community organizing in the inner city to the "new working class," the professionals who served the capitalist system. As the training ground for professionals, the university became a legitimate focus for organizing. Moreover, SDS perceived the university as deeply enmeshed with the political and economic structure through its corporate and real estate investments, government contracts, military research, ROTC, and personal ties to Washington. Early demonstrations sought to create the moral society by changing university or government policy. Later protests were actions staged by radicals to educate idealistic collegians about what radicals regarded as the true nature of the university and its collusion with the capitalist imperialist system.[19] In some cases, these tactics worked, transforming the consciousness of many students, even of those who only observed.

But far more important in altering the minds of significant numbers of undergraduates than the activities of radical students were the war and the draft. The Vietnam War changed the meaning of authority to many college youth. Not only was the nation fighting a war they judged evil; the national administration was waging it on the backs of young men. Protected for four years by student deferments, college men felt threatened by the death sentence that awaited them upon graduation. This threat became greatly magnified in the mid-1960s when the government—with the intention of ending student deferments for those with low grades—asked colleges and universities to supply rank lists of students. As each young man confronted his future, what might have remained distantly "out there" became immediate and intensely personal. The rational pleadings of parents—to study rather than demonstrate—felt strangely irrational in the face of this future. The numbers of students opposed to the war swelled. In 1967, 35 percent of students identified themselves as "doves"; by 1969, the proportion had grown to 69 percent.[20] For many, especially the privileged, their opposition to the war led to broader questioning of their government, their university, their education, their lives. In the late 1960s, to a lot of students in elite institutions, everything seemed up for grabs.

In April 1968 Columbia erupted. The degree of calculation of radical groups who precipitated the conflict, the level of violence, and Columbia's impact on students at other colleges and universities demonstrate the changes on American campuses since the Berkeley crisis of 1964. In 1968 SDS was deeply and bitterly divided. At its national level it focused now on foreign policy and its connection to the political and economic system. Its national leadership was evolving more extreme interpretations of American malaise that led them into what Matusow has appropriately called "guerrilla fantasy." But new recruits and the far larger discontented band on which it drew differed on questions of both ideology and tactics.[21] At Columbia, led by Mark Rudd, the faction of SDS committed to direct action gained control and precipitated conflict. SDS had staged repeated demonstrations to point to university racism and collusion with the military through the Institute for Defense Analysis (IDA), but had not attracted broader student support.

When the university began building a gymnasium on leased park property that Harlem activists claimed properly belonged to the black community, Columbia SDS found its issue. It called a protest. Radicals occupied Hamilton Hall, a university classroom and administration building. Kicked out by militant blacks, the whites moved on to seize Low Library. A tumultuous week followed: over a thousand students joined in taking over three more buildings; Harlem blacks demonstrated support for the brothers in Hamilton Hall; conservative counter-protesters threatened to oust their radical classmates; faculty tried various strategies to mediate and to buffer student factions from each other and from police. Ultimately in what stands as one of the most terrifying moments in the history of American higher education, police violently restored Columbia to university authorities. Columbia students went on strike. Classes stopped; the university canceled final exams.[22]

Radical success at Columbia led to the cry "two, three, many Columbias" and to similar radical actions on other campuses. Protest reached its height during the 1969–70 academic year: there was a total of 9,408 outbreaks; 731 of them led to the intervention of police and arrests; 410 involved damage to property; and 230, physical violence. Many actions occurred off campus, at places such as banks, corporate offices, government buildings, and induction centers. Many of the actors were not enrolled students. But there were 197 attacks against ROTC buildings on campus. And radicalism appealed to a significant segment of the undergraduate community: 19 percent of college youth surveyed the year before either "strongly" or "partially" agreed on the need of a "mass revolutionary party."[23] The national television networks and the major news magazines reported from the college battlefront with the same seriousness and urgency as from Vietnam.

The media undoubtedly exaggerated the degree of student radicalism. Commentators have correctly pointed out that in the 1960s membership in radical organizations and participation in demonstrations (before 1970) was actually smaller than in the 1930s. However, this comparison with the 1930s fails to measure both the intensity of dissent and its quality in the 1960s. Led by Berkeley, Columbia, and Harvard, the college campuses that erupted in strikes before the Cambodia crisis were those high on the rank order of prestigious institutions. The students who struck often included the best and the brightest. Especially at smaller elite liberal arts colleges and the great research universities, the radical group emerged as the catalytic force that drew in support from the most prestigious undergraduates, many of whom would once have been conventional college men and women.

This was the new element that made the 1960s different from the 1930s. In the earlier era rebellion attracted the iconoclastic and the radical among those whose socioeconomic position might have led them into college life. But their numbers had remained few, and their supporters were found largely among the outsiders. In 1932 fraternity members had thrown eggs at Columbia demonstrators protesting the expulsion of Reed Harris. They began the same way in the 1960s, harassing Berkeley participants in the Free Speech Movement. But as the decade progressed, a shift occurred. While the Greek system continued to attract the more affluent undergraduates of a conservative bent, some of its members—and more of its potential recruits —went over to the camp of the rebels. With the barriers between contending campus groups lowered, an even greater number of college men and women began to wonder if perhaps their rebellious contemporaries were not right after all.

A careful study of student participants in protest suggests that by the mid-1960s they were those who in earlier decades had been the mainstays of college life. Like the initiating radicals of the 1960s, they tended to be prosperous children of middle-class parents.[24] However, unlike the early protesters, activists of a few years later were not high academic achievers. They were well-adjusted youth, oriented toward power and service. "Aggressive, self-confident, purposive, and well organized," they had been student leaders in high school and sought to be leaders in college.[25]

No single explanation suffices as to why, in many prestigious institutions, collegiate rebellion triumphed. The shift in power among contending campus groups involved a decade-long interaction between events on and off campus. The 1960s began with a small, though significant, number of cultural and political radicals on campus, stimulated by adult mentors. The civil rights movement propelled some of them into political action and taught them the techniques of protest and the pleasures of solidarity. Cultural change divided young from old and created a new sense of connectedness among youth. Political rebels banded together to create the New Left, ground it in statements of philosophy and tactics, and extend it on campus. The Movement offered to sympathetic college youth a radical community with a sense of collective meaning and a plan of purposeful action. But American society proved far more complicated and intractable than early optimism warranted. The New Left turned angry; Marxism in its extreme forms appealed to some, violence and mayhem to others. To one faction, the university in its ties to the wider society became the appropriate target for actions to demonstrate to students the structure of the society. The Vietnam War and the draft posed a direct threat to college men, changing for them the meaning of authority. In this context, traditional college life looked to many like fun and games in the middle of war. College life had also become tainted by its ties to the college administration and appeared to be the student side of the establishment. Many shunned the world of the organized altogether. Those who continued to run for office in student government and vie for positions on the newspaper increasingly did so in the name of change.[26]

Adults in and out of the academy engaged in protest. This was appropriately perceived as an extension of their politics in a time of national crisis. In contrast, student dissent was treated as a special case that demanded explanation. A plethora of studies examined the psyche and character, as well as the socioeconomic background, of protesters. Were they rebelling against their fathers or imitating them? Were young radicals healthy or sick? Morally more highly developed or unwilling to grow up? The forerunners of a new era or modern-day Luddities? The answers offered depended a great deal on the politics of the questioner. Those who sympathized found their subjects to be living out their parents' ideals, healthy, more highly developed morally, and in the avant-garde. Those who opposed them tended to see them as rebelling against paternal authority, sick, unwilling to face adulthood, the machine-smashers of the contemporary world. Thus although the connection of dissent with socioeconomic position is clear, its relation to moral and psychological drives remains ambiguous.[27] This is because the pressures were less personal than cultural.

Understanding the ways that contending undergraduate cultures have operated in the past clarifies that protesters in the 1960s were acting not merely out of individual conscience but from within a collegiate culture with its own ethos and codes of behavior. In an earlier era, the power of college life on individual students was such that the president of Amherst perceived collegians as temporarily insane, to be restored to health only upon graduation. Such was the distance in the mid-nineteenth century between the culture of college men and that of college presidents. What was at work was not individual psyche, but the hold of college life.[28]

College life has normally been politically neutral or even conservative, intent on separating the campus from the rest of the society. Its adherents usually won undergraduate elections, although on some campuses, especially in the 1930s, rebels rallied enough outsiders to take office for a time. At Bennington, however, collegiate rebels had no real opposition. Thus Theodore Newcomb's study of Bennington students in the 1930s gives us some clues about the 1960s. Bennington students came from affluent, sheltered households whose politics tended to be conservative. Freshmen entered a society that valued political action and liberalism. During their college years, those who wanted to belong and to lead became progressively more conscious politically and moved to the Left. The higher their degree of conformism on personality tests, the greater the probability that they were informed about the Spanish Civil War and supported the Loyalists.[29]

By the late 1960s just such a dynamic had been created in many colleges and universities across the country. In these places undergraduates entered a new social order in which the authority of college life had given way to collegiate rebellion. Traditional college life had lost its appeal to many. While only a small minority belonged to radical organizations, many more had come to question the established order. The softening of boundaries

Students gathered in the quadrangle at Duke for a protest vigil, 1968 (INSET: close-up). *Duke University Archives.*

between competing undergraduate cultures allowed increasing numbers of students to identify with radicals personally, even when they disagreed with their politics. Prestige and power were in the hands of those who opposed or at least questioned the established order. Affluent, ambitious youth implicitly knew where the wind blew.

James Simon Kunen was just such an undergraduate. Following the Columbia strike of 1968 he published *The Strawberry Statement.* These witty jottings linked politics and style into one irreverent whole. A graduate of Andover, Kunen was a junior when the demonstrations began. He offered this self-description: "Although not altogether straight, I'm not a hair person either, and ten days ago I was writing letters to Kokomo, Indiana, for Senator McCarthy; my principal association with the left was that I rowed port on the crew." As the protests began, he quickly joined in the sport of seizing and occupying Columbia buildings. To his dismay, the life of an instant revolutionary proved largely boring. He tried to find ways to be useful and to amuse himself. One morning he shaved with Grayson Kirk's razor and splashed on his after-shave, "grooving on it all. I need something morale-building like this, because my revolutionary fervor takes about half an hour longer than the rest of me to wake up."[30] His principal relief came when he secretly climbed out the window of Low Library to make crew practice and a meet at MIT.

Kunen seldom let down his iconoclastic guard, which he turned on his own leaders as well as the police and the administration. "Tom Hayden is in Chicago now. As an Outside Agitator, he has a lot of outsiders to agitate in. Like the Lone Ranger, he didn't even wave good-bye, but quietly slipped away, taking his silver protest buttons to another beleaguered campus." But despite his humorist's distance, Kunen became something of a true believer. To the disgust of his father, he grew his hair. In the summer that followed the spring of protests, he found he could not stay home because his long hair aroused intense hostility. His father told him that other people made "bad associations" when they saw long hair. But Kunen found those to the good: "I want the cops to sneer and the old ladies swear and the businessmen worry. I want everyone to see me and say 'There goes an enemy of the state,' because that's where I'm at, as we say in the Revolution biz." Long hair repelled the bad guys, but attracted the good. "I like to have peace people wave me victory signs and I like to return them, and for that we've got to be able to recognize each other."[31]

In the summer as he roamed around attending demonstrations and radical gatherings, falling in love, and getting material to pad his book, he assumed many of the attitudes that fit his anti-establishment persona. He picketed

Hubert Humphrey. He interviewed an assortment of people, and was kind if they were down and out, ridiculing if they smacked of position or money. Somehow it seemed worthy to include such random summer non-thoughts as his reaction to the familiar ad " 'GM—Mark of Excellence.' I started laughing, thinking of an emendation: 'GM—mark of bullshit.' It struck me as funny."[32]

Yet Kunen only toyed with such talk. He was both too independent and too loyal to basic institutions to be a true radical. He liked the honest Columbia dean he intended to hate. Despite his misgivings about Eugene McCarthy, Kunen continued to support him. When told to leave a meeting between Hayden and Columbia radicals, he noted that "the concepts of participatory democracy and of the revolutionary vanguard are not easily reconciled." He closed his book by announcing, "I have a statement to make at this time, gentlemen. Since the First Republic of the United States is one hundred ninety-two years old and I am nineteen, I will give it one more chance."[33]

Kunen was hardly a true radical. *The Strawberry Statement* is a testament to the force of collegiate rebellion in the late 1960s, a force strong enough to draw into its net large numbers of students who in an earlier era would have been the mainstays of college life. Yet, although a good many potential college men and women went over to the camp of rebellion, not all did so. Fraternities and sororities declined in membership, but they continued to draw new recruits into the houses. On some campuses, counter-protesters emerged, dedicated to defending their institutions against the radicals. The socioeconomic profile of the counter-protesters is quite similar to that of their rebellious counterparts, and they share an orientation to power and service. The two differ, however, in that the counter-protesters tended to come from conservative rather than liberal homes; they remained in the fraternity houses; and they were more likely to be engineering rather than liberal arts students.[34] They also often included the athletes, who tended to think of themselves as institutional guardians, there to protect their administration and the good name of the university.[35]

Up to now, discussion of undergraduates in the 1960s has focused on shifts within the rebel and collegiate subcultures. What about the outsiders? They divided according to their purposes in college as well as their politics. Some, particularly those in the humanities, influenced by liberal or radical faculty, supported protest. Yet among outsiders there was a higher likelihood that support might be limited to ends, but not to means, or that sharp ideological disagreement might prevent engagement. An outsider such as Steven Kelman, a member of YPSL at Harvard, kept his gaze fixed less on other

In the late 1960s black students and faculty experienced a new sense of common cause. *Duke University Archives.*

As feminist speakers came on campus, undergraduates struggled to understand their messages: University of Texas, 1970. *Eugene C. Barker Texas History Center, The University of Texas at Austin.*

students than on his faculty mentors and on politics outside the campus.[36]

In contrast, a good many of the students for whom college provided a set of professional competencies—future engineers and technicians—imitated their conservative professors and eschewed politics or took cautious positions. Membership in ROTC declined sharply, but it retained the loyalty of some of those dependent upon its fellowships. The large numbers of commuter students in community colleges and the lesser branches of state universities—who, like generations before them, went to school to enter the middle class—frequently paid no attention to protest.

In the course of the 1960s the black student movement and the women's movement intersected with the New Left and then moved on independent trajectories. As non-black colleges and universities responded to the imperatives of the civil rights movement, many of them rethought their admissions and financial-aid policies to open their institutions to greater numbers of black students. Faculty and administrators found, however, that this just began the process of rethinking. In the early 1960s the demand for civil rights had fired the imagination of politically awakening students, but the movement's force was directed outward to luncheon counters, public facilities, and voting booths. As calls within the black community turned from integration to Black Power, the concerns of black undergraduates came on campus. At those institutions that had recently opened their doors to greater numbers of blacks, student organizations demanded black studies programs, black houses, and an increase in black ratios. At the historically black colleges, students sought greater institutional commitment to black culture and politics. Campuses erupting in protests over the war had secondary conflicts—sometimes connected, sometimes separate—as black students forced colleges to confront their agenda. SNCC, which had begun within the elevated Christian rhetoric of the civil rights movement, shifted in the mid-1960s to the language of hate and guns. The bravado of the Black Panthers appealed to both black and white radicals. Black collegians, torn between personal aspirations for mobility and the new demands for identification with the ghetto, seized buildings and threatened violence.[37]

By the late 1960s black students felt under intense pressure to identify themselves with other blacks and to adopt a militant posture. For some this came naturally. For others it added to the strain of going to college, especially when earlier schooling had not fully prepared them for college work. The combination of high visibility, elevated ambition, academic insecurity, and militancy made these complicated and difficult years for black collegians, especially those on largely white campuses.[38] But it had never been easy for blacks, and for those attending campuses that had formerly admitted only a few blacks, the presence of significant numbers of their own kind may have more than compensated for the anguish. For the first time they began to create their own college world. On a good number of campuses, protest or the threat of protest, combined with varying mixes of genuine faculty interest, led to the creation of black studies programs, offering courses that described and analyzed the Afro-American experience in a variety of disciplines.

As blacks struggled to define their own life on campus, white students responded with varying degrees of sympathy, indifference, and hostility. After the intense early years of working for civil rights, white undergraduate radicals, like their adult counterparts, found themselves in the awkward position of being unwanted, reduced to an unquestioning support of black militants at a distance. Students outside radical circles could only observe. Gradually many white undergraduates returned to old ways. In the early 1960s the moral legitimacy of integration had forced many to confront racism. The turn to Black Power enabled them to return to business as usual. As black students ate at their own tables, socialized in their own organizations, and took courses in black studies, white undergraduates could ignore both their own prejudices and discrimination on and off campus.

The civil rights movement and the New Left attracted both intensely religious Southern women and the Northern daughters of radical parents. Except at the women's colleges, however, radical leaders on campus were men. The ranks of college rebels had always included women, and early collegiate iconoclasm contained a healthy dose of feminism. But many women who joined the Movement in the 1960s found themselves more camp followers than full participants. As they graduated and committed their lives to the struggle, these women realized their own subordination both within the Movement and in the broader society. In the process, they rediscovered feminism and recast it in the language of the New Left.[39]

Betty Friedan had published *The Feminine Mystique* in 1963, but this was read more by suburban matrons and professional women than by college students. The National Organization for Women, created in 1966, seemed to female collegians distantly out there. But in 1965 Casey Hayden (then married to Tom Hayden) and Mary King spoke directly both to radical women and to students. White veterans of SNCC, in their mid-twenties, and active in SDS, both women had established credentials in the Movement. In their "kind of memo" they wrote about applying the lessons "of the movement to think radically about the personal worth and abilities of people whose role in society had gone unchallenged before" to their lives as women and their relations with men. This document reverberated

May 1970: University of Texas. *Eugene C. Barker Texas History Center, The University of Texas at Austin.*

throughout New Left circles, and women began to organize in groups to talk about what it meant to be female. This new wave of feminism originated with those a few years out of college, but it touched women on campus, especially the ones who perceived themselves as radical, and they formed consciousness-raising groups among themselves. By the late 1960s some women students were adding questions about the structure of gender in the society to those of race, class, and power.[40] A small ground swell began that in the next decade would lead to courses and programs in women's studies.

As the media reported on campus protests, they informed (and misinformed) incoming students of what to expect in college. By the late 1960s freshmen were arriving primed by television for the battles to come. The New Left had captured high school imaginations, and some secondary school students were becoming experienced demonstrators. In the fall of 1970 freshmen—who were eleven and twelve at the time of the Berkeley Free Speech Movement—assumed that protest was the established college mode.

Established, but suddenly dangerous. In May 1970 sixty colleges and universities went on strike to protest the United States invasion of Cambodia. On May 4, as approximately two hundred unarmed Kent State University students milled in protest on campus, twenty-eight members of the National Guard at a distance fired sixty-one random bullets at them. Four students, a football field away, died instantly. On May 14, state and local police shot into an unarmed crowd of Jackson State College students, killing two. On campuses across the country, students expressed their horror and their anger.

The freshman class of September 1970 regarded protest as normal. And it was deadly. Suddenly the 1960s became banal. The hold of undergraduate rebellion quickly evaporated. Committed radicals continued to raise issues, but they could no longer bring out the troops.

The campus of the past did not return in the same form, however. The 1960s had reshaped the college world. Fraternities and sororities lost their appeal. For the first time in their history, they declined both in membership and in prestige. Many houses at the lower end of the pecking order closed. Schools suspended college rituals, due to lack of interest. Student government seemed passé. The hegemony of college men and women and the prestige of their activities ended. Divisions still existed between students, but no longer operated to sort them out hierarchically. The structural consequences of the 1960s remained on campus after students had turned from protest to serious study.

# The Nerds Take Revenge

"Grim professionalism" is how Yale president Kingman Brewster characterized the style of college students in the 1970s. The 1970s followed the thesis
of the 1960s as its antithesis. Students were not only quiet; they were
unnaturally quiet. Young high school radicals arrived on campus ready for
action, to find little there. No one was interested in protest. A few diehards
joined the newspaper or public interest groups on campus to find that both
held little respect. Not only had radicalism ebbed, but the formerly secure
place of the college rebel seemed in jeopardy. Despite commentators' analo-
gies, the 1920s and the 1950s had not returned. Although fraternity and
sorority appeal gradually widened throughout the decade, the power on
campus of the Greek system was gone and the hold of the extracurriculum
had evaporated.

What was left? With rebels and college men and women subdued, what
triumphed in the 1970s was the world of the outsider. Long scorned as grinds
who worked for themselves, not for the college, outsiders moved into their
own to claim the campus. Their familiar pursuit in college of their futures
through correct public behavior and hard study became the dominant mode
in colleges and universities across the country. Yet, because the outsiders
now came to college from affluent homes in a conservative era, they would
be outsiders with a difference.

Repression had worked. The death of six students at Kent State University and Jackson State College had a chilling effect. Kent and Jackson State
gave the signal that anyone who participated in protest—not just the radicals
or the leaders—was vulnerable. After the widespread student explosion in

witness to these meaningless killings, undergraduates retreated back to their rooms.

In fact, the killings were only the most dramatic statement of the repression that had battled college radicals for years. This, as well as the seemingly immutable nature of the American political and economic structure and the succession of assassinations that had removed creative leaders, had its effect on student radicalism. In addition, internal destructive forces—perhaps closely linked to adolescent impatience—ate at the heart of the student Movement, turning radicals into revolutionaries bent on symbolic violence. When the draft ended and the Vietnam War wound down, the motive forces that had fueled liberal support of protest evaporated.

The economy went sour. In the 1960s seemingly boundless opportunities had promised challenging futures to college graduates. By the 1970s rising unemployment rates coupled with soaring and relentless inflation put pressures on college students not seen since the 1930s. In addition, undergraduates of the 1970s had the misfortune to fall at the middle and end of the post–World War II population spurt known as the baby boom. This meant that a huge age cohort entered a job force already saturated by those lucky enough to have been born a few years before. Annual reports emanating from career placement offices indicated that there were far more seekers after white-collar employment than there were jobs. Saturation of the academic market ended for all but a very few the chance to draw out education in graduate school as a preparation for scholarship.

Parents began to pressure their progeny to aim for the sure berths to upper-middle-class status, the professions. Undergraduates of the 1970s were the first college generation born largely of college-educated parents. A fair number of fathers had gone to college under the GI Bill after World War II. The veterans had disdained college life and had placed a high value on the utility of the curriculum. They had entered college to gain professional and vocational skills. Now they insisted that their children follow their lead. They had been in a hurry. Now they hurried their children. Gone was the once-honored moratorium after college that gave youths two years or so to experiment, do good, or find themselves before embarking on a career. Instead, parents of the 1970s insisted that their children immediately secure their futures with professional school or a remunerative job.

Part of the pressure came at least implicitly from the negative examples that many collegians of the 1960s set for younger relatives. Students entering college in the 1970s had brothers and sisters and cousins who had become the seeming victims of the 1960s. To their aspiring parents and relations, the knowledge that once-talented children now languished in low-paying jobs

Students of the 1970s tried to balance academic seriousness with personal freedom: a University of Texas coed reads the Cliff Notes to *Crime and Punishment* in her carefully decorated room. *Eugene C. Barker Texas History Center, The University of Texas at Austin.*

cut deep. In elders' eyes the real direction in which the student Movement had led was downward social mobility. Each family had its exemplary characters: the hippy or radical dropout eking out a modest living in Chicago; the hardworking engineer who had ignored protest and now lived the good life, with two cars and a boat, in Winnetka. The bad student and the good. Some undergraduates tried to resist the messages that their elders were sending them, but many succumbed to the lessons. They came to college as serious as any immigrant commuter in 1910. College was the place for courses. If one chose subjects well, studied hard, and stayed out of trouble, then college would enable advancement to the next level—medical or law school. Hard work there meant a good life to come. Defer pleasure. Be good, at least in the presence of professors. Julian Sturtevant, the Jewish grinds, and the veterans would have felt at home: in the 1970s the outsider won.

A critical difference, however, was that college students in the 1970s did not need to protect their private lives. The ending of curfews and parietal rules in the 1960s meant that professors and deans no longer involved themselves in monitoring students outside of class. The emergence into the academy of younger professors whose formative experiences had been in the 1960s meant that some faculty were accepting of student hedonism and available for personal counseling. The potential for a new, sympathetic relationship between teachers and taught largely remained unrealized, however. Just as college men in the late nineteenth century had failed to perceive that their professors no longer felt themselves combatants in a war against students, so, too, did 1970s undergraduates presume that their professors were as straitlaced as their parents.

The Pill and the sexual revolution did not disappear in the 1970s. In fact, in 1979 college students were socially more liberal than in the 1960s. Roughly half believed that sex was "ok if people like each other," and approved of couples living together before marriage.[1] An intensive study at Cornell of cohabitation—defined as "having shared a bedroom and/or bed with someone of the opposite sex (to whom one was not married) for four or more nights a week for three or more consecutive months"—found that 31 percent of the sample had cohabited. Of these, 90 percent had sensed no disapproval of their choice from other students or from the university's administration. Even more striking, only 7 percent of those who had not cohabited had been constrained by their feeling that to do so was "morally wrong."[2] College students of the 1970s resembled other Americans. The broader society began to catch up with America's youth as polls reflected both increasing disinterest in female virginity and growing acceptance of premarital sexual intercourse.[3] In some college dormitories and apartments only the presence of roommates limited heterosexual cohabitation.

Yet exploitation and anarchy lay on the other side of freedom. College women in the 1970s experienced new dilemmas as they tried to find their way through the sexual minefield. September of Joyce Maynard's freshman year gave a brief "catching-up period" to the sexually inexperienced, as young men and women frantically grabbed each other and rushed into bed. "It was maybe the last chance to be clumsy and amateurish and virginal. After that, you entered the professional league where, if you weren't a pro, you had a problem." As she staggered sleeping hours with her roommate and her roommate's boyfriend she realized that she, "the one who slept alone . . . was the embarrassed one."[4] To make young women's choices even more complicated, on some campuses lesbianism emerged not just as an alternative possibility but as a politically correct choice. In the highly charged college atmosphere, this linkage confused undergraduate women not only about their sexuality but about their politics. Some heterosexual female collegians began to shun feminism because of their fear that asserting it might brand them as lesbian.

Colleges generally did not attempt to police the drug traffic on or off campus. Christopher Buckley, later an *Esquire* editor and Republican speechwriter, recalled that at Yale in the early 1970s, "eventhough marijuana smoke grew so thick that it set off fire alarms, no one was kicked out for smoking pot or dropping acid. . . . The rumor was that New Haven cops had to notify the campus cops if they were going to bust any students, and that the campus cops always notified the student in time for him to clean out his room. I suspect this was nonsense. . . . But I don't think anyone was ever busted."[5] Drug use was hardly confined to campus. A comprehensive survey of high school seniors in the late 1970s found that six in ten had tried marijuana, and one of three had used it at least twenty times. More than a third of the seniors had also sampled another illicit drug. Drug use was heaviest among those not bound for college.[6] Although half the students surveyed in 1979 favored the legalization of marijuana, undergraduates seeking escape made a shift during the decade from illegal drugs to legal alcohol—and learned of its potency.[7] In 1979 a survey of the students at four Florida universities found that more than 80 percent of them drank, 40 percent "specifically 'to get high,' " and 13 percent to excess.[8] Collegians had always wanted college authorities to get off their backs and let them conduct their private lives. In the 1970s they got their wish. As a result, classroom docility contrasted even more sharply with raising hell on the weekends.

College students could feel that because they had control over their "life style," they had not sold out to the system.

The curious nature of the undergraduate community speeded up the transition from the 1960s to the 1970s. Over one quarter of the college student body turns over each year. What in other societies would have gradually seeped in came with a flood of freshmen. Commentators noted a change beginning in 1970–71; by the following year, the 1960s were decisively over. In the fall of 1972, when the future *New York Times* writer Michiko Kakutani entered Yale, "the banners spray-painted 'Shut Down' and 'Solidarity,' which had hung from the rafters, were gone from the dining halls, and most of the old SDS leaders had graduated. . . . A visiting reporter characterized the student mood as 'disappointed, disillusioned, drained and exhausted,' and Kingman Brewster began to decry 'grim professionalism' instead of the inability of black revolutionaries to get a fair trial."[9]

Demographic changes reinforced this sea change in the tone of undergraduate life. Just as the middle class is always rising in the history of modern Europe, so, too, are the non-traditional students always gaining in number in American colleges and universities. During the decade of the 1970s more Americans than ever before attended college. In 1979 almost 11.7 million entered, 42 percent more than the almost 8 million ten years before. More than half held jobs; over 40 percent went to some classes at night. A greater proportion were black, female, and adults over twenty-five. Only roughly one-third of all students lived either in dormitories or in fraternity or sorority houses; a greater proportion resided on their own in rooming houses, apartments, or houses; 28 percent lived with their parents or members of their family. Community colleges and the less prestigious branches of state institutions took many of these less affluent, less conventional students.[10] Such undergraduates have never shown much interest in college life, of either the traditional or the rebellious variety. They have come to college with vocational goals and have generally stayed within the culture of their homes. College has been for them a steppingstone to becoming somebody in the world. Students out to make it have often expressed their hopes for the future in monetary or materialistic terms.

The goals of students in college shifted significantly after 1970. By 1976 students thought it more important to acquire "training and skills for an occupation" and get a "detailed grasp of a special field" than to get along with people or formulate life goals, their strongest preferences in 1969. As they chose courses, they turned to business, engineering, and scientific and technical fields, rather than the humanities and the less career-oriented of the social sciences.[11]

Earlier generations of upwardly mobile students had shared this vocational perception of higher education, but collegians in the 1970s seemed distinctively selfish. Arthur Levine, one of their most astute observers and critics, has called this a "lifeboat mentality": "Each student is alone in a boat in a terrible storm, far from the nearest harbor. Each boat is beginning to take on water. There is but one alternative: each student must singlemindedly bail. Conditions are so bad that no one has time to care for others who may also be foundering." Unlike undergraduates in earlier eras, collegians in the 1970s held high hopes for personal achievement at the same time that they were deeply pessimistic about the future of the society. In describing this, Levine shifted his nautical analogy: 1970s students wanted to go "first class on the *Titanic.*"[12]

Since 1966 millions of college freshmen have been subjected to an annual survey conducted by Alexander W. Astin and sponsored by the Graduate School of Education at UCLA and the American Council on Education. During the 1970s the survey recorded their growing withdrawal from political concerns. Follow-up surveys of seniors showed them to be even more focused than freshmen on personal success. Astin called 1970s undergraduates "the new realists."[13]

When a team of researchers headed by Dean R. Hoge replicated the Cornell Study of 1952 in 1968–69 and again in 1974 and 1979, it found a striking contrast between the 1960s and the 1970s. Like students in the 1950s, those of the 1970s had, to a significant degree, returned to "privatism": they were committed to family, leisure, and career, but "oblivious to broader social or ideological interests." Though to a lesser degree than in 1952, in the 1970s undergraduates returned to religious belief (though not formal practice), "faith in government and the military," and "support for free enterprise." Respondents in the 1970s valued personal freedoms, but they showed "no sign of much moral obligation for the environment or for over-population and no sign of new commitment to work for social betterment." In their "weakened sense of social responsibility" Hoge perceived that students of the 1970s were not a return to the 1950s.[14]

The aspirations of college students in the 1970s reflected their outsider mentality. When queried, they unhesitatingly expressed their overriding interest in their own careers and the desire to make money. In 1979, 63 percent of entering freshmen gave as an "essential or very important objective" the desire to be prosperous, in contrast to only 45 percent a decade before. Far less concerned with developing a philosophy of life than in 1969, students looked to careers in the professions and in management. They were attracted to such jobs not by notions of public service, but because they held glitter and offered "perks." Overwhelmingly, students surveyed in 1979 stated that they "would rather become authorities in their field or obtain recognition from their colleagues than make a theoretical contribution to science, create artistic works, achieve in the performing arts, or write original works."[15]

This nature of the outsider mentality explains their political temper. Unlike the college men who willfully ignore the politics and conflicts of the broader society to focus on struggles for prestige on campus, outsiders never cushion themselves from the world. They retain their cultures of origin in college. Their attitudes reflect those of the adult society. When times have been hopeful, they have been hopeful. For example, in the Progressive period around 1910, many outsiders imagined careers linking professions and public service. When the hard times of the Depression came, reporters found such students to be grim, worried about their personal futures or determined to change the broader society. In the 1970s they faced an adulthood endangered by rising inflation and unemployment. Moreover, with the re-emergence of political conservatism, they confronted the collapse of federal commitment to broader social welfare and the return of an ideology emphasizing the patriotism of personal selfishness. College students did not create the "Me-ism" of the decade; it merely came with them to campus.

What made the college world in the 1970s so different is not only that it drew conservative messages from American society but also that the mentality of the outsider, shaped by the broader culture, was not effectively balanced either by traditional collegiate culture or by its rebellious alternative. In contrast to earlier periods, outsiders emerged as the dominant voice. The other types of students continued to exist, but they were now subordinate. Most significant of all, the ranks of outsiders spread to include those who in preceding decades were college men and women or rebels.

Why and how did this happen? Three elements are critical to the answer. Processes of the 1960s left traditional college life in disarray. The women's movement began to have a profound impact on college students. And the claims of the meritocracy now appeared invincible.

As increasing numbers of students moved out of fraternity and sorority houses in the 1960s to engage in protest or to enjoy a more independent life, the balance of power on many campuses shifted. The old collegiate culture never died, but it shrank precipitously, and as it did, it lost its hold. Some institutions, such as student government and the campus newspaper, came out from under the dominance of the Greek or club system, changed their content to the issues of the times, and persisted. Those so identified with the old ways that they could not be altered were often abandoned. Many colleges gave up rituals that smacked of sentimentalism or traditionalism. Those that remained to satisfy alumni, such as homecomings at large universities, seemed merely silly to most undergraduates; and their queens and kings, jokes. As undergraduates moved into the 1970s only fragments of collegiate culture remained, and these had lost much of their potency.

At the tail end of the 1960s, women's liberation emerged on college campuses as a part of the broader critique of American society. Its greatest impact on students, however, awaited the 1970s. As a result, most college women received feminism in only a limited, narrow way. Although a small minority opened themselves up to radical concerns, the bulk of female students read feminism's message as a call to enter the traditional professions. For them feminism blended into the prevailing ethos of getting ahead. In the context of the 1970s they decided not that men and women should rethink the nature of careers and family, but that women should put on gray flannel suits. By 1979 more freshman women aspired to be business executives than elementary school teachers. Like the men around them, greater numbers aimed at medicine and law, the professions that assured upper-middle-class status. Although the totals still remained relatively small, during the 1970s the number of female freshmen hoping for medical school tripled; for law school, the number increased ninefold.[16] Their applications altered the possibilities for men: a formerly all-male law school that did not grow in size as it admitted an entering class of whom 40 percent were women cut admission by 40 percent to men who applied.

Meritocracy—once one of two basic routes to financial success in American society—now appeared, for all but a handful, the only way. Only the most privileged children destined to inherit great wealth felt free of its demands. Even the sons and daughters of the upper middle class, once aided by the right style and connections or the assurance of marrying well, felt the insistent pressure of getting into law or business school. The signals parents gave to the young changed dramatically. The only advantages a parent could pass on to a child were those in his or her head. The test of proper parenting became children's acceptance into the right college and ultimately the right professional school.

The number of students intending to follow college with professional training soared in the 1970s. In 1979 two out of three freshmen aspired to a professional career, and one out of five hoped to become a doctor or lawyer.[17] In the decade between the mid-1960s and the mid-1970s, the number of students applying to medical school more than doubled: 45,000 for fewer than 16,000 places.[18] Thus the role of the college as the gatekeeper to the professions magnified. Students became increasingly grade-conscious. The behavior that Becker had found in the late 1950s—making the grade —returned with a vengeance.

A Yale alumnus of these years, a remnant of the old collegiate mentality, described the triumphant culture of "Weenie-ism." He recalled a vision of his more serious classmates at midterms "trekking en masse up Science Hill,

Dressed for success: Stanford University student, 1970s.
*Stanford University Archives.*

reciting aloud their ketone syntheses on the way to Orgo, the Homeric-sounding, beastlike nickname for Organic Chemistry, the premed prerequisite that only the dedicated passed, and that meant the difference between a Park Avenue practice and . . . oblivion!"[19] A less hostile reporter put it thus: "In some minds the mere fraction of a grade became the nail-in-the-horseshoe that could wreck life's best laid battle plan: for want of a high enough fraction, a student's semester grade point average could suffer, which in turn could impair his year-end GPA, ruining his chance to be accepted by a top law school and, later, by a prestigious firm that would make him a partner within ten years, assuring him a minimum salary of $100,000 a year and lifetime security."[20]

We have seen this mentality before, reflected through eyes equally critical. What we have not seen, however, is its powerful growth among privileged groups during an era of ascendant conservatism. Until the 1970s outsiders tended to come from poor or upwardly mobile elements in the society. In the 1970s these mainstays were joined by prosperous collegians fearful of downward social mobility. Behavior once linked to the promise of American life took on a new, sour quality, as the nation's privileged children adopted it in an era permeated by a conviction of national failure. Affluent newcomers imitated characteristics of older outsiders, but they brought new elements to the fore. Because of their reworking of older codes, the characteristic students of the years after 1970 are best understood as the *New Outsiders.*

The classroom had long been the battlefield where many students sparred with their professors to find out what would nail an A. But in the 1970s the atmosphere changed. The grade inflation that took place in the 1960s increased many students' belief that they were entitled to high marks. Though such students did not necessarily believe that grades really measured what they knew, they did believe that grades were important. The pressure to make high grades increased competition between students. Four out of five undergraduates surveyed in 1976 described other students in their major as very competitive.[21] Afraid of alienating their professors, fewer students raised basic questions in class. New reports surfaced about cheating. At Stanford 30 percent admitted to cheating at least once; at Amherst, 43 percent. At Dartmouth and the University of Michigan, between 50 and 60 percent admitted to violating the honor code.[22] As students vied against each other in premed courses, rumors circulated about the intentional wrecking of classmates' scientific experiments to improve the curve.

For a time in the mid-1970s an ugly mood descended on many campuses. Lansing Lamont, returning from five years abroad as a reporter, felt the contrast between the newspaper accounts of the return of normalcy to the university and the anguish in his friends' voices as they talked of their college children. He traveled to a dozen campuses to interview students and those who worked closely with them. His hyperbolic chronicle, *Campus Shock,* lacked both perspective and discrimination, but contained disturbing examples of 1970s malaise. In a telling phrase, he described the problem students faced as "Lost Civility," a self-centered disregard for others' rights. This manifested itself in both dramatic and quiet ways. The campus and its environs no longer felt safe, as rapes and muggings occurred with disturbing

For many undergraduates in the 1970s, examinations loomed like Judgment Day: final at Berkeley, 1973. *University Archives, The Bancroft Library.*

regularity. Urban institutions could attribute this to their locations, but not all crime in colleges could be blamed on non-students. Harvard estimated that 20 to 40 percent of its thefts came from inside.[23] Undergraduates locked their doors as carefully as any city apartment dweller. Signs warning patrons not to leave possessions on library desks insistently reminded them that the old codes no longer held. If students were brothers, they were now Cain and Abel.

But the trouble went deeper than crime statistics. Since the years following World War II, many college students had taken pride in crossing racial and class barriers. In the 1970s the walls went up again. Increased minority enrollment meant one thing when the economic pie was growing larger. But as it shrank, some white undergraduates felt that their privileges were being eroded by opening up admission and financial aid to blacks and browns and by compensatory programs; and they turned hostile to any indication of reverse discrimination. Feeling insecure academically and unwelcome, many minority students withdrew from social interactions with whites to focus on their own groups and on making the grade. Women at formerly all-male colleges, such as Dartmouth, or the male-dominated coeducational campuses, such as the University of Michigan, felt pressures comparable to those on minorities, because they, too, were challenging privileges assumed to be prerogatives. As ethnic pride surfaced, it became confused with ethnic isolation. College social life began to resemble that of early-twentieth-century American urban neighborhoods where immigrants from Pinsk did not mix with those from Minsk.

As the sense of community eroded, many undergraduates felt themselves engaged in the war of each against all. Required books were stolen from libraries, assigned articles torn out of journals. A Yale student recalled the "academic skirmishes in the Cross Campus Library: staking out a study carrel before thy neighbor did; hiding Closed Reserve books where no one else could find them."[24] Some malicious acts came from competitive drives that knew no limit, but more, I am convinced, came out of a sense of entitlement. Some undergraduates felt their families were paying big money for college, and here they were standing in line for a book on reserve. The goods were just too scarce. And they were impatient to get their due. So take, don't wait. Such feelings and such acts do not make for community, but for Hobbesian anarchy.

One result of the college climate were the disturbing reports of psychic distress among undergraduates. Unable to cope with the shame of failure and parental disappointment, a few students resorted to suicide. In January 1976 a University of Michigan senior encouraged his parents to attend his midyear graduation. No trace of him could be found at the ceremony or for the week following. He had shot himself, rather than let his parents know that he had received failing grades and could not graduate on schedule.[25] College counseling services had increased traffic. Two of Michiko Kakutani's suitemates at Yale left within the first year. Another friend withdrew; yet another, an excellent swimmer, drowned over the summer. She described her freshman year at Yale as pervaded by a "sense of free-floating unhappiness." She reported that in the fall of 1972 the *Yale Daily News* summarized the findings of the Student Committee on Mental Health. Twenty percent of Yale women sought counseling at the university's mental health clinic. The *Daily* announced, "Despair, suicidal depression and emotional crises seem to characterize the Yale experience as much as college seminars, Mory's and mixers."[26] In that same period Christopher Buckley visited friends so frequently at the Yale Psychiatric Institute that he "knew some of the doctors by their first names."[27]

As observers looked around, they found that not all political interest died in the 1970s. Constant warnings appeared throughout the decade that, given sufficient provocation, undergraduates would take to the streets again. Such observers were both right and wrong. They correctly judged that students felt a clear sense of grievance and alienation from college authorities. Yet the sources of undergraduate concern, as they surfaced in college government meetings or in editorials in the campus press, were of a different nature from those of earlier decades. As Arthur Levine has pointed out, moved by their sense of entitlement, students created a campus consumer movement. They fought against the raising of fees, restricted library hours, the inability of teaching assistants to speak comprehensible English.[28] A Yale undergraduate in the early 1970s recalled that "the first campus-wide controversy . . . one month into freshman year, wasn't about Vietnam but rather a plan to cut back on the hours of Sterling Library. There followed such an uproar that it was withdrawn."[29]

The cynical tone of Alan Schoonmaker's *A Students' Survival Manual: Or How to Get an Education Despite It All* reflected the decade's temper. The educational "system is archaic, inefficient, and inhuman, but you're stuck with it," Schoonmaker declared. He outlined the reasons why the system cannot change: social inertia increased by academic traditionalism; oligarchic control by professors interested in retaining power even at the cost of the university's essential purposes; bureaucrats' fear of disrupting procedures; and the sad fact that teaching costs money, but research brings it in. Then he counseled against open confrontation. However bad the system, to counter it with violence could only lead to repression and the substitution of ineptitude by dictatorship. "We professors are no bargain. We are unaware of your needs, unable to respond to them, and more than a little incompetent. But we are *infinitely* better than the men who would replace us after a violent revolution. . . . I therefore suggest that you play it cool." What is intriguing about Schoonmaker's guide is that linked to his radical critique of American higher education is a set of suggestions to students (for freeing themselves from social pressures to become autonomous, making conservative decisions about sex and drugs, and learning elemental study skills) so traditional that no college dean trained in 1920 could disapprove.[30]

"Drinks available": Stanford University. *Stanford University Archives.*

Predictors also erred about the manner of student protest. Most undergraduates merely grumbled and felt vaguely disaffected. Those who decided to represent them as student leaders acted in the manner of future lawyers and legislators, not of demonstrators. Out to prove their sense of responsibility, they argued that, in contrast to the students of the 1960s, they had learned how to address questions effectively.

What initially troubled many adults as they looked at college students in the early 1970s was that they were having little fun. Despite the popularity of *Animal House,* social life appeared on the decline. In many places formal dating (though certainly not coupling) had largely stopped in the

1960s, replaced by informal group partying and moviegoing. When under-graduates stopped hanging out together in the 1970s in quite the same mass way, many young people found themselves studying on Saturday night. College rituals ceased or became déclassé, but appropriate new forms did not take their place. Drugs and sex remained, and drinking resumed with a vengeance, but more cautious collegians felt threatened and withdrew.

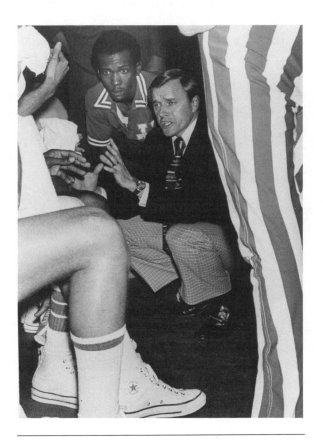

College athletics remained serious business: Coach Leon Black discusses game strategy at SMU-Texas basketball game. *Eugene C. Barker Texas History Center, The University of Texas at Austin.*

Gradually during the 1970s college life revved up again. Essentially some collegians—wanting more, but not understanding how to create it—re-verted to the old standbys of college life: the Greek system, organized athletics, pranks. As early as 1973 at Yale, students regaled themselves with laughing-gas parties, midnight swims, and costume galas. "One student, imitating Harold Acton perhaps, read *The Waste Land* aloud from the top of Harkness Tower, and another tried unsuccessfully to steal the Yale Banner and ransom it to Harvard."[31] Streaking captured the imagination of fun-loving undergraduates as clearly a more provocative act than swallowing goldfish. When Elliot Richardson spoke at Yale "several hundred Yale men and women streaked through the Old Campus, watched mutely by President Brewster and Mr. Richardson from the steps of Battell Chapel, holding on-to their brandy snifters for dear life."[32] As attendance at games and pep rallies increased and as membership in sororities and fraternities grew, famil-iar divisions reappeared on campus. Alumni returning to alma mater felt reassured: the 1950s had returned.

But they had not. For the realities of the 1970s would not go away. Young men and women in college still aimed for professional careers, and this required sustained academic achievement. Fraternities tried to reinforce the message that *who* you knew was important (the fraternity provides valuable "contacts"), but law school applications insisted on *what* you knew. Fraternities gained back the members lost in the late 1960s, yet, because of the growth in the number of undergraduates, their percentage of the total student population declined.[33] More importantly, the old power of the Greek system was gone: it was for some people, certain types, but it was hardly a mark of prestige. College government no longer claimed leaders, but the "politicos"; campus newspapers, those with journalistic ambitions; athletics, those looking to the pros. The organizations that proliferated offered professional or personal help, religious answers, or physical fitness: intramural athletics, meditation, evangelical Christianity.[34] Each activity became justified only in terms of a particularistic career or individual goal. One no longer worked for Michigan or Carolina, but only for oneself.

The hold of the extracurriculum had not returned. Student governments held elections to which nobody came: student leaders cheered a 40 percent turnout; more typical was the 6 percent of the student body at the University of Michigan who even bothered to vote. College students no longer read campus newspapers, causing some publications to come upon hard times. The only common ground was the football stadium, where, for a few hours on Saturday afternoon, booze-filled undergraduates felt a sense of unity; but even here some stayed away to study or because they felt alienated.

For a time in the late 1970s college ceased to be a definable place. It became simply a setting where individuals acted out their private dramas of personal fulfillment and ambition. By choice or force of circumstance, college outsiders have always experienced the campus in this manner. But until the 1970s they have seldom been dominant. Upwardly mobile, they have largely felt confident and optimistic about the nation's future. In the

Stanford University, 1971. *Stanford University Archives.*

1970s such students, often from minority groups, still came to college, and remained outsiders; but now they were joined by privileged youth terrified that they might fail to attain the material well-being of their affluent parents. The New Outsiders brought to the campus their conservatism, sense of entitlement, and hostility to classmates seeking to take their places in the economic and social order. They helped to create the harsh college world that today's students inherit.

# 12

## The New Outsiders,

## College Men and Women,

## and Rebels Today

It is time to return to the black freshman at the University of Michigan who in the spring of 1983 was having "no fun." He informs us that much of the campus mood of the 1970s continues in the 1980s. No sharp divide separates the decades. Yet paradoxically this very fact makes the present different. Rather than the abrupt swings in mood and behavior of the 1960s and early 1970s, the present sees a settling down.

We can now assess the worlds that late-twentieth-century undergraduates make and distinguish between the faddish and the enduring. The Michigan freshman's criticism helps us to see that not every student likes the way things are.

The primary fact in undergraduate life today is not that the 1960s are over or that Reagan appeals to the young. It is that the imperatives of the twentieth century will not go away. Institutions of higher education committed to the whole person, especially well-endowed small colleges and private universities, try to moderate the force of these imperatives, but "grim professionalism" remains to dominate contemporary college experience. As a Stanford senior editorialized, "like the T-shirt says, the basic philosophy of many students here seems to be work, study, and get rich."[1]

In one way the last two decades have heightened the impact of these imperatives. A quarter-century ago the campus was divided into clear and separate worlds of college men and women, outsiders, and rebels. During the 1960s the boundaries between students softened. Distinctions that once had mattered deeply ceased to count as much. While some students revived elements of college life in the 1970s, undergraduate culture did not go back to the 1950s. No Maginot Line returned to separate Greek from Barb. In

ways unthinkable before, sorority membership or politics does not determine college friendships today. No domestic ideology has sent women back
to the kitchen: contemporary female students share the career goals and the
personal hopes of male classmates.[2] Thus much of the mentality of the New
Outsiders who dominate the campus affects those who nominally regard
themselves as college men and women or rebels. In 1920 an outsider going
to Yale could be relatively immune from the values of the college men. In
the 1970s or 1980s no student can remain unaffected by the ethos of the New
Outsiders.

Contemporary students are therefore more alike today than different.
Although at the fringes of each modality, one finds students who fit the old
patterns quite exclusively, these are the exceptions. At the center, students
—whether outsider, organized, or iconoclastic, male or female—share many
attitudes about life and learning.

As I conversed with a quiet, graceful junior biology major hoping to
become a doctor like her parents, I found it difficult to get her to talk about
anything other than courses and studying.[3] I kept straining to find a common
ground on which we could discuss her roommates, social life, extracurricular
activities, or intellectual interests, but there seemed to be none. At one point,
I decided that she stuck to academic matters because she was shy. Only later
did I realize that she had focused on class preparations, labs, lectures, and
examinations because they were essentially all that mattered to her. It was
a profoundly disturbing realization, but one that I would have repeatedly.

Such students today are facing up to the sobering truth that outsiders have
understood all along: they go to college for a formal education. Their four
years are less a special time than a continuation of past study and a preparation for professional school. They know that the four years are crucial ones.
They enter with opportunity seemingly open, but how they rank as they
leave will set their chances for the future—for their jobs and incomes. The
subjects that they take and the grades that they make will determine the
course of their lives.

Of course, this caricatures a reality that in actuality allows for the play
of chance, non-academic skills, capital, and connections. But undergraduates
receive from their parents and educational institutions the message of the
meritocracy in all its purity, and many of them believe it whole.

As we have seen, the message does contain much truth. Academic achievement in college has been a significant path of social mobility throughout
the twentieth century. As the society has required more technological and
professional skills, this path has widened, opening more positions to the
highly trained. Increasing numbers of jobs require graduate degrees. Colle-

gians who want to minimize risk rightly see engineering, medicine, and law as assuring them position and income. Admission to professional schools has becomé more highly competitive, and qualification depends less on your face or your father than on standardized test scores and grades.

Of course, the message today's students receive is refracted through the lens of a particular economic and political situation. For undergraduates the 1970s have not gone away. Although the economy has moved upward and the sense of expanding opportunity has begun to filter down to students, rough shoals lie ahead. By late November 1983 roughly one-half of the Princeton class that had graduated in June had tried to enter the job market: 24 percent had found work, but 23 percent were still looking.[4] Thus with some reason middle-class children remain stuck on attaining professional positions requiring graduate school. Ninety-five percent of Harvard students plan some form of advanced education.[5] Thus intense anxiety over grades continues to control the lives of students in a wide social circle.

When the culture of the outsider emerged triumphant in the 1970s, it was a particular version of a phenomenon we have traced since the early nine-teenth century. As we have seen, outsiders have always been important numerically, often the majority. Unlike their organized colleagues, how-ever, they have been a motley collection, joined less by positive traits than by the negative fact of not being included. Outsiders today comprise a wide range of students—from commuters who work and go to college part-time to blacks seeking social mobility to returning women who need credentials. In addition, into their ranks have come a new group, the economically privileged in elite institutions.

A Duke senior reflected on the mood on campus: "There's a lot of paranoia around here about coming from affluent families and not being able to maintain that. Students are scared of slipping or being unable to begin a generation of affluence. It sounds selfish but if you don't look out for yourself, no one will."[6] Here speak the New Outsiders who have dominated campus life since 1970. Unlike the optimistic children of modest back-grounds who have come to college in order to rise in the world, the New Outsiders are the frightened sons and daughters of the middle and upper middle class who fear downward social mobility. Affluent students were originally the mainstays of traditional college life. In the 1960s many of them experimented with rebellion. When they became the New Outsiders in the 1970s and turned to serious study, they altered the college environ-ment. Today the New Outsiders continue to shape the college world in their own image.

One evening as I talked with a group of prosperous suburban students sharing a comfortable house off campus, I felt that I found the truly Representative Students of the present. It was deeply depressing. I had taught one of them the semester before, and she had impressed me as very able, but rather wary. She agreed to gather her housemates for a long conversation about their lives and hopes. I do not know what I expected of the seven attractive and intelligent young men and women I met that evening, but I did expect more.

They quickly informed me of their pride in creating around them the comforts and security of home. They were not only pleased with their house; they were pleased with finding each other. They had been acquaintances before college. After a freshman year in which they had mixed randomly with the hoi polloi in different dormitories, they reconstituted as sophomores their friendship world of high school. In the present they studied and played with those from their past.

I asked them to try to clarify the nature of the pressures they felt. A handsome junior had no hesitation: "It's fear of not having what you have right now. I'm living in a house right now. I have just about everything that I have ever wanted. . . . Soon as I graduate, the phones [to his parents, i.e. their economic support of him] are cut. What happens then? . . . It's really scary, I've never felt this way. One of my other roommates said to me, . . . 'This is your last summer coming up.' Oh my God, it is. What's after school? I have to work. I guess you don't get summers off. . . . I mean my heart just trapped [sic]. So, yeh, I think it's important to do well." He later tried to define what he was working for: "What I consider to be successful . . . is maintaining the comfort level that you grew up with, basically. . . . Now there is a lot of pressure because we're starting out at this level and now we have to say this is where we want to be. . . . We're running six figures for married people with two children." In imagining their futures, none could go beyond the hope to re-create his or her parents' house and its material possessions.

These students were exceedingly cautious in talking to me, not only because I represented authority to them but also because caution had become their accustomed mode. Nothing, especially not a rebellious act, should get in the way of their dreams. "I know when I get out I want to have a ski-boat. I want to do this. And to be radical right now . . . now's not the time. With the economy, however it is. If I want to get a job now, I have to follow everybody's rules." This young man's suppressed rebellion was echoed by the others. A junior woman put her inner conflicts this way: "I respect [it] when people get out of line. I like to see somebody taking things into his own hands and doing what he wants to do. I like to look at it from the outside. I would never do it myself. . . . If I have a complaint I think that I would do something about it. I mean I don't have any really strong feelings at this point about things. . . . At that point [after she viewed *The Day After,* the television special on nuclear holocaust] I really thought that I was going to do something about it. But then, I talked to my father. I talked to friends. They all laughed at me and said, 'What are you going to do?' "

As I listened to them I sensed a pervasive undercurrent of fear that they might not earn enough to reproduce the luxurious world of home. One of them had an older sister who had lived out the rebellion of the 1960s. She had not finished college, and she now worked in a bookstore while her husband picked up odd jobs. She "definitely settled for much less comfort than she grew up with. And it's really hard for anybody in my family . . . to think that she can be happy . . . she might be, which is impossible for me to imagine myself." Such an example drove the younger sister to prepare conscientiously for law school. A close friend of the roommates, who had joined the conversation, also planned to become a lawyer. Not because he wanted to, but "for the security. . . . I think I would enjoy practicing law, but I am not what you would call a scholar type. I like to learn, I enjoy to read but I don't enjoy to have it to learn on a conformist basis where you learn to do this and this. . . . Had you talked to me when I was in high school the last thing I would ever say I might consider doing would be law; the only thing behind that would be a doctor."

What drove these young people to suppress their adolescent stirrings and to work so hard? "Money," they agreed in chorus. "It seems like all we talk about is money." "That's the bottom line." "We talk about it all the time." "You hear people talk about it constantly." "I try to say that it's not that important. But it's really important to be comfortable and you can't be comfortable without money."

They all connected their ability to earn with their college marks. For this they studied very hard. Yet I could sense in them little desire to know or understand, to experience, or to do. Though, with two exceptions, liberal arts majors, they could have been studying arcane or technical fields, for all the difference a college education was making in their lives.

I have thought a lot about these housemates since. They are important not only in themselves but because they speak for many others in their generation. In going to college they have not so much left home as taken home with them. They clearly admit their pleasure in being away from their parents' rules about curfew and alcohol, but they dutifully follow their parents' advice and plan their futures in their parents' image. They insist that college not change their goals, perspectives, or style of life. They live among their friends, and they study. College offers neither the group pleasures of college life nor the individualist expressions of rebellion. Though richer, they are in many ways like generations of outsiders before them.

They lack, however, the sparks of intellectual life that were the saving grace of many earlier outsiders. While college men and women in the early twentieth century played the games of the extracurriculum, some of the outsiders discovered the university. They were open to the empirical modes of thinking that changed higher education. In class and out, they made real connection with new ideas and approaches that opened to them the life of the mind of the twentieth century. Despite their seriousness, the New Outsiders have little in common with these enthusiastic seekers of knowledge: they hold themselves as aloof from real learning as did the college men and women of the past. What is going on? Why do such hardworking students divorce education from life?

As I ponder this, I recall the phenomenon that Howard Becker studied in the 1950s. At the University of Kansas he found a classroom culture that he called the "GPA perspective." In the setting of a large state university that could not be selective in its student body, he discovered the extent to which grade-consciousness shaped the behavior of undergraduates and prevented them from learning. He called it "making the grade." Today, in the mid-1980s, this phenomenon has spread to include those once seemingly immune from it—privileged college youth in elite institutions. Becker's descriptions of two decades ago capture the mentality of today's New Outsiders. In their anxiety to achieve marks that will get them into professional school, the New Outsiders go to college less to learn than to "make the grade."

As I try to connect today's New Outsiders, Becker's research, my own experience as a professor, and undergraduate experience of the last two hundred years, I sense the roots of today's dilemmas in the traditions of college life of the nineteenth century, more precisely in the misperceptions of the outsider by the college man. In the nineteenth and early twentieth centuries college men saw two alternatives: college life and the realm of the outsider. Intellectual achievement was valued largely by poor country boys, who came to college to become ministers, and by Jews, who saw college as the steppingstone to the professions. Just as the secularism and urbanity of the nineteenth century obscured the vision of emerging campus leaders, so the anti-Semitism of the clubmen of the twentieth century made them misperceive the outsiders and the real nature of their academic success. Out of this conflict—more social and political than intellectual—college men in the past created a hostile image of serious students and of their achievement.

They saw outsiders as grinds—rote learners and apple polishers. As it became clear to increasing numbers of students in the twentieth century that the collegiate way no longer offered the sure road to success, they looked to its flip side and sought to achieve through grinding the hoped-for future. The New Outsiders have simply accepted the terms of the past, only turning that which had once been despised into something dominant and positive.

Some of the original needs that led to college life in the first place underlie grinding. Although the nature of the twentieth-century university and its relation to society make it no longer possible for most students to believe in the power of the extracurriculum, like workers and prisoners, they still need to defend themselves against those in authority. Confronted with the awesome weight of faculty power, early-nineteenth-century collegians turned from open rebellion to the covert war of the classroom. The New Outsiders merely retreat to a deeper cover. Blocked from a frontal or even side attack, they do an end run. They create the culture of grinding.

College life had declared marks valueless. The New Outsiders reverse the judgment: grades are the ultimate value. Yet in making this shift, such students keep many of the elements of the old conception. Grades do not reflect innate differences in intelligence; rather they result from figuring out what their professors want, spending long hours in study, and currying favor with their instructors. The terms derive from the nineteenth century. The only difference lies in the attitude taken toward them. Whereas college men scorned both the techniques and the goals of grade-grubbing, the New Outsider turns them into valued strategies and admirable ends.

The psychology of the New Outsider is more complicated than that of the college man. Nineteenth-century collegians owed individual professors respect, but could openly scorn them as a class. College men controlled the allocation of status because they chose those who led in sports and clubs. In the late twentieth century, professors hold the one judgment that matters to the New Outsiders—grades. They must therefore check any signs of open rebellion, even to the point of not allowing themselves to feel it. Hero worship has come to replace denigration. Professors assume an exalted status in such students' eyes. In the classroom they accept all the terms that the professor sets. Privately they may grumble or criticize faculty eccentricities, but their words sound like the grousing of a monarch's subjects, an indirect means of confirming his or her power. They reserve real scorn for the teaching assistants, the royal ministers. Yet cheating remains rampant.

Cheating has been a notoriously difficult question to research, for college students have known of the broader culture's disapproval of it and, when questioned, have consistently underreported its incidence. A survey at Indiana University in November 1983 found that 32 percent admitted to looking at another's test during an exam, 12 percent to using notes during a test, 20 percent to looking at copies of a test before taking it, 55 percent to asking someone in an earlier section what was on a test, and 6 percent to buying a term paper from a service.[7] At Princeton, two undergraduates openly cheated on a physics exam—using crib sheets, consulting a text, and whispering—to test the honor code. No one turned them in.[8] As the *Daily Princetonian* editorialized, though the conception of honor on which the system was based may have worked "when academic achievement meant less than social standing, when a straight C student like Adlai Stevenson '22 could still go to Harvard Law School," times had changed. "Today's students see only too keenly that a grade on a single exam could mean the difference between medical school acceptance and rejection and that the pressure to cheat can sometimes be overwhelming." Thus a recent poll reported that although only 9 percent of Princeton undergraduates cheated, few students would turn another in.[9]

Students report mixed feelings about cheating. On the one hand, it violates the code of fair play among them: the cheater creates an unfair advantage for himself vis-à-vis other students, especially serious when grading is on a curve. Yet some also admire one who wrests a high grade from a professor.

Cheating, in fact, only extends the normal transaction of the classroom. A few dramatic cases have surfaced in which students have stolen exams from professors' offices or trash baskets, but students find legal channels to achieve the same ends. Files of back exams, once the guarded treasure of fraternity houses, are, in this more democratic age, kept by counseling centers. In the era of the New Outsider the classroom becomes a sparring field where students try to learn the questions on examinations and how they are to be evaluated.

They also seek the certainty of the right answers. Although in some subjects, especially at an elementary level, there are clear right and wrong answers, in many fields, as students advance, the question of interpretation or perspective enters. Students can take either side of a debate or a position in between. Professors judge the integrity of the argument—its logic, clarity, subtlety, and documentation. Here is where grinding often fails. For here students can no longer rely merely on memorized information or on the judgment of the professor, but must make imaginative connections on their own and create intellectual structures to support them. Although a few students accept and even welcome intellectual adventure, many become frightened by uncertainty and angry because they believe that the professor is withholding knowledge.

The New Outsider puts all responsibility for learning in the professor's hands. Course reading becomes an assignment or even "homework." Learning turns into cramming for exams. Such students do not seek to understand the nature of the universe or even to master a discipline or to deepen their knowledge in one of its areas. They are after grades. Courses provide a set of mental exercises performed on cue to get a grade.

Some voices in the higher educational system have reinforced the culture of grinding. Perhaps inadvertently, they have helped students ignore the claims of inquiry and the free play of ideas and the nagging possibility that intellectual excellence cannot be acquired simply by application. In the effort to encourage study, some professors have suggested to students that only hard work brings academic success, without being candid about the differences in individuals' mental powers. Some educators have obscured the potentially subversive quality of intellectual life. They have emphasized their role as gatekeepers to the professions and, in the process, have helped students forget about learning in the games of grade-seeking that they play.

Students entering college in the mid-1980s receive the New Outsiders' message to grind as surely as their nineteenth-century counterparts received the canons of the college man. It has high personal costs.

As limiting as it was, traditional college life did create a time and place away from home where young men and women could try to define themselves. Distinctive dress marked the collegian; hedonism offered new experiences; rejection of professorial standards allowed a sublimated form of adolescent rebellion; and, for some, struggle among peers opened new opportunities. College rebels pushed themselves to make a sharp break not only with the standards and politics of their peers but also with those of their parents. Even the old-fashioned outsiders struggled in a quiet way to leave home: education offered their chance to rise in the world and that meant adopting the language and style, as well as the skills, of one's future professional niche.

In different ways undergraduates in the past worked for autonomy. But today's New Outsiders seem content to remain emotionally and economically dependent on their parents. College neither provides an alternative world of its own nor promises one in the future. Since they aspire to imitate their parents, the New Outsiders struggle in college to maintain the standards of home.

Undergraduates today insist that long before coming to college they became independent of their parents. When pressed, they review the conflicts of their mid-teens over sex, alcohol, and drugs. They assume that because these battles were won years before, no more remain, and they can now claim their parents as their best friends. They fail to see that their struggle to grow up has only begun.

The result is deep dependency. Phone bills give testimony to the need of many undergraduates living away from home to discuss the details of their lives with their parents. They involve their parents in a new set of decisions. Mother and father not only monitor grades; they help choose majors and even courses. Sons and daughters assume their parents' cost-accounting perspective and demand of courses a return on the financial investment. As a result, undergraduates are enrolling increasingly in vocationally oriented subjects, rather than in the less easily justifiable liberal arts.

The real danger lies in the future. Like the young man fearful of losing his phone line to his father, some students face the prospect of supporting themselves with dread. They may join the increasing number of graduates who return home to the safety of the parental roof and kitchen. Some parents who faced the empty nest four years before are finding to their dismay that it is refilling. Reporters have assumed that only tough times have forced young adults home, but my own conversations with dependent undergraduates have pointed to inner needs behind "nesting."[10]

Vocational choice suffers the most serious consequences. One of the saddest voices I heard was that of the youth girding himself up for the law school that he did not want. I was disturbed not only by his resignation but also by his failure to make a true choice. Much of grim professionalism today is mindless professionalism. And it can be enthusiastic as well as resigned. What characterizes both is calculation rather than experience.

When undergraduates perceive college as mere preparation for professional school, they hold themselves in. They push themselves to make high grades and present an unblemished portrait before an admissions committee. This means that they do not let themselves explore their inner selves or their world. How can they afford the luxury of contemplation when they are accumulating the grade point average necessary for application forms? How can they ask themselves the painful questions of youth? Real growth might knock them off the ladder to success.

Thus they fail to make a genuine choice. However messy for a grade point average, facing life during college gives a basis on which to make important decisions about the future. As today's New Outsiders calculate whether they want to be lawyers or bankers, they use language as abstract as high school seniors in a college interview committing themselves to a major.

For the choice of vocation to be meaningful, it must grow out of deeply felt needs and intense interests. A true vocation comes out of a long and intricate process of maturation that the New Outsiders feel they cannot risk. Thus they prematurely commit themselves to an image, a career without content.[11]

The New Outsiders dominate the campus of the 1980s, setting the terms of undergraduate discourse. They are not, however, the only group on campus. Old outsiders still remain, little affected by shifts in college power relations and culture. Their situation has become more straitened since 1981, however, with the sharp decline in federal financial aid of the Reagan years.[12] This has hit black students especially hard. From a 1978 high of 10.4 percent of the college population, black students had slipped by 1982 to 9.8 percent.[13]

In addition to the now familiar cadre of engineering students, women in continuing education programs, and blacks, two new groups have come to the fore. Especially in the South and Midwest, evangelical students gather not only to pray but also to question contemporary morality and the secular curriculum. In the manner of their outspoken preachers, they set themselves against the dominant social and intellectual trends of the twentieth century. In college they insistently retain the culture of their home and church.

In increasing numbers the children of Asian immigrants are entering institutions of higher education. In a manner that recalls the Protestant ministers of the early nineteenth century, the Jews of the early twentieth, and the veterans of World War II, they bring intellectual gifts, intense drive, and the hope for social mobility to study. They are encountering the resistance to their special seriousness that the others faced. The most prestigious private institutions set criteria for admission other than test scores and grades, criteria that discriminate against Asians. As proportions of Asian applicants are weighed against proportions of Asians accepted, rumors of quotas circulate. Against Asians the rhetoric of college life resounds anew: their only interest is in study and professional achievement; what about the college's need for athletes, actors, and alumni children?[14]

Old outsiders remain sealed off from cultural currents on campus, but this is not the case for other undergraduates, both those who have ventured to college determined to be—even in this era—college men or women and those who assume the mantle of college rebels. In this post-1960s world, boundaries are permeable. Thus the consciousness of the New Outsider shapes the terms by which today's college men and women and rebels define themselves.

This is true even at a time when Greek life appears more appealing. In

1983 newspapers focused on the abolition of the Greek system at Colby and Amherst, but the real story was the quieter one reported in the campus press: the resurgence of organized life. Fraternities and sororities are seeing a new rush on campus as increasing numbers of students choose to be members. Colleges and universities are recognizing new chapters. In the fall of 1983 the *Stanford Daily* gave regular updates on the successful efforts of Alpha Kappa Alpha and Sigma Alpha Mu to gain official status.[15]

Who joins fraternities and sororities today? Students perceive that their numbers come from the ranks of wealthier students, and point to expensive and stylish dress and haircuts for confirmation. "Preppy" clothing has lost its connection to Eastern preparatory schools and has, in many places, become the uniform of the organized student. In a survey of 182 students in an introductory economics class at Northwestern, the income of the Greek students' parents was one-third higher than that of all students.[16] However, not all such students choose Greek life. From visits to sororities and conversations with organized students I sense that those join who feel that they need a ready-made group life with a clear identity and who are willing to accept structure and rules. For this they will give up personal freedoms, privacy, and time. The report to trustees on fraternities by Amherst's College Council confirms this. It judged that fraternities "respond to a need many have to join groups and form strong attachments to organizations," a need felt by some students but not those who perceive themselves as "more independent."[17]

When students today join fraternities and sororities, do they take on the traditions of Greek life? They consistently argue that, in becoming brothers and sisters, they accept only the positive virtues—service and leadership. Yet there are many indications that organized students continue to assume the culture of college men and women, embedded deep within Greek life. Because the male and female cultures are distinct, they need to be dealt with in turn.

As we have examined the world of the college man, created in the revolts of the early nineteenth century, we have learned of its hedonism, its violence, its elitism, its belief that the real life in college was that built out of the competition among peers, and its assumption that faculty and students were at war. The 1960s and 1970s altered much, but certain elements have remained unchanged.

Many of the reasons that earlier generations of male collegians joined fraternities and clubs have now evaporated. Hedonism, once their exclusive prerogative, is now shared by any college student who chooses it. The main places for campus indulgence and fun lie off campus in bars, rather than in the fraternity houses. Certain groups claim their turf on certain nights in certain places, but local business interests ensure access to alcohol, music, and dancing to all who can pay. (This may change, however. As new state laws go into effect raising the drinking age to twenty-one, the fraternity may regain its appeal, less as a brotherhood and more as a private club unencumbered by restrictions.) The ending of parietal regulations in dormitories and the lessening commitment of many universities to house even female students on campus give undergraduates easy entry to each other's bedrooms. Students find pleasure as easily outside the fraternity house as in.

Elitism, like hedonism, is no longer the preserve of the college man. It is everywhere. Students divide themselves into groups based on wealth, ethnicity, and social status. Few undergraduates need confirmation of this in a club structure. However, in many places the Greek system still provides a highly visible framework of discrimination. At the University of Texas, the Panhellenic sororities moved off campus rather than sign a non-discrimination agreement. In 1984 three remained all-Jewish. In the Inter-fraternity Council fraternities at Texas, only one black was a member, and he was forced on his brothers because he brought his membership to Austin when he transferred from another school.[18] Harvard's Porcellian Club only selected its first black member in 1983, after 192 all-white years.[19] Even in the 1980s the national fraternity Kappa Alpha continues its Old South Week. In 1985 at the University of North Carolina, the Confederate flag adorned the KA house throughout the week; its racist imagery was not lost on black students on campus.[20]

Yet today the status offered by the Greek and club system differs somewhat from that of early decades. Not only are the boundaries between the organized and the independents less distinct than in the 1950s, but contemporary fraternity members no longer feel confident that they are one with their brothers; they find the fraternity divided from within into cliques, divisions that can be as powerful as those between chapters or between the initiated and the outsider.

As students' perceptions of the extracurriculum has changed, the power of the fraternity has ebbed. Most undergraduates today continue to hold themselves aloof, believing that only grades count. Interest in the extracurriculum is returning, but, as in the 1970s, it carries a meaning different from that of earlier generations. Although football and basketball call out large and enthusiastic crowds of undergraduate spectators, those who join an organization do so either because they perceive a particular activity as potentially useful in their future lives or because it offers personal help. This approach continues to undermine the prestige of college organizations.

College athletics continued to draw out intense fighting spirit in players and crowd alike: Coach Bill Foster, members of the team, and fans. *Duke University Archives, courtesy Scott Berg.*

Alcohol resumed its respected place in the canons of college life: fraternity house interior. *Courtesy Northwestern University Archives.*

Rituals have never recovered their hold among many undergraduates. Northwestern still seems to conduct a serious contest for Homecoming Queen, but at a number of universities, to spoof the occasion, males have vied for the post and won. To protest the dishonor of meeting William and Mary on the gridiron, University of North Carolina student Steve Latham assumed the alias Yure Nmomma (pronounced "your momma") and ran for 1983 Homecoming Queen. Taking advantage of widespread student apathy, he won the election and was duly crowned, much to the embarrassment of the North Carolina administration.[21]

Thus the fact that fraternities and sororities serve as important bases for power and honors has ceased to be important. Greek enthusiasts still argue that their membership participates more actively in college organizations and even garners the most offices and titles, but the great unwashed do not care. The organized may control elections on many campuses, but few students outside or inside the system regard these elections as having any significance.

Yet certain elements remain identified with the fraternity. Although hedonism has become generalized and there are many reports of violence on campus that have nothing to do with fraternities, the brotherhood still offers special opportunity for engaging in both as a group activity.

At a time when colleges and universities are beginning to crack down on underage drinking in college buildings, the fraternity drunk is receiving more attention. Specific incidents point to a broader phenomenon. Harvard disciplined the Pi Eta Club after ten members got so drunk and violent that they required medical care.[22] The Amherst report cited that in the fraternities "exclusive drinking to the point of vomiting was tolerated and even celebrated."[23]

Fraternity violence, once mitigated by the presence of housemothers and the rules of energetic deans, has turned nasty. As in the past, it takes a variety of different forms. Some is connected to alcohol or drug consumption, such as furniture and window smashing during parties. Although fraternity hazing has largely shifted from physical to mental abuse, reports of deaths (forty since 1970) and injuries point to the persistence of older torments. Because college life officers generally do not give details of student misdemeanors, information about violent hazing usually leaks out when particular fraternities are barred from campus and individual students are suspended, the actions taken by the University of Florida in the spring of 1983 against Omega Psi Phi and by the University of Texas in February 1986 against Alpha Tau Omega.[24] Finally, the older tradition associated with violent rushes remains at places like Princeton, where the Tiger Inn stages an annual Trees and Trolls brawl.[25]

A particular variant of violence associated with fraternity life has recently come out into the open. Young women who are sexually abused in the houses no longer necessarily maintain their silence. In the fall of 1983 a Cornell student filed a complaint with the Ithaca police department charging sexual harassment when Delta Chi fraternity members blocked her from leaving a party, exposed themselves, and backed her into a corner.[26] In the spring of 1983 a board at the University of Pennsylvania temporarily suspended the Alpha Tau Omega fraternity after investigating the charge that an estimated six members had successive sexual intercourse with a female student. One of the most disturbing elements of the testimony was the fraternity's defense that it was "common for multiple consensual sexual intercourse to occur in one evening on the University campus approximately one to two times per month."[27] In the last few years, over fifty acquaintance gang rapes have come to the attention of Bernice Sandler, director of the Association of American Colleges' Project on the Status and Education of Women, and staff associate Julie K. Ehrhart. Of these, "nearly all [of recently reported incidents] . . . have involved fraternities." Many cases are unreported and unacknowledged by victims and assaulters. Acquaintance gang rape appears to occur regularly, even every weekend, on a few campuses. Ehrhart and Sandler describe the typical scenerio: "A fraternity holds a party. In many cases but by no means in all, a young woman often has had too much to drink and/or too many drugs. Therefore she may be unaware that the 'friendly' persuasion of the brothers is actually a planned pursuit of easy prey. By the time she recognizes her predicament, her confusion has changed to fear and panic, and escape seems impossible. She is unable to protest or her protests are ignored. Anywhere from two to eleven or more men rape her."[28]

The fraternity house also serves as a base for a certain kind of cheating. As we have seen, students cheat for different reasons. The New Outsiders cheat to make the grade, in the hope that they may better their chances for professional school. They cheat in secret. The cheating of the college man is of a more casual and public kind that springs from the old assumption that faculty and students are at war. No undergraduate would ever admit to a professor or a poll-taker such a state of mind. I got a sense of it only from clues. When I mentioned to a fifth-year design student and fraternity loyalist how intrigued I was with the 1920s distinction that Daniel Katz had found between cheating and "cribbing," he laughed aloud and almost exploded with "I have always known that the last time a lab report was actually written was in 1910!" Bewildered, I asked him to clarify. His fraternity brothers, he patiently explained, might not "cheat," but they certainly felt comfortable in using back files in the house to fill in their lab assignments.

Do sorority members assume the status-consciousness and social conservatism of their predecessors? Over and over again I was told that they do not, that their real purpose in the 1980s is to provide leadership skills and an "old-girl network" valuable for future careers. And yet, certain clues suggested the hold of the past. Several college women who had rushed admitted that they were queried in certain houses on the occupations of their fathers and on the extent of their travel abroad. Although sorority rules about sexual behavior have eased, limits on actions within the house are still drawn, and sorority officers must monitor them. The expelling of a bulimic sister from her house at the University of Michigan in the spring of 1983 occasioned intense discussion there about the timidity of sororities when confronted with complex problems. The unwillingness of houses to discuss publicly anorexia nervosa, a serious problem in certain instances, is another indication of sororities' fear of any issue that might detract from their social standing.

But the reign of the New Outsider in the post-1960s world has altered much in Greek life. It, too, has absorbed the concern for grades and for getting into graduate school. Although the promise of living among one's own kind in a sorority or a fraternity house remains the dominant appeal of the system to contemporary students, the Greek system is trying out utilitarian arguments to win new members. Fraternities and sororities promise to contribute to future chances by giving undergraduates useful connections both among their peers and through their alumni/ae network. At the University of Michigan, Gerald Ford's face appeared on Delta Kappa Epsilon rush posters. In the fall of 1985 Psi Upsilon announced its return to the Berkeley campus after an absence of thirteen years by fliers which billed the fraternity as "YOUR OPPORTUNITY TO BECOME A LEADER." In addition, academic achievement has become a new mark of house status. Brothers once stressed the number of varsity letters in the house. Now they advertise the house GPA and promise tutoring.

If the dominance of the New Outsider has changed college men and women, what has it done to college rebels? Because of the intricate relation between politics and rebellion, a word is in order about contemporary student politics. The confusing issue is labels. Students today like to characterize themselves as middle-of-the-road. But when queried about particular issues, not about self-image, they are a distinctly liberal group. In Alexander

Astin's comprehensive survey of 1984 entering freshmen, 57.4 percent declared themselves in the middle politically, but 77.7 percent judge the federal government as not adequately controlling pollution, and 61.4 percent support a national health insurance program.[29]

In keeping with their avoidance of an appearance of radical leanings, the numbers of self-proclaimed rebels are slight. On certain campuses they have retained their positions on college newspapers, but this can put the publications at risk. The University of Michigan's *Daily,* for example, perceived

On many campuses, the college newspaper remained the location of undergraduate rebels: *Daily Northwestern* staff, 1971–72. *Courtesy Northwestern University Archives.*

by many undergraduates as to their left, had a 1985 press run roughly one-third what it was in the 1960s. Circulation and advertising fell so low in 1985 that the paper found itself deeply in the red, ironically able to survive because it could draw on the surpluses of its radical heyday.[30] On some campuses, contemporary rebels have established alternative publications, such as *The Missing Link* at Duke.[31]

Consumer issues have aroused students in the 1980s as in the 1970s. In 1983 the campus press reported student efforts at the University of Nebraska, Stanford, and the University of Pittsburgh to get the university libraries open, respectively, during Saturday football games, on Saturday night, and after midnight.[32] At the University of Maryland over 1,300 students signed a petition asking the university to require English proficiency tests of foreign teaching assistants.[33]

Conservative students have adopted rebel strategies and have waged successful campaigns at several universities to remove from student activity fees the dollar or two that finance the Ralph Nader-inspired student public interest research groups (PIRGs). Assisted by the adult-led Accuracy in Academia, Inc., right-wing truth squads have appeared in classes at Arizona State University and the University of Washington to challenge the politics of liberal or radical professors.[34] In January 1986 the Young Conservatives of Texas maintained that they monitored University of Texas classrooms to prevent liberal professorial bias from lowering the grades of conservative students.[35]

The early years of the decade found many students personally supporting such issues as the nuclear freeze (which won at Princeton by almost two to one), but only a few involving themselves in protest. Where radicals mounted demonstrations, such as at the University of Michigan, these seemed to serve, as did interfraternity contests, largely to reassure participants of their own existence. By the mid-1980s protests began to mount in number and to attract more undergraduates. Brown students voted a request to the university to stock suicide pills in the case of nuclear war. A number of Brown students attempted to put recruiters from the CIA under citizen's arrest.

On April 4, 1985, Columbia University activists gained national attention when they barricaded a building and demanded that the institution divest itself of stock in companies doing business with South Africa. Campus protests for divestiture have grown since their beginnings in the late 1970s. The National Anti-Apartheid Protest Day, April 24, 1985, brought thousands of student protesters out on an estimated seventy campuses throughout the country.[36] These demonstrations impressed observers with their commitment to non-violence, the efficiency of their computer-assisted organization, and their essential respect for the academic calendar, ending as they did before the examination period. In 1985–86 students on many campuses erected shantytowns to dramatize South African oppression. At Dartmouth, violence erupted as conservative students attempted to destroy the structures; at Berkeley, arrests of demonstrators by police provoked a violent response. At Wellesley, students dressed as "living corpses" gained national attention as they partially blocked the entrance to the college library, where the board of trustees was meeting. During the month of April 1986, 322 protesters at Yale were arrested "on or near the campus."[37]

Radical campus activists also found local issues around which to organize demonstrations. At the University of Texas in the spring of 1986, to protest racism and the working conditions of fraternity service staff, the Alliance of College Students for a Unified Left picketed Pi Kappa Alpha's "Big John's 6th Annual Porter Party," named for a PKA porter who died in 1983. The fraternity promised free drinks to all fraternity porters, who are normally black. A protester noted the six hundred partygoers included only three blacks, one of them the PKA porter.[38]

While it would be foolhardy to predict the shape and direction of the new student movement, at the very least, its existence—as well as the simultaneous growth of the Greek system—suggests that some undergraduates are beginning to mediate pressures for academic success to make room in college for non-careerist commitments.

It would be a mistake, however, to see political activism as the only important alternative to the ethos of the New Outsider. Far greater in number today than the political rebels are those who question basic assumptions. A few assume a quite visible presence. On certain campuses they gather in cooperative houses where they share a communal life according to their principles. A handful of them adopt some of the outward signs of bohemia, such as tie-dyed clothing and beads. I listened as one of them, in dress and jewelry reminiscent of the early 1960s, thoughtfully raised many of its questions. She continually contrasted herself with conventional women in sororities who lived, as she saw it, within a clear structure of expectations. She saw herself as aloof from their stylized and competitive world. She had had to struggle for independence from home. Her parents had gone to college in the belief that they would have jobs when they graduated, a "reward at the end of the line." In contrast, she had no such expectations. "I don't feel like that at all. . . . On the one hand I just know that there aren't jobs that I'm interested in." In addition, her very existence seemed problematic. What does it mean to go to college, she asked, when one has the question "What if the world blows up tomorrow? What is the point?"

Yet although a few contemporary college rebels recall the 1960s in both their dress and their language, most do not. As a result, they initially caught me off guard. They can look quite conventional and even join in some of the pursuits of traditional college life. This is because they have a different enemy from the one in the past. They no longer direct their gaze at college men and women, but rather at the New Outsiders. The alternative world that they seek to construct in college today breaks with new canons, not old.

It has taken me a long time to comprehend the meaning of a conversation that I had with a lively group of seniors at an Eastern university. One thing about them was immediately apparent. Beneath the comfortable version of preppy clothing that they all wore, they looked quite different from each other. Unlike the suburban living group of old friends, these undergraduates had chosen not to live among their own kind. These six suitemates were male and female; Jew, Gentile, Asian; a self-proclaimed intellectual, a free spirit, an athlete, a politico, a committed psychologist. As we talked, they seemed to enjoy the fact of their variety.

From the outset they told me frankly that they did not like my effort to sort students into types. They felt themselves and most other undergraduates to be composites with elements of each. They felt that it was perfectly possible to be both academically oriented and rebellious or an intellectual committed to "Old Ivy." Involvement in the college's extracurricular life did not mean buying traditional values. The campus newspaper was worthless and college government merited scorn for accomplishing nothing, but some activities meant a lot to them, especially those that they could pursue at low, amateurish levels.

When I asked them about "Old Ivy," I sensed less antagonism than distance. They showed little interest in the subject of honor societies, which they saw as pertinent only to a small group on campus. Only one of them had seen herself in the running. She took her failure to be tapped with good grace. When they thought of the last remnants of college men on campus, they were less angry than amused. They broke out into spontaneous group laughter when they described the antics of the "Apes"—wealthy, hard-drinking, macho types—and the "Jane Goodalls" who hung out with them.

Their real antagonists were not the bull-necked college men, but their ambition-driven classmates, those they called the "grasping" types. Voices rose when they turned to the career counseling and appointments office and described classmates striding there in suits. Each in his or her own way was trying to come to terms with those I have called the New Outsiders.

All of them felt the message of the dominant ethos that they should secure their futures by present academic achievement. None of them accepted it in its original purity. They differed significantly among themselves in how they approached grades and vocation. One clear-thinking woman had known from the beginning that she wanted to study psychology and had applied herself with consistent dedication to her work. Because she had taken what she liked, she "felt like there is no reason why I shouldn't get good grades." Although accused half-jokingly by her suitemates of being a conventional grade-grubber, she loved her chosen field too much to be labeled such. An American studies major with a more mixed record did not study for grades or a future career but because she was deeply interested in particular courses: "I felt a sort of an immediate gratification from enjoying a class." Her spotty transcript demonstrated where her keen interests lay. An economics and political science major mixed his interest in courses with concern about their connection to career or graduate school. This contrasted markedly with his anti-vocational roommate, who had transferred from another campus so that he might study and talk philosophy and literature, wherever this might lead him. The one premed among them normally hid her major because it suggested to others the wrong thing about her, that she cared only about study and grades. Two of them experienced academic life with a special intensity. Asian women from immigrant backgrounds, they described the "pressure to know things, pressure to be educated." Each had felt ill equipped to enter college, but had come to feel that she could hold her own, learn, and do.

The six differed on whether college had involved a sharp break from their past or a continuation. One woman felt that because leaving home was something she "had planned to do all my life," it was "no big deal." Another felt she had entered a completely different world. But all agreed that whatever the degree of discontinuity, the college years involved a critical period of growth in their lives. When one of the men stated that he had wasted some of his chances for an education by taking courses along the lines of his interests, rather than building a solid core that contained more philosophy and history, the others moved in to fight him. The one who held the floor argued that specific courses did not matter, for the content would not stick; rather "just learning about yourself" through courses counted.

At first I thought that these six seniors were free from the patterns of the past, for they did not fit into any established groove. But as I reflected on their independence of mind, I kept connecting them with lively collegians of earlier eras. Margaret Mead could have been in that room or Willie Morris or the optimistic seekers of the early 1960s.

And then it became clear. These are the cultural rebels of the present. Like the rebels of the past, they seek to break through social and psychic boundaries. They do not look like earlier counterparts, however, or use their vocabulary. They do not fight in public with college men to control college organizations. They battle in their own minds the New Outsider. Today's rebels seek to distance themselves these days, not from the Greek and club system, but from the grade-consciousness of their careerist colleagues. Given the nature of contemporary college experience, the conflict they wage is quiet, reflective, and cautious.

A later conversation at a Southern university with a lively group of students confirmed this perception of contemporary undergraduate rebellion. These students did not form a friendship group, but had been prompted by their professor in an evening seminar to talk with me after class. They had read for the class a book about student life in the 1960s, and it had started them thinking about the differences between that era and today. Whatever their politics, they felt the gap between the decades: in the late 1960s student government posed questions about the war and the draft; in the mid-1980s the questionnaire their college council had just sent them dealt with the issue of the ideal length for breaks.

The evening was a lively one because they grew less interested in informing me than in getting to know each other. Although all of them were the children of college-educated parents, they differed from each other in important respects, for they included Greeks and independents and a self-proclaimed radical who belonged to the remnant of a cooperative house. While one was comfortably conformist, accepting both the undergraduate environment and the mainstream future, the rest felt at some remove from their classmates. What set them apart was their self-criticism. They had read about their college generation and were troubled to the degree that they fit the descriptions. One articulate young man knew his GPA to the thousandth decimal place. He was self-admittedly obsessed with academic achievement and derived from it his "whole self-esteem." He could not figure out why, however. His parents did not pressure him, he had no immediate career or graduate school plans, and "no one to atone to." He felt himself struggling to unshackle himself from the clutches of grade-consciousness. Others agreed that in the college environment there was a strong "pull to be obsessed," a pull that they were trying in various ways to resist. A young woman questioned the quantitative cast of her parents' minds that continually led them to place her in some rank order. She spoke with pride of her decision to take a course that mattered to her even though she anticipated a low grade. Another who had attended a competitive preparatory school decided that in college she would "learn to learn." When she encountered a class she felt was "stupid," she boycotted it and took, as a result, a less than satisfactory grade. In today's pressured college environment these small acts constitute a form of undergraduate rebellion.

As we turned to their futures, the most articulate talked of their hope for meaning in work. A few thought they had found what they wanted to do. "What is your personal relation to what you know?" was the way that one young man phrased the grounds of his choice. He had just decided to take a fifth year to get the premed courses he needed to become a psychiatrist. Religion courses had opened to him the possibility of becoming a counselor. The radical had just convinced herself that she could become a full-time political activist, but a moment later she was talking about documentary filmmaking. The grade-obsessed young man spoke of his regret that he had not yet found his calling. The junior Phi Bete had gotten a job as a reporter for the summer following graduation; he had no set goals, but felt confident that they would emerge in time. These collegians spoke in many voices, but, in different ways, each was attempting to create some distance from the careerist claims of the present.

In some respects the present favors them. Unlike their counterparts of a decade ago, these undergraduates have lived with talk of jobs and professions since a young age, and for some this has a way of building immunities from pressures in college. The inflated hopes of law and medicine have begun to fade as reports circulate that, at least in desired urban areas, firms are saturated and doctors are scrambling for patients. For the first time since the 1960s the number of applications for law school and medical school are down. Some undergraduates are beginning to look to business immediately after graduation, where presumably no admissions board demands high grades or degrees from prestigious colleges. Job opportunities are improving slightly. Corporate leaders are talking about the need for good liberal arts students.

There is evidence, however, that rhetoric is partially obscuring reality. The job market remains tightly competitive. Recruiters are on the prowl, but they are seeking to hire engineers and computer technicians or those with strong programs in accounting or economics. Placement offices report that employers screen prospects by grade point average, looking only at those with a 3.0 and above.[39] Schoolteachers are desperately needed, but young people know too well the working conditions and pay that those in education garner. The public sector that fed the idealistic hopes of the 1930s and 1960s remains dry. Thus although the squeeze of the 1970s may be starting to ease, undergraduate rebels of the 1980s remain appropriately wary and cautious.

One last voice from the 1980s, full not of the certainty of the New Outsider, but of the honest doubts of today's quiet rebels. In "Confessions of a Pre-med Dropout," Amherst junior Rand Cooper described his inner struggle to break with his family's expectations that he follow his father into brain surgery. The change felt like a death: "The symptoms were there— my decision to major in English rather than neuroscience, my abandonment of Genetics after two weeks—but I ignored them. Then one night it happened. I woke from a nightmare with a frightening presentiment of change. I knew, as I lay there kicking and sweating. . . . *I didn't want to be a doctor anymore.*" As Cooper faced up to his decision, he encountered elders

Rand Cooper. *Amherst College Archives.*

who reminded him of the importance of staying on track. He risked "derailment." As a caution, they told him of a local doctor's son who went to New Hampshire to make leather pouches and, when he decided to become a doctor, could get no closer to medicine than taking a job as a janitor at a med lab. Cooper answered that he "wanted to get off the track for a while, in order to see more of the surrounding countryside"; perhaps he would find another means of transportation. As he reflected on what had led to the death

Some undergraduates keep their sense of humor: unidentified undergraduate, no date. *Stanford University Archives.*

of his "doctor self," he saw it as "a disease that must be suffered by every person here. If we do not reconsider the labels we have stuck on our foreheads—the stock responses to the question 'what do you want to be when you grow up'—then we will fail to do the growing that can be done at this place and time in life."[40]

On campus today the New Outsiders call the shots. They control no organized life, which remains unimportant. They do, however, provide the dominant model of how to be an undergraduate. As they hunger to reproduce the material world of their parents, they work in college to achieve, and they hold themselves in.

Against them today's rebels struggle, less for political than for psychic independence. They fight, not over the *Daily,* but over the right to choose in college to learn and grow, to work and enjoy, and—despite the pressures —to become themselves. As Rand Cooper put it, "anything is possible for the ex-pre-med."[41]

# Coda

Predictions about college students invariably miss the mark. In 1960 it seemed undeniable that Sputnik had ordained an era in which the demands of technology and government would dominate higher education. In 1970 the cultural revolution and widening protest signaled the dawning of the post-industrial world that allowed youths lengthened periods in which to find meaning and develop a heightened individuality. As I write this in late 1985 the imperatives of the twentieth century with their insistence upon disciplined training for a profession seem likely to persist. And yet I know better.

Part of the difficulty in imagining undergraduate futures has been the monolithic way that students have been perceived. In any decade since 1920, single images of collegians have dominated the public consciousness; it is implicitly assumed that no other kinds of students have existed. Thus all students in the 1920s are seen to wear raccoon coats and carry hip flasks, while those of the 1930s march in demonstrations against war. The problem has been the failure to recognize that undergraduates have been divided into contending cultures. In any one era, one of these appears to be dominant and catches the public eye: in the 1920s it was college life; in the 1930s, rebellion; between 1948 and 1955, the world of the outsider; from 1955 to 1965, college life again; from 1965 to 1970, rebellion once more; since 1970, the ethos of the New Outsider. Other student worlds did not vanish, however. They were simply less visible or less interesting to reporters. In our political system, the triumph of one party or ideology in an election does not destroy the opposition; the losing side persists and tries to build strength for the next encounter. Just as there were Republicans alive and well during the New Deal, so were there college men and women in the 1930s and 1960s.

I have argued that, in the 1960s, the power of traditional college life was broken, ending the hegemony of the college man. Morever, the boundaries between groups became more permeable, making the dominant voice carry greater resonance. When the New Outsiders triumphed in the 1970s, therefore, they had a greater impact than the victors of earlier decades. Their assertion did not, however, end the existence of college life or rebellion.

Thus, whatever imperatives underlie the ethos of the New Outsider, it seems likely that it will soon come under attack either by the resurgence of college life or by rebellion. The claims of the Greek system to be a school for success increase its attractiveness at a time when interest in business is reasserting itself. In undergraduates' renewed competition for scarce goods, social exclusiveness for its own sake is becoming appealing. Moreover, as state laws prohibit alcohol at open campus parties, the organized hedonism of the fraternity—and its darker side of group violence—draws young men to the houses.

As traditional college life gears up once again, it will have to compete with a strengthened rebellious culture. The children of the 1960s rebels are now entering college. From first reports, they are bringing both their assertive independence and their heightened consciences on campus.

Moreover, new cultural forms may appear. Nothing ordains that the tripartite division that I have traced contains the only possibilities. Do the quiet rebels of the present, in fact, represent the development of a fourth undergraduate culture? Might one connect them to a separate tradition that began with David Riesman at Harvard in the late 1920s and continued in the independent-minded of the decades that followed? I have looked at cultural rebels as a variant within the rebel tradition. They may now be emerging as a distinct modality in their own right: clear individualists who mediate the complex pressures of undergraduate worlds, struggling for self-definition against the backdrop of contending college cultures.

I have met a few of these students, both in class and outside. They are unusual in their ability to perceive me—either as professor, interviewer, or acquaintance—not as a force, but as a person. In the best tradition of pre-1960s rebels, they seem unconstrained by the conventions of the war between student and faculty. Like the most interesting of earlier outsiders, they concentrate intensely on their academic work and sustain a high degree of engagement in class. They share with college men and women of the past the ability to enjoy the pleasures of undergraduate society. Yet unlike college men or women, past or present, they keep their own counsel, setting their own limits.

Those of us teaching women's history talk often of the pleasure of our women's history classes and the unusual students that they draw—or, more precisely, drew in the early 1970s. We believed then that it was the subject itself and the complex struggle to which it was intrinsically linked that made this difference. It is clear now that it was, at least in part, the unusual mentality of the students who walked in the classroom door. Their independence and intellectual play sprang from the way in which their emerging comprehension of sexism, on and off campus, empowered them as they mediated the counterclaims of undergraduate cultures.

My own prejudices, sympathies, and hopes for the future should now be clear. As historically necessary as male college life once was and as enjoyable as it has continued to be, it has erected a cultural barrier that has prevented its partakers from encountering ideas and taking them seriously. Embedded within the fraternity system is the implicit understanding that faculty and students are at war, and, therefore, that higher education is not a process of discovery, but a series of battles to be won. College life has devalued academic and intellectual attainment. As higher education has increased in its importance in the culture, the negative effects of college life have borne more serious implications for the society. The vicious excesses of contemporary fraternities should be curbed. Far better for education and the nation would be the fraternity's dissolution.

I have admired college life in the women's colleges in an earlier period because of its ability to break through the gender system to teach women the routes to power. Now that the society is changing, the question for women's colleges is: power to what end? The generation at the turn of the century turned their newfound skills to social service. If this is lost in the current generation—if college women merely learn to play effectively the games of men—then the lessons are futile. Our society has little need to double the number of persons in gray flannel suits.

Although college life in the women's colleges has had some claim to be of value, at least in an earlier time, that in coeducational institutions is more questionable. The plight of young women excluded in the late nineteenth century from male college life on their campuses calls for sympathetic understanding. They needed to band together. Sadly, however, the auxiliary order that they created contained intolerance and social conservatism, narrowing their members' visions. In the period between 1920 and 1965—and continuing to this day on some campuses—college women allowed themselves to be bought by social honors that accrued from their appeal to men, rather than seeking to attain and do in their own right. Unlike the fraternity system, that of the sorority is not inherently hostile to the academic enterprise. It is, however, by its very definition, discriminatory, intent on retaining archaic social distinctions that warp the personal and intellectual growth of its members.

My sympathies for the outsiders should be obvious. Not only have outsiders been the underdogs of the campus; they have been those most capable of connecting to its central purposes. Outsiders have not partaken in the mentality of male or female college life. Thus they have been free to engage fully in their courses and in the serious discussions of young adults. Moreover, outsiders have looked to the college or university as the way to rise in the world. This has pushed them to achieve intellectually and to make contact with professors as mentors. The world of outsiders is a residual category. It contains many subgroups—all left out of college life—and therefore many different ways of coping with the demands of college. But it includes within it those capable of serious study, eager for academic attainment, and open to ideas. From the ranks of the outsiders have come many of our most important scholars, scientists, engineers, and professionals.

I have tried to make a distinction between genuine outsiders—who exist even today—and those I have called New Outsiders, a creation of our own time. While outsiders have generally come from lower-income families or from ethnic groups excluded from college life, the New Outsiders are typically affluent collegians who have turned their backs on college life because they do not see its value for their futures. My quarrel with them is that they have failed to perceive the real achievement of outsiders, which has been less the pursuit of high grades than the quest for knowledge. New Outsiders carry the assumption of college life that students are at war with faculty, but they have shifted the strategy. They have imitated behavior that they think leads to academic success. They have concentrated on the husks of grade-grubbing, ignorant that kernels of knowledge exist. In their competitive struggle for high grades, they do not allow themselves the time or the risks necessary for personal growth.

Unquestionably, I feel a sense of common cause with certain rebels, at least those in college before 1964 or after 1971. They have continually opposed college life—for good reason. They have raised important questions about the relation of higher education to politics, economics, society, and gender. They have insisted that the world outside college gates come onto campus. Their courage and spunk have enlivened debate, both in class and out.

Yet I know that there is another side. Collegiate rebellion has not always been independent of adult causes that have sought to manipulate youthful idealism for political ends beyond the campus. Moreover, even when independent, undergraduate rebellion carries great risks. When it is responsible, it can enable college students to make the critical connections between their educations and their lives. It can help the institutions of higher education themselves to act responsibly in their investments, in their involvements with the national defense and security establishments, and toward their

With graduation, farewell. *Duke University Archives.*

surrounding communities. When collegiate rebellion becomes irresponsible, as it did in many places from the mid-1960s through 1970, it endangers higher education and provokes sharp conservative backlash. As members of the next generation of potentially rebellious undergraduates enter the university, they must guard against the forces of violence and irrationality that ultimately helped undo the causes for which their parents stood.

Although I must remain conflicted about political rebellion, given the excesses that I have witnessed, I am unambivalent about the quiet rebels of the past and present. My heart is as much with them as it is with the true outsiders. Their independence, maturity, and quiet courage make them a joy to teach and to know. Although I cannot predict, I can hope that they are, in fact, the avant-garde of an emerging consciousness.

Will they always be so few and so guarded? Might we be entering an era in which their insights and questions will come to the fore?

As I write these questions, I now have a partial explanation of what has pushed me to explore the many facets of undergraduate cultures as they have emerged from the late eighteenth century to the present. I have written about the past not only because it fascinates me but also because I want to release its hold on the present. If we—students, parents, professors, and administrators—who are actors in the college dramas of the present, understand the complex cultural world of undergraduates as it has evolved from past to present, perhaps we can gain the necessary insight and distance to foster change.

The anger at undergraduate dependence that led me to begin this inquiry three years ago has found its proper object in the New Outsiders. I have learned much about the past and present that I had not known. The long process of discovery has revealed to me many troubling aspects of college life, male and female. At the same time, it has given me the unanticipated pleasure of a new possibility and, therefore, unexpected grounds for hope. I have found contemporary undergraduates who are transcending the tired plots of the past to create new scenarios. I have called them the quiet rebels of the present. Perhaps they will find for themselves a new name, appropriate to their special mentality. May their numbers and strength increase.

# Notes

CHAPTER ONE

1. To ensure the confidentiality of these interviews, I do not attribute the source. A more general word is in order about this introductory chapter and its documentation. The chapter has two parts, treated differently. Where it attempts to establish the socioeconomic and psychological grounds for college-going and collegiate styles, citations point to sources of statistics and analyses. Where it introduces themes developed in the book, citations await the chapters that follow.

2. Seymour E. Harris, *A Statistical Portrait of Higher Education,* A Report for the Carnegie Commission on Higher Education (New York: McGraw-Hill Book Company, 1972), p. 924. It is surprisingly difficult to find out who American college students were. The best study, Colin B. Burke, *American Collegiate Populations: A Test of the Traditional View* (New York: New York University Press, 1982), pp. 90–136, emphasizes the diverse backgrounds of undergraduate populations from 1800 to 1860 and the important role of antebellum colleges in educating the ministry.

3. Harris, *Statistical Portrait of Higher Education,* p. 924. One of the most interesting and provocative pieces to shape my thinking on higher education is Richard Angelo, "The Students at the University of Pennsylvania and the Temple College of Philadelphia, 1873–1906: Some Notes on Schooling, Class and Social Mobility in the Late Nineteenth Century," *History of Education Quarterly* 19 (1979): 179–207.

4. U.S. Bureau of the Census, *Historical Statistics of the United States: Colonial Times to 1957* (Washington, D.C.: U.S. Government Printing Office, 1960), pp. 210–11.

5. Ibid., pp. 207, 210–11.

6. One of the most telling statistics is that in 1880, 54.3 percent of male junior and senior students at the University of Illinois came from farm households; only 15 percent of them ever returned to farming (Joseph R. DeMartini, "Student Culture as a Change Agent in American Higher Education: An Illustration from the Nineteenth Century," *Journal of Social History* 9 [1975–76]: 529).

7. Joseph F. Kett, *Rites of Passage: Adolescence in America, 1790 to the Present* (New York: Basic Books, 1977); specific citation, p. 151; I rely more generally on the broader discussion, esp. pp. 144–72.

8. David F. Noble, *America by Design: Science, Technology, and the Rise of Corporate Capitalism* (New York: Alfred A. Knopf, 1977), p. 310.

9. This statement should not be misconstrued as an argument that higher education supports a meritocracy unrelated to parents' socioeconomic position. Samuel Bowles and Herbert Gintis, *Schooling in Capitalist America: Educational Reform and the Contradictions of Economic Life* (New York: Basic Books, 1976), have argued that schools serve to reproduce the existing structure of class relations. Burton R. Clark, *Educating the Expert Society* (San Francisco: Chandler Publishing Company, 1962),

pp. 58–69, has established that the decision to attend college and the choice of the college attended are clearly related to the wealth and educational level of parents. Undoubtedly, this is true for a large percentage of American youth. However, there is evidence from autobiography and biography and collective data on professions that suggests that academic success within college has been a significant means of social mobility, especially for some intellectually talented sons from urban families who have respected educational attainment and have been able to survive without the added income from adolescent labor.

10. Frederick Rudolph, *Curriculum: A History of the American Undergraduate Course of Study Since 1636,* Carnegie Council Series (San Francisco: Jossey-Bass, 1977), p. 210.

11. Harris, *Statistical Portrait of Higher Education,* pp. 926–27.

12. Ibid., p. 288.

13. Clark, *Educating the Expert Society,* p. 211.

14. For the blatant discrimination of earlier decades, see Jerold S. Auerbach, *Unequal Justice: Lawyers and Social Change in Modern America* (New York: Oxford University Press, 1976), passim, esp. pp. 25–26, 100–1, 185–88.

15. *Historical Statistics of the United States,* pp. 75–78.

16. B. Bruce-Briggs, "Appendix: Enumerating the New Class," in *The New Class?,* ed. B. Bruce-Briggs (New Brunswick, N.J.: Transaction Books, 1979), p. 220. I am aware that, to some readers, my discussion of the changing nature of careers and alternative collegiate cultures will support theories of the emergence of a New Class, as articulated, for example, by Alvin W. Gouldner, *The Future of Intellectuals and the Rise of the New Class* (New York: The Seabury Press, 1979). My own position, however, is more eclectic: professionals and intellectuals constitute one of the sectors of power and privilege in the society, but they continue to contend with older elites, corporation managers, and entrepreneurs, who may or may not have educational credentials or professional expertise.

17. *1981–82 Fact Book for Academic Administrators,* compiled by Charles J. Andersen (Washington, D.C.: American Council on Education, 1981), tables 57 and 59 (no page numbers).

18. Human differences are clearly delineated in David Keirsey and Marilyn Bates, *Please Understand Me: Character and Temperament Types* (Del Mar, Cal.: Prometheus Nemesis Books, 1979).

19. I have learned much from Philip Greven, *The Protestant Temperament: Patterns of Child-Rearing, Religious Experience, and the Self in Early America* (New York: Alfred A. Knopf, 1977).

20. Henry Seidel Canby, *Alma Mater: The Gothic Age of the American College* (New York: Farrar & Rinehart, 1936), pp. 23–25.

CHAPTER TWO

1. Charles H. Haskins, "The Earliest Universities," in *Student Activism: Town and Gown in Historical Perspective,* ed. Alexander De Conde (New York: Charles Scribner's Sons, 1971), pp. 19–32.

2. Samuel Eliot Morison, *Harvard College in the Seventeenth Century,* Part 2 (Cambridge, Mass.: Harvard University Press, 1936), pp. 458–71; Morison, *Three Centuries of Harvard, 1636–1936* (Cambridge, Mass.: Harvard University Press, 1936), pp. 27, 78, 109.

3. James McLachlan, "The *Choice of Hercules:* American Student Societies in the Early 19th Century," in *The University in Society,* vol. 2, ed. Lawrence Stone (Princeton: Princeton University Press, 1974), pp. 449–94; Morison, *Three Centuries of Harvard,* pp. 181–82.

4. Steven J. Novak, *Rights of Youth: American Colleges and Student Revolt, 1798–1815* (Cambridge, Mass.: Harvard University Press, 1977), passim; for discussion of the revolt at the University of North Carolina, see pp. 110–13.

5. Thomas Jefferson Wertenbaker, *Princeton, 1746–1896* (Princeton: Princeton University Press, 1946), p. 137.

6. Ibid., pp. 138–42.

7. " 'The Great Rebellion' at Princeton," *William and Mary Quarterly* 16 (1907): 119–21.

8. Wertenbaker, *Princeton, 1746–1896,* pp. 140, 142, 167.

9. Novak, *Rights of Youth,* p. 19.

10. David F. Allmendinger, Jr., *Paupers and Scholars: The Transformation of Student Life in Nineteenth-Century New England* (New York: St. Martin's Press, 1975), p. 108.

11. The following discussion of the curriculum is based on Frederick Rudolph, *Curriculum: A History of the American Undergraduate Course of Study Since 1636,* Carnegie Council Series (San Francisco: Jossey-Bass, 1977), pp. 25–54.

12. Ibid., p. 53.

13. The following discussion is indebted to Novak, *Rights of Youth.* I do not, however, accept Novak's central argument that the rebellions were externally caused by a generation which needed to prove its manhood by repeating the battles of the Revolution within the college context.

14. Philip Greven, *The Protestant Temperament: Patterns of Child-Rearing, Religious Experience, and the Self in Early America* (New York: Alfred A. Knopf, 1977).

15. E. Merton Coulter, *College Life in the Old South,* 2nd ed. (Athens: University of Georgia Press, 1951), p. 65.

16. McLachlan, "The *Choice of Hercules.*"

17. William Raimond Baird, *American College Fraternities* (Philadelphia: J. B. Lippincott & Co., 1879), p. 16.

18. Frederick Rudolph, *Mark Hopkins and the Log: Williams College, 1836–1872* (New Haven: Yale University Press, 1956), pp. 101–18.

19. B. H. Hall, *A Collection of College Words and Customs* (Cambridge, Mass.: John Bartlett, 1856), pp. 159, 188, 243, 30–31.

20. Kathryn McDaniel Moore, "Freedom and Constraint in Eighteenth Century Harvard," *Journal of Higher Education* 47 (1976): 649–59; Moore, "The War with the Tutors: Student-Faculty Conflict at Harvard and Yale, 1745–1771," *History of Education Quarterly* 18 (1978): 115–27.

21. Coulter, *College Life in the Old South,* pp. 103–33, 257, 271–73.

22. William Gardiner Hammond, *Remembrance of Amherst: An Undergraduate's Diary, 1846–48,* ed. George F. Whicher (New York: Columbia University Press, 1946), passim; re: Jenks, pp. 132, 191, 239.

23. [Lyman Hotchkiss Bagg] *Four Years at Yale* (New Haven: Charles C. Chatfield & Co., 1871), pp. 657, 650.

24. Ibid., pp. 657, 620–58; final statement, p. 647.

25. Ibid., p. 650.

26. Ibid., pp. 594, 618–19; quote from p. 619.

27. Andrew Dickson White, *Autobiography of Andrew Dickson White,* vol. 1 (New York: The Century Co., 1905), pp. 26–27.

28. Ibid., p. 29.

29. [Bagg] *Four Years at Yale,* p. 658.

30. Hall, *College Words and Customs,* pp. 34, 81, 200, 22; quote from p. 201.

31. S. C. Bartlett, "College Disturbances," *Forum* 4 (Sept. 1887–Feb. 1888): 424–31.

32. Virginius Dabney, *Across the Years: Memories of a Virginian* (Garden City, N.Y.: Doubleday & Company, 1978), p. 81.

33. Rudolph, *Mark Hopkins,* pp. 101–5.

34. Ibid., p. 112, including footnote 45.

35. Hall, *College Words and Customs,* pp. 65–79; quote from p. 78.

36. Rudolph, *Mark Hopkins,* p. 112.

37. Codman Hislop, *Eliphalet Nott* (Middletown, Conn.: Wesleyan University Press, 1971), pp. 389–90; quote from p. 389.

38. Rudolph, *Mark Hopkins,* pp. 116–17.

39. Edward Hitchcock, *Reminiscences of Amherst College* (Northampton: Bridgman & Childs, 1863), pp. 321–25.

40. Faculty report quoted in Wilfred Shaw, *The University of Michigan* (New York: Harcourt, Brace and Howe, 1920), p. 37; Howard H. Peckham, *The Making of the University of Michigan, 1817–1967* (Ann Arbor: University of Michigan Press, 1967), pp. 27–28.

41. E. Wendy Saul and R. Gordon Kelly, "Christians, Brahmins, and Other Sporting Fellows: An Analysis of School Sports Stories," *Children's Literature in Education* 15 (Winter 1984): 234–45;

Benjamin G. Rader, *American Sports from the Age of Folk Games to the Age of Spectators* (Englewood Cliffs, N.J.: Prentice-Hall, 1983), pp. 20–86.

42. Frederick Rudolph, *The American College and University: A History* (New York: Alfred A. Knopf, 1962), pp. 144–50.

43. Charlotte Williams Conable, *Women at Cornell: The Myth of Equal Education* (Ithaca: Cornell University Press, 1977), pp. 115–17.

44. James Gardner Sanderson, *Cornell Stories* (New York: Charles Scribner's Sons, 1898).

45. Cornelius Howard Patton and Walter Taylor Field, *Eight O'Clock Chapel: A Study of New England College Life in the Eighties* (Boston: Houghton Mifflin Company, 1927), pp. 237–42.

46. Henry Seidel Canby, *Alma Mater: The Gothic Age of the American College* (New York: Farrar & Rinehart, 1936), p. 29.

47. David F. Allmendinger, Jr., "The Dangers of Ante-Bellum Student Life," *Journal of Social History* 7 (1973–74): 75–85.

48. [Bagg] *Four Years at Yale*, pp. 527–30; quote from p. 527.

49. Canby, *Alma Mater*, pp. 32–33.

50. Dabney, *Across the Years*, p. 81.

51. [Bagg] *Four Years at Yale*, p. 521.

52. Rudolph, *Mark Hopkins*, p. 103.

53. Carleton Putnam, *Theodore Roosevelt*, vol. 1 (New York: Charles Scribner's Sons, 1958), pp. 129–97; Roosevelt quoted on p. 136.

54. Ibid.; Theodore Roosevelt to Anna Roosevelt, Oct. 13, 1879, reproduced in *The Letters of Theodore Roosevelt*, vol. 1, ed. Elting E. Morison et al. (Cambridge, Mass.: Harvard University Press, 1951), pp. 41–42; quote from p. 42.

55. William Roscoe Thayer, quoted in Putnam, *Theodore Roosevelt*, vol. 1, p. 140.

56. Theodore Roosevelt to Anna Roosevelt, Nov. 10, 1878, reproduced in *Letters of Theodore Roosevelt*, p. 35.

57. Henry Adams, *The Education of Henry Adams* (New York: The Modern Library, 1931 [originally published 1918]), pp. 54–69, quote from p. 67; *The Bernard Berenson Treasury*, ed. Hanna Kiel (New York: Simon & Schuster, 1962), p. 209 (Berenson changed the spelling of his given name in later life); Robert Morss Lovett, *All Our Years* (New York: The Viking Press, 1948), pp. 39–43.

58. [Bagg] *Four Years at Yale*, p. 521.

59. Canby, *Alma Mater*, pp. 27–29.

60. Ibid., pp. 37–38.

61. Ibid., pp. 74–75. Walter Camp, Yale's great football coach, repeatedly made these connections explicit. For example, he stated in an undated manuscript: "Football has come to be recognized as the best school for instilling into the young man those attributes which business desires and demands" (quoted in David L. Westby and Allen Sack, "The Commercialization and Functional Rationalization of College Football," *Journal of Higher Education* 47 [1976]: 644).

62. Canby, *Alma Mater*, p. 72.

63. See, for example, Richard Holbrook, *Boys and Men: A Story of Life at Yale* (New York: Charles Scribner's Sons, 1900).

64. Lincoln Steffens, *The Autobiography of Lincoln Steffens* (New York: Harcourt, Brace & Company, 1931), p. 117.

65. Ibid., p. 119.

66. Ibid., pp. 117–18, 120.

67. Ibid., p. 121.

68. Hitchcock, *Reminiscences of Amherst College*, p. 320.

69. J. Edmund Welch, *Edward Hitchcock, M.D.: Founder of Physical Education in the College Curriculum* (Greenville, N.C.: East Carolina College, pub. J. E. Welch, 1966).

70. Wertenbaker, *Princeton*, p. 138.

71. Rader, *American Sports*, pp. 75–86.

72. *Yale Courant*, Dec. 8, 1877, pp. 78–79.

73. Westby and Sack, "The Commercialization and Functional Rationalization of College Football," pp. 638–39.

74. Paula S. Fass, *The Damned and the Beautiful: American Youth in the 1920s* (New York: Oxford University Press, 1977), p. 142.

CHAPTER THREE

1. Edward Hitchcock, *Reminiscences of Amherst College* (Northampton: Bridgman & Childs, 1863), p. 321.

2. The following discussion is based on David F. Allmendinger, Jr., *Paupers and Scholars: The Transformation of Student Life in Nineteenth-Century New England* (New York: St. Martin's Press, 1975).

3. Quoted from Hawthorne's notebooks in ibid., p. 2.

4. *Julian M. Sturtevant: An Autobiography,* ed. J. M. Sturtevant, Jr. (New York: Fleming H. Revell Company, 1896), pp. 55, 78.

5. Ibid., p. 102.

6. Ibid., pp. 86, 90, 91.

7. Ibid., pp. 94–95.

8. Ibid., pp. 95, 97–98.

9. Ibid., p. 100.

10. Wilson Smith, "Apologia pro Alma Matre: The College as Community in Ante-Bellum America," in *The Hofstadter Aegis: A Memorial,* ed. Stanley Elkins and Eric McKitrick (New York: Alfred A. Knopf, 1974), pp. 146–52; quote from p. 147.

11. Andrew M. Greeley, *From Backwater to Mainstream: A Profile of Catholic Higher Education* (New York: McGraw-Hill Book Company, 1969), pp. 9–10; although from a later period, the account of an 1881 graduate conveys the respect Boston College evoked in the public reminiscences of one of its clergy sons (William Cardinal O'Connell, *Recollections of Seventy Years* [Boston: Houghton Mifflin Company, 1934], pp. 72–73).

12. Robert Samuel Fletcher, *A History of Oberlin College: From Its Foundation Through the Civil War,* vol. 2 (Oberlin: Oberlin College, 1943), p. 507, including footnote 2.

13. Allmendinger, *Paupers and Scholars,* pp. 8–12.

14. William F. Galpin, *Delta Upsilon: One Hundred Years, 1834–1934* (Camden, N.J.: Delta Upsilon Fraternity, 1934), pp. 7–8.

15. Ibid., p. 16.

16. Diary entries July 22, 1854, and Nov. 8, 1855, reproduced in *The Diary of James A. Garfield,* vol. 1, ed. with intro. Harry James Brown and Frederick D. Williams (East Lansing: Michigan State University Press, 1967), pp. 268, 274–75.

17. Frederick Rudolph, *Mark Hopkins and the Log: Williams College, 1836–1872* (New Haven: Yale University Press, 1956), pp. 108, 109.

18. George Rugg Cutting, *Student Life at Amherst College: Its Organizations, Their Membership and History* (Amherst: Hatch & Williams, 1871), pp. 192, 181.

19. Quoted in Rudolph, *Mark Hopkins and the Log,* p. 114.

20. Bailey B. Burritt, *Professional Distribution of College and University Graduates,* U.S. Bureau of Education Bulletin, no. 491 (Washington, D.C.: U.S. Government Printing Office, 1912), documents the increasingly varied career choices made by undergraduates from college beginnings to the early twentieth century. Law is one profession that attracted both the established and the aspiring, although their career lines might take different paths. The scions of wealth created the prestigious firms closely allied with business, while the upwardly mobile sought clients outside the establishment and often served to represent members of their own ethnic group.

21. Abraham Flexner, *I Remember: The Autobiography of Abraham Flexner* (New York: Simon & Schuster, 1940), p. 59.

22. Ibid., pp. 52–63; quote from p. 59.

23. William L. Langer, *In and Out of the Ivory Tower: The Autobiography of William L. Langer* (New York: Neale Watson Academic Publications, 1977), pp. 43–66; quote from p. 48.

24. Ibid., p. 65.

25. Henry D. Sheldon, *History of University of Oregon* (Portland: Binfords & Mort, 1940), p. 220; Smith, "Apologia pro Alma Matre," pp. 149–50.

26. Alvin Johnson, *Pioneer's Progress: An Autobiography* (New York: The Viking Press, 1952), pp. 81–89; quote from p. 88.

27. Ibid., pp. 90–94; quotes from pp. 90, 92.

28. Edwin E. Slosson, *Great American Universities* (New York: The Macmillan Company, 1910), p. 35.

29. Charlotte Williams Conable, *Women at Cornell: The Myth of Equal Education* (Ithaca: Cornell University Press, 1977), p. 117.

30. Howard H. Peckham, *The Making of the University of Michigan, 1817–1967* (Ann Arbor: University of Michigan Press, 1967), p. 41.

31. *Yale Courant,* May 26, 1877, p. 200.

32. The following discussion of the curriculum is based on the comprehensive and excellent study by Frederick Rudolph, *Curriculum: A History of the American Undergraduate Course of Study Since 1636,* Carnegie Council Series (San Francisco: Jossey-Bass, 1977), pp. 99–150. My debt to Rudolph extends to the best source for university development, Laurence R. Veysey, *The Emergence of the American University* (Chicago: University of Chicago Press, 1965).

33. Hugh Hawkins, *Between Harvard and America: The Educational Leadership of Charles W. Eliot* (New York: Oxford University Press, 1972); Samuel Eliot Morison, *Three Centuries of Harvard, 1636–1936* (Cambridge, Mass.: Harvard University Press, 1936), pp. 329–99.

34. Morison is particularly good on these distinctions; see ibid., pp. 420–22.

35. Again, my indebtedness to Rudolph, *Curriculum,* pp. 99–150, and Veysey, *Emergence of the American University,* pp. 121–79.

36. Walter B. Pitkin, *On My Own* (New York: Charles Scribner's Sons, 1944), p. 196.

37. Ibid., pp. 198–99, 228–34; quotes from pp. 229, 230.

38. Ibid., p. 228.

39. Harry Barnard, *The Forging of an American Jew: The Life and Times of Judge Julian W. Mack* (New York: Herzl Press, 1974), pp. 24–27.

40. George Biddle, *An American Artist's Story* (Boston: Little, Brown and Company, 1939), pp. 116, 117.

41. Quoted in H. N. Hirsch, *The Enigma of Felix Frankfurter* (New York: Basic Books, 1981), p. 21.

42. Quoted in ibid.

43. Selma C. Berrol, "School Days on the Old East Side: The Italian and Jewish Experience," *New York History* 57 (1976): 201–13, esp. pp. 206–7. While the colleges received the sons of Jewish immigrants in significant numbers, these were a minority, however, within the immigrant Jewish community. The primary routes to economic improvement for Jews were manual labor, white-collar occupations (requiring schooling only to the eighth grade), and commerce (Selma C. Berrol, "Education and Economic Mobility: The Jewish Experience in New York City, 1890–1920," *American Jewish Historical Quarterly* 66 [1976]: 257–71).

44. Marcia Graham Synnott, *The Half-Opened Door: Discrimination and Admissions at Harvard, Yale, and Princeton, 1900–1970* (Westport, Conn.: Greenwood Press, 1979), p. 16. More generally, I have found this a most useful source.

45. Maurice Hindus, *A Traveler in Two Worlds* (Garden City, N.Y.: Doubleday & Company, 1971), pp. 124–44, esp. p. 141.

46. Francis Biddle, *A Casual Past* (Garden City, N.Y.: Doubleday & Company, 1961), p. 219.

47. Harry Starr, "The Affair at Harvard: What the Students Did," *The Menorah Journal* 8 (1922): 266.

48. Ibid., p. 23; Heywood Broun and George Britt, *Christians Only: A Study in Prejudice* (New York: Vanguard Press, 1931), pp. 72–124.

49. Morris J. Escholl, "The Perennial Burden of the Jew," *The Menorah Journal* 1 (1915): 222.

50. Mortimer J. Adler, *Philosopher at Large: An Intellectual Autobiography* (New York: Macmillan Publishing Co., 1977), pp. 23, 24, 26–29; quotes from pp. 26, 28.

51. Synnott, *Half-Opened Door,* p. 98.

52. William T. Ham, "Harvard Student Opinion on the Jewish Question," *The Nation* 115 (1922): 225–27; quotes from p. 225.

53. Quoted in Synnott, *Half-Opened Door,* p. 159.

54. Owen Wister, *Philosophy 4: A Story of Harvard University* (New York: Macmillan Company, 1903), p. 23. (It originally appeared in 1901.)

55. Ibid., pp. 14, 15.

56. Ibid., p. 24.

57. Ibid., p. 87.

58. *The Letters of Theodore Roosevelt,* vol. 1, ed. Elting E. Morison et al. (Cambridge, Mass.: Harvard University Press, 1951), p. 16, footnotes, and pp. 16–45 passim.

59. *Fiftieth Anniversary Report of the Harvard Class of 1907* (Cambridge, Mass.: Harvard University Printing Office, 1957), pp. 251–52, 327, 392–95.

CHAPTER FOUR

1. Vincent Sheean, *Personal History* (New York: The Literary Guild, 1934, 1935), p. 9.

2. Ibid., pp. 11, 12. The fraternity was not actually a Jewish one, but because it contained Jews as well as Christians it was identified as Jewish by some University of Chicago students (footnote, p. 13).

3. Ibid., pp. 19, 19–20, 21.

4. Ibid., p. 23.

5. Ronald Steel, *Walter Lippmann and the American Century* (Boston: Little, Brown and Company, 1980), pp. 12–29.

6. Van Wyck Brooks, *Scenes and Portraits: Memories of Childhood and Youth* (New York: E. P. Dutton & Co., 1954), pp. 98–104.

7. John Reed, "Almost Thirty," *The New Republic* 86 (April 29, 1936): 333. The article was originally written in 1917. Standing in clear contrast to Reed's enthusiasm is the criticism of Harvard's radicals by a member of the class of 1913 for lacking a sense of history and of humor, for failing to be Christians, and for being intolerant of the mentality "of the undergraduate who wants to do his work, do his athletics, have a boys' club, go into them all hard and leave the future until he gets there" (Francis B. Thwing, "Radicalism at Harvard," *Harvard Undergraduate Magazine* [1911]: 260–63; quote from pp. 261–62).

8. Steel, *Walter Lippmann,* pp. 16–22. It is intriguing that at the end of his long, controversial, and productive life, these were the moments that Lippmann wanted to recall (Ronald Steel, "The Biographer as Detective: What Walter Lippmann Preferred to Forget," *The New York Times Book Review,* July 21, 1985, pp. 3, 16).

9. Max Eastman, *Enjoyment of Living* (New York: Harper & Brothers, 1948), pp. 133, 134.

10. Ibid., pp. 223, 228–29.

11. Richard Walser, *Thomas Wolfe Undergraduate* (Durham: Duke University Press, 1977).

12. Quotes from ibid., pp. 18, 52.

13. Paul Scott Mowrer, *The House of Europe* (Cambridge, Mass.: The Riverside Press of Houghton Mifflin Company, 1945), p. 85.

14. Ibid., p. 106.

15. Ibid., pp. 82–95; quote from p. 94.

16. Robert A. Caro, *The Power Broker: Robert Moses and the Fall of New York* (New York: Alfred A. Knopf, 1974), pp. 38–47.

17. Lee Simonson, "Varied Outlooks: V.," *Harvard Advocate,* Jan. 1908, pp. 99–101; quote from p. 99.

18. Bruce Clayton, *Forgotten Prophet: The Life of Randolph Bourne* (Baton Rouge: Louisiana State University Press, 1984), pp. 32–95; quote from Jinx Roosevelt, "Randolph Bourne: The Education of a Critic: An Interpretation," *History of Education Quarterly* 17 (1977): 257–74; Bourne to Prudence Wimterrowd, March 2, 1913, quoted on p. 265.

19. Randolph S. Bourne, "The College: An Undergraduate View," *Atlantic Monthly* 108 (1911): 668–69.

20. Ibid., p. 670.

21. Ibid., pp. 671, 672. In a later essay, Bourne suggested that the real problem of the college lay

in the contrast between its values and the strength of the sporting philosophy of the undergraduate, brought from home and school, which understood life and work as a game to be won or lost (Randolph Bourne, "The Undergraduate," in *Education and Living* [New York: The Century Co., 1917], pp. 222–29).

22. Margaret Mead, *Blackberry Winter: My Earlier Years* (New York: William Morrow & Co., 1972), p. 90.

23. Ibid., pp. 94, 100.

24. Ibid., pp. 102, 100–9; quote from p. 108.

25. Ibid., pp. 114, 115. Mead's relationship with Benedict ultimately became a lesbian one (Mary Catherine Bateson, *With a Daughter's Eye* [William Morrow & Co., 1984], pp. 115–27).

CHAPTER FIVE

1. Owen Johnson, *Stover at Yale* (New York: Collier Books, 1968 [originally published by Frederick A. Stokes Company, 1912]), p. 10.

2. Ibid., p. 187.

3. Ibid., p. 202.

4. Ibid., p. 232.

5. Ibid., p. 308.

6. The following discussion draws on Frederick Rudolph, *Curriculum: A History of the American Undergraduate Course of Study Since 1636*, Carnegie Council Series (San Francisco: Jossey-Bass, 1977), pp. 151–244.

7. JB Lon Hefferlin, *Dynamics of Academic Reform* (San Francisco: Jossey-Bass, 1969), cited in Rudolph, *Curriculum*, p. 245. Although Hefferlin's data came from a statistical study of 110 college catalogues between 1962 and 1967, his work has broader applicability.

8. Abraham Flexner, *The American College: A Criticism* (New York: The Century Co., 1908); quote from p. 11.

9. Woodrow Wilson, "What Is a College For?" in *The Papers of Woodrow Wilson*, vol. 19, ed. Arthur S. Link (Princeton: Princeton University Press, 1975), pp. 344, 346, 344. (The article originally appeared in *Scribner's Magazine* 46 [1909]: 570–77.)

10. Woodrow Wilson, "The Spirit of Learning," an address at Harvard, July 1, 1901, quoted in ibid., p. 287.

11. Henry Wilkinson Bragdon, *Woodrow Wilson: The Academic Years* (Cambridge, Mass.: The Belknap Press of Harvard University Press, 1967), pp. 15–46, 269–352.

12. Woodrow Wilson to Mary Allen Hulbert Peck, July 3, 1901, quoted in *Papers*, vol. 19, p. 290.

13. Charles William Eliot, "The Potency of the Jewish Race," *The Menorah Journal* 1 (1915): 141–44; quote from p. 144. Eliot's remarks have been criticized by others for his stereotyping of Jews, losing sight of the general positive cast of his remarks.

14. Quoted in Henry Aaron Yeomans, *Abbott Lawrence Lowell, 1856–1943* (Cambridge, Mass.: Harvard University Press, 1948), pp. 128, 129.

15. A. Lawrence Lowell, "Competition in College," *Atlantic Monthly* 103 (1909): 823.

16. Harold S. Wechsler, *The Qualified Student: A History of Selective College Admission in America* (New York: John Wiley & Sons, 1977), pp. 131–67.

17. Marcia Graham Synnott, *The Half-Opened Door: Discrimination and Admissions at Harvard, Yale, and Princeton, 1900–1970* (Westport, Conn.: Greenwood Press, 1979), pp. 85–124; specific reference on p. 110.

18. Quoted in ibid., p. 67.

19. The discussion of Reed relies on the excellent work by Burton R. Clark, *The Distinctive College: Antioch, Reed & Swarthmore* (Chicago: Aldine Publishing Company, 1970), pp. 91–168; Foster quoted on p. 94.

20. Foster quoted in ibid., p. 105.

21. Joseph R. DeMartini, "Student Culture as a Change Agent in American Higher Education: An Illustration from the Nineteenth Century," *Journal of Social History* 9 (1975–76): 526–41, is an excellent study of this process at the University of Illinois.

22. Merle Scott Ward, *Philosophies of Administration Current in the Deanship of the Liberal Arts College*, Contributions to Education, no. 632 (New York: Teachers College Bureau of Publications, 1934), pp. 14–15.

23. E. E. Lindsay and E. O. Holland, *College and University Administration* (New York: The Macmillan Company, 1930), pp. 487–538; quote from p. 531.

24. DeMartini, "Student Culture as a Change Agent," p. 535.

25. Thomas Arkle Clark, *The Fraternity and the College* (Menasha, Wis.: George Banta Publishing Company, 1915), pp. 7–28; quote from p. 27.

26. Clarence Cook Little, *The Awakening College* (New York: W. W. Norton & Company, 1930), p. 73; Howard H. Peckham, *The Making of the University of Michigan, 1817–1967* (Ann Arbor: University of Michigan Press, 1967), pp. 157–68.

27. Rudolph, *Curriculum,* pp. 276–77; Alexander Meiklejohn, *The Experimental College* (Madison: University of Wisconsin, 1928).

28. The discussion of Swarthmore relies on Clark, *The Distinctive College,* pp. 171–230.

29. Quoted in ibid., p. 186.

30. Aydelotte quoted in ibid., p. 196; second quote from p. 198.

31. Speech by C. A. Prosser, quoted in *Yale Daily News,* Oct. 3, 1922.

32. Robert C. Angell, "The Trend toward Greater Maturity among Undergraduates Due to the Depression," *School and Society* 38 (1933): 391–96.

33. John R. Tunis, *A Measure of Independence* (New York: Atheneum, 1964), pp. 90–94; quote from p. 90.

34. John R. Tunis, *Was College Worth While?* (New York: Harcourt, Brace & Company, 1936).

35. Tunis, *Measure of Independence,* pp. 226, 225.

CHAPTER SIX

1. The best source here is James S. Coleman, "The Adolescent Subculture and Academic Achievement," *The American Journal of Sociology* 65 (1960): 337–47; and Coleman, "Peer Cultures and Education in Modern Society," in *College Peer Groups: Problems and Prospects for Research,* ed. Theodore M. Newcomb and Everett K. Wilson (Chicago: Aldine Publishing Company, 1966), pp. 263–67.

2. Paula S. Fass, *The Damned and the Beautiful: American Youth in the 1920s* (New York: Oxford University Press, 1977), treats in great detail many of the themes of this chapter, although in the particular context of youth in the 1920s. While I agree with Fass about many specifics, we differ in that I see college life in the 1920s more in terms of its continuities than its new facets. Many elements of the male college life that she describes can be found as early as 1830. In addition, I see male and female college life as only one alternative path, dominant in political power on campus, but not in its hold over the majority of undergraduates, who remained, both in fact and in consciousness, outsiders. The primary sources that Fass uses—undergraduate newspapers—were largely controlled in the 1920s by fraternity men and thus reflect their perspective. The few editors who were rebels would tend to dramatize the hold of the Greek system on the rest of the campus. Specific reference for fraternity growth, p. 143.

3. Frank B. Gilbreth, Jr., *I'm a Lucky Guy* (New York: Thomas Y. Crowell Company, 1951), pp. 31–62.

4. Ibid., pp. 77–92; quotes from pp. 82, 86.

5. Walter L. Wallace, *Student Culture: Social Structure and Continuity in a Liberal Arts College* (Chicago: Aldine Publishing Company, 1966).

6. Ibid., p. 185.

7. F. Scott Fitzgerald, *This Side of Paradise* (New York: Charles Scribner's Sons, 1948 [originally published 1920]), pp. 58, 58–59.

8. Letter to *Illini,* May 14, 1922, reproduced in *An Illini Century: One Hundred Years of Campus Life,* ed. Roger Ebert (Urbana: University of Illinois Press, 1967), p. 118.

9. Fass, *The Damned and the Beautiful,* pp. 262–70.

10. Hoagy Carmichael, with Stephen Longstreet, *Sometimes I Wonder: The Story of Hoagy Carmichael* (New York: Farrar, Straus and Giroux, 1965), pp. 61, 61–62.

11. Ibid., pp. 63–64, 68.

12. Willard Waller, "The Rating and Dating Complex," *American Sociological Review* 2 (1937): 727–34.

13. Lynn Montross and Lois Seyster Montross, "When Greek Meets Barb," *Town and Gown* (New York: George H. Doran Company, 1923), p. 264.

14. Joe Kapp, selection in *There Was Light: Autobiography of a University: Berkeley: 1868–1968,* ed. with intro. Irving Stone (Garden City, N.Y.: Doubleday & Company, 1970), p. 174.

15. W. H. Cowley, "Significance of Student Traditions," in *Higher Education and Society: A Symposium* (Norman: University of Oklahoma Press, 1936), pp. 33–36.

16. Daniel Katz and Floyd Henry Allport, *Students' Attitudes: A Report of the Syracuse University Reaction Study* (Syracuse: The Craftsman Press, 1931), pp. 128–33; quote from p. 131.

17. Robert Cooley Angell, *The Campus: A Study of Contemporary Undergraduate Life in the American University* (New York: D. Appleton and Company, 1928), p. 85.

18. Ibid., pp. 80–81, and Appendices, pp. 229–34. A survey of students at the University of Indiana in 1951 came to the same conclusions: Raymond A. Mulligan, "Socio-economic Background and College Enrollment," *The American Sociological Review* 16 (1951): 188–96.

19. Angell, *The Campus,* p. 6.

20. Montross and Montross, "Peter Warshaw," *Town and Gown,* pp. 19–20, 26, 30–31.

21. Ibid., p. 33.

22. Ibid., p. 35.

23. Melvin M. Belli, with Robert Blair Kaiser, *My Life on Trial: An Autobiography* (New York: William Morrow & Co., 1976), pp. 40–49; quote from pp. 43–44.

24. Mary M. Crawford, *Student Folkways and Spending at Indiana University, 1940–1941: A Study in Consumption* (New York: Columbia University Press, 1943), p. 215.

25. Ibid., p. 148.

26. Rose K. Goldsen et al., *What College Students Think* (Princeton: D. Van Nostrand Company, 1960); quote from p. 69.

27. Ibid., pp. 69–71.

28. Ibid., pp. 6–15.

29. Angell, *The Campus,* p. 139.

30. Ibid., pp. 127, 6.

31. Ibid., p. 80.

32. Ibid., pp. 128, 2–3.

33. For example, Basil H. Peterson, "The Scholarship of Students Housed in Various Living Quarters," *School and Society* 57 (1943): 221–24.

34. Angell, *The Campus,* pp. 2–3.

35. Ibid., p. 44.

36. Katz and Allport, *Students' Attitudes,* p. 161.

37. Ibid., pp. 162–65.

38. Ibid., p. 160.

39. Ibid., p. 48.

40. Goldsen, *What Students Think,* p. 66.

41. Otto Butz, ed., *The Unsilent Generation: An Anonymous Symposium in Which Eleven College Seniors Look at Themselves and Their World* (New York: Rinehart & Company, 1958), p. 70.

42. F. Stuart Chapin, "Research Studies of Extracurricular Activities and Their Significance in Reflecting Social Changes," *Journal of Educational Sociology* 4 (1930–31): 491–98; Albert Beecher Crawford, "Extra-Curricular Activities and Academic Work," *The Personnel Journal* 7 (1928–29): 121–29.

43. Goldsen, *What Students Think,* p. 72.

44. Ibid., p. 73.

45. Butz, *Unsilent Generation,* p. 71.

46. Junius A. Davis and Norman Frederiksen, "Public and Private School Graduates in College," *Journal of Higher Education* 6 (1955): 18–22.

47. For example, Carl C. Seltzer, "Academic Success in College of Public and Private School Students: Freshman Year at Harvard," *Journal of Psychology* 25 (1948): 419–31.

48. Charles McArthur, "Subculture and Personality during the College Years," *Journal of Educational Sociology* 33 (1960): 260–67; quotes from pp. 260, 261.

49. Ibid.; quote from p. 262.

50. Goldsen, *What Students Think,* pp. 78–80.

51. John Harp and Philip Taietz, "Academic Integrity and Social Structure: A Study of Cheating among College Students," *Social Problems* 13 (1966): 365–73; William J. Bowers, *Student Dishonesty and Its Control in College* (New York: Bureau of Applied Social Research, Columbia, 1965), pp. 109–10.

52. Goldsen, *What Students Think,* p. 79.

53. Such studies are the most common form of inquiry into student populations between 1930 and 1970. Many of these studies were summarized in Philip E. Jacob's controversial *Changing Values in College: An Exploratory Study of the Impact of College Teaching* (New York: Harper & Brothers, 1957). A full review of the literature is Kenneth A. Feldman and Theodore M. Newcomb, *The Impact of College on Students,* 2 vols. (San Francisco: Jossey-Bass, 1970). The genre continues on a massive scale in the work of Alexander Astin.

54. Hilding B. Carlson, "Attitudes of Undergraduate Students," *Journal of Social Psychology* 5 (1934): 202–12.

55. Hanan C. Selvin and Warren O. Hagstrom, "Determinants of Support for Civil Liberties," *British Journal of Sociology* 11 (1960): 51–69.

56. Goldsen, *What Students Think,* pp. 97–124.

57. Ibid., pp. 119–24.

58. Katz and Allport, *Students' Attitudes,* pp. 146–47; for information about Syracuse University in this period, see Harvey Strum, "Louis Marshall and Anti-Semitism at Syracuse University," *American Jewish Archives* 35 (1983): 1–12.

59. Gilbert W. Gabriel, *The Seven-Branched Candlestick: The Schooldays of a Young American Jew* (New York: Block Publishing Co., 1925); quotes from pp. 66, 80.

60. Lee J. Levinger, "Surveying the Jewish Students," *B'nai B'rith Magazine* 51 (1937); *Campus Activities,* ed. Harold C. Hand (New York: McGraw-Hill Book Company, 1938), p. 148.

61. Heywood Broun and George Britt, *Christians Only: A Study in Prejudice* (New York: Vanguard Press, 1931), p. 79.

62. Katz and Allport, *Students' Attitudes,* pp. 186–87.

63. This effort is documented in Alfred McClung Lee, *Fraternities without Brotherhood: A Study of Prejudice on the American Campus* (Boston: Beacon Press, 1955). Lee uses as a chapter title "Schools for Prejudice?" (p. 102).

64. G. M. Gilbert, "Stereotype Persistence and Change among College Students," *Journal of Abnormal and Social Psychology* 46 (1951): 245–54.

65. Ian C. Ross, "Group Standards Concerning the Admission of Jews to Fraternities at the University of Michigan," *Social Problems* 2 (1955): 133–40.

66. Alfred S. Romer, "The Color Line in Fraternities," *Atlantic Monthly* 183 (1949): 27–31.

67. Lee, *Fraternities without Brotherhood,* passim.

68. Lawrence Bloomgarden, "Our Changing Elite Colleges," *Commentary* 29 (1960): 150–54.

69. James S. Davie and A. Paul Hare, "Button-down Collar Culture: A Study of Undergraduate Life at a Men's College," *Human Organization* 14 (1956): 13–20; quote from p. 16.

70. Ibid.; quote from p. 16.

CHAPTER SEVEN

1. Upton Sinclair, *The Goose-step: A Study of American Education* (Pasadena, Cal.: Upton Sinclair, 1923).

2. J. E. Kirkpatrick, *The American College and Its Rulers* (New York: New Republic, Inc., 1926), pp. 197–224; quote from p. 224. Raymond Wolters' excellent study of the 1920s campus revolts of black students found that the central goals were the attainment of self-determination and a liberal arts curriculum, in institutions that were controlled paternalistically by philanthropists and that promoted industrial education (*The New Negro on Campus: Black College Rebellions of the 1920s* [Princeton: Princeton University Press, 1975]).

3. Horace M. Kallen, *College Prolongs Infancy* (New York: The John Day Company, 1932).

4. *The Students Speak Out! A Symposium from 22 Colleges* (New York: New Republic, Inc., 1929).

5. Philip G. Altbach, *Student Politics in America: An Historical Analysis* (New York: McGraw-Hill Book Company, 1974), pp. 34–39.

6. "News About Fraternities, Student Government," *The New Student* 3 (April 26, 1924): 9.

7. "An Ouster Epic," *The New Student* 7 (Oct. 12, 1927): 6.

8. George D. Pratt, Jr., "Amherst Men Take the Lead," *The New Student* 3 (Oct. 6, 1923): 2.

9. Quoted in "Students Ask Profs to Be Iconoclastic," *The New Student* 4 (March 28, 1925): 1.

10. Earl Schenck Miers, *The Trouble Bush* (Chicago: Rand McNally & Company, 1966), pp. 107, 108.

11. Ibid.

12. Ibid., pp. 113–14.

13. Ibid., pp. 116–17; 128–32; quote from p. 128.

14. Doris Kearns, *Lyndon Johnson and the American Dream* (New York: Harper & Row, 1976), pp. 46–52; Johnson quoted on p. 49.

15. Ibid., pp. 46–52. Robert A. Caro gives a far less sympathetic reading to Johnson's college years, but his essential story does not dispute that of Kearns (*The Years of Lyndon Johnson: The Path to Power* [New York: Alfred A. Knopf, 1982], Chapter 11).

16. Profiles of 1930s Communist Party members and of liberal-left students found them to be the children of professional, liberal parents, often Jewish or non-religious (Seymour Martin Lipset, *Rebellion in the University* [Chicago: University of Chicago Press, 1976], p. 182).

17. "Harvard Stirred by Attack on Cliques, Lamont and MacVeagh Try to Bridge Student Chasm," *The New York Times*, Dec. 9, 1923, section 10, p. 3.

18. See, for example, John Erskine, *The Memory of Certain Persons* (Philadelphia: J. B. Lippincott Company, 1947), pp. 70–101.

19. Eileen Eagan, *Class, Culture, and the Classroom: The Student Peace Movement of the 1930s* (Philadelphia: Temple University Press, 1981), pp. 42–44; James Wechsler, *Revolt on the Campus* (New York: Covici, Friede, 1935), pp. 108–20; *The New York Times*, April 3, 1932; Tudor Harris quoted in "Students to Fight Harris Expulsion," *The New York Times*, April 3, 1932.

20. David Riesman, "Educational Reform at Harvard College: Meritocracy and Its Adversaries," in Seymour Martin Lipset and David Riesman, *Education and Politics at Harvard* (New York: McGraw-Hill Book Company, 1975), p. 298.

21. Ibid., pp. 298–99.

22. George Anthony Weller, *Not to Eat, Not for Love* (New York: Harrison Smith and Robert Haas, 1933).

23. Ibid., pp. 98, 108–15, 321–26; quotes from pp. 110, 113, 324.

24. Ibid., pp. 126–27.

25. Ibid., p. 166.

26. Ibid., pp. 141, 400.

27. Altbach, *Student Politics in America*, pp. 58–72; Wechsler, *Revolt on the Campus*, pp. 166–81, 287–347; Eagan, *Class, Culture, and the Classroom*, passim.

28. Eric Sevareid, *Not So Wild a Dream* (New York: Alfred A. Knopf, 1946), p. 51.

29. Ibid., p. 65.

30. Ibid., pp. 66–67; quote from p. 66.

31. Ibid., pp. 63, 68.

32. Ibid., pp. 49, 50, 51.

33. Joseph R. DeMartini, "Student Activists of the 1930s and 1960s: A Comparison of the Social Base of Two Student Movements," *Youth and Society* 6 (1975): 395–422.

34. Pauline Kael, "Campus Life," in Studs Terkel, *Hard Times: An Oral History of the Great Depression* (New York: Pantheon Books, 1970), pp. 346–47.

35. James A. Wechsler, *The Age of Suspicion* (New York: Random House, 1953), pp. 21, 22.

36. Ibid., p. 25.

37. Ibid., pp. 36, 40–41, 51–52.

38. Ibid., pp. 61, 62–64.

39. Irving Howe, *A Margin of Hope: An Intellectual Autobiography* (San Diego: Harcourt Brace Jovanovich, 1982), pp. 64–65.

40. Ibid., pp. 64, 62, 68.

41. Richard H. Rovere, *Arrivals and Departures: A Journalist's Memoirs* (New York: Macmillan Publishing Co., 1976), p. 44.

42. Ann Charters, *Kerouac: A Biography* (San Francisco: Straight Arrow Books, 1973), pp. 31–62; John Tytell, *Naked Angels: The Lives and Literature of the Beat Generation* (New York: McGraw-Hill Book Company, 1976), pp. 36–94.

43. Kenneth Keniston's research on Harvard College students for *The Uncommitted: Alienated Youth in American Society* (New York: Harcourt, Brace & World, 1964) began in the late 1950s.

44. Roy Heath, *The Reasonable Adventurer: A Study of the Development of Thirty-six Undergraduates at Princeton* (Pittsburgh: University of Pittsburgh Press, 1964); quotes from pp. 30, 36. Heath studied undergraduates from the class of 1954. The critical foreword by David Riesman, written in 1963, is of particular interest.

45. Willie Morris, *North Toward Home* (Boston: Houghton Mifflin Company, 1967), p. 153.

46. Ibid., pp. 155, 156, 155.

47. Ibid., pp. 164, 165, 149–50.

CHAPTER EIGHT

1. Albert Beecher Crawford, *Incentives to Study: A Survey of Student Opinion* (New Haven: Yale University Press, 1929); specific reference, p. 42.

2. Ibid., p. 70.

3. Ibid., p. 156.

4. Clara M. Brown, "The Social Adjustment of College Students," *Journal of the American Association of University Women* 30 (1937): 162–63.

5. Ibid., p. 163.

6. Louis Tendler, "For Those Who Toil," *Chimes* 6 (1925): 21, 49.

7. *Report of the Faculty-Student Committee on the Distribution of Students' Time* (Chicago: University of Chicago Press, 1925), p. 26. The study also showed that students who belonged to the male fraternities and the female clubs made fewer low grades than the student population as a whole, perhaps because of grade minimums set by the organizations or because of mutual aid (ibid., p. 43).

8. Thomas Bergin, "My Native Country," in *My Harvard, My Yale,* ed. Diana Dubois (New York: Random House, 1982), pp. 163–64, 162.

9. Ibid., p. 164.

10. George F. Kennan, *Memoirs: 1925–1950* (Boston: Little, Brown and Company, 1967), pp. 9, 10, 11.

11. Ibid., pp. 11, 12, 13.

12. Langston Hughes, *The Big Sea* (New York: Hill and Wang, 1963 [original copyright, 1940]), pp. 83–85; quotes from pp. 83, 85. As a student at Lincoln, Hughes surveyed student views on the questions of its all-white faculty and its failure to include courses on the literature and history of

Afro-Americans (ibid., pp. 306–10, and Raymond Wolters, *The New Negro on Campus: Black College Rebellions of the 1920s* [Princeton: Princeton University Press, 1975], pp. 281–82).

13. Theodore H. White, *In Search of History: A Personal Adventure* (New York: Harper & Row, 1978), p. 43.

14. Ibid., p. 44.

15. James B. Conant, *My Several Lives: Memoirs of a Social Inventor* (New York: Harper & Row, 1970), pp. 22–25; quote from p. 24.

16. White, *In Search of History,* p. 43.

17. Ibid., pp. 47, 49, 54.

18. Ibid., p. 43.

19. Murray Kempton, *Part of Our Time: Some Ruins and Monuments of the Thirties* (New York: Simon & Schuster, 1955), pp. 302–3.

20. Hal Draper, "The Student Movement of the Thirties: A Political History," in *As We Saw the Thirties: Essays on Social and Political Movements of a Decade,* ed. Rita James Simon (Urbana: University of Illinois Press, 1967), p. 188.

21. James Wechsler, *Revolt on the Campus* (New York: Covici, Friede, 1935), p. 179.

22. Irving Howe, *A Margin of Hope: An Intellectual Autobiography* (San Diego: Harcourt Brace Jovanovich, 1982), p. 66.

23. Keith W. Olson, *The G.I. Bill, the Veterans, and the Colleges* (Lexington: The University Press of Kentucky, 1974), pp. 43–44.

24. Edith Efron, "The Two Joes Meet—Joe College, Joe Veteran," *The New York Times Magazine,* June 16, 1949, p. 21.

25. Norman Fredericksen and W. B. Schrader, "The Academic Achievement of Veteran and Nonveteran Students," *Psychological Monographs: General and Applied* 66, no. 15, whole no. 347 (1952): 1–55. Olson, *G.I. Bill,* ably summarizes these studies, pp. 50–55; quote from Fredericksen and Schrader on p. 55.

26. Janet Agnes Kelley, *College Life and the Mores* (New York: Bureau of Publications, Teachers College, 1949), pp. 219–20.

27. Efron, "Two Joes Meet," p. 21.

28. Ibid.

29. Ernest Havemann and Patricia Salter West, *They Went to College: The College Graduate in America Today* (New York: Harcourt, Brace & Company, 1952), pp. 31, 178–85.

30. Ibid., pp. 35–37.

31. Ibid., p. 159.

32. Ibid., pp. 162–63.

33. Ibid., pp. 172, 182–89. A summary of recent studies that have attempted to take differences in ability, motivation, and parental position into account concludes that "three fourths (more or less) of the [income] difference [between those who went to college and those who did not] represent a real economic benefit of higher education" (Dael Wolfle, "To What Extent Do Monetary Returns to Education Vary with Family Background, Mental Ability, and School Quality?" in *Does College Matter? Some Evidence on the Impacts of Higher Education,* ed. Lewis C. Solmon and Paul J. Taubman [New York: Academic Press, 1973], pp. 65–74; quote from p. 67).

34. This is most fully stated in Burton R. Clark, *Educating the Expert Society* (San Francisco: Chandler Publishing Company, 1962); quote from p. 50.

35. The clarification of college subcultures is most clearly expressed in Burton R. Clark and Martin Trow, "The Organizational Context," in *College Peer Groups: Problems and Prospects for Research,* ed. Theodore M. Newcomb and Everett K. Wilson (Chicago: Aldine Publishing Company, 1961), pp. 17–71; quote from p. 28.

36. Randall Collins, *The Credential Society: An Historical Sociology of Education and Stratification* (New York: Academic Press, 1979).

37. This was most fully worked out in Howard S. Becker, Blanche Geer, and Everett C. Hughes, *Making the Grade: The Academic Side of College Life* (New York: John Wiley & Sons, 1968).

38. Ibid., pp. 63, 82.

39. Ibid., p. 98.

40. Ibid., p. 99.

CHAPTER NINE

1. Barbara Miller Solomon, "Alice Elvira Freeman Palmer," *Notable American Women,* vol. 3, ed. Edward T. James (Cambridge, Mass.: The Belknap Press of Harvard University Press, 1971), pp. 4–9.

2. Olive Anderson, *An American Girl and Her Four Years in a Boys College* (New York: D. Appleton and Company, 1878), p. 52.

3. Patricia Foster Haines, "Climates of Expectation: The Ecology of Coeducation at Cornell University, 1868–1900," unpublished paper, April 1983.

4. Florence Kelley, "When Co-education Was Young," *The Survey* 57 (1927): 557, 559.

5. *The Making of a Feminist: Early Journals and Letters of M. Carey Thomas,* ed. Marjorie Housepian Dobkin (Kent, Ohio: Kent State University Press, 1979), 101–19.

6. College culture in the women's colleges is discussed at greater length in the author's *Alma Mater: Design and Experience in the Women's Colleges from Their Nineteenth Century Beginnings to the 1930s* (New York: Alfred A. Knopf, 1984).

7. F. Stuart Chapin, "Extra-Curricular Activities of College Students: A Study of College Leadership," *School and Society* 23 (1926): 215.

8. Mary E. Cookingham, "Bluestockings, Spinsters and Pedagogues: Women College Graduates, 1865–1910," *Population Studies* 38 (1984): 349–64.

9. Mary E. Cookingham, "Combining Marriage, Motherhood, and Jobs before World War II: Women College Graduates, Classes of 1905–1935," *Journal of Family History* 9 (1984): 178–95.

10. Richard H. Klemer, "Factors of Personality and Experience Which Differentiate Single from Married Women," *Marriage and Family Living* 16 (1954): 41–44; quote from 44.

11. Don Brown, interview, Jan. 31, 1984.

12. Kathryn M. Kerns, "The Ladies Speak: Women's Literary Clubs at Alfred University, 1850–1861," unpublished paper, Conference on the History of Education, Oct. 1983.

13. Haines, "Climates of Expectation."

14. Charlotte Williams Conable, *Women at Cornell: The Myth of Equal Education* (Ithaca: Cornell University Press, 1977), pp. 62–97.

15. Dorothy Gies McGuigan, *A Dangerous Experiment: 100 Years of Women at the University of Michigan* (Ann Arbor: Center for Continuing Education of Women, 1970).

16. Joan G. Zimmerman, "Daughters of Main Street: Culture and the Female Community at Grinnell, 1884–1917," in *Woman's Being, Woman's Place: Female Identity and Vocation in American History,* ed. Mary Kelley (Boston: G. K. Hall & Co., 1979), p. 160.

17. Vincent Sheean, *Personal History* (New York: The Literary Guild, 1935), p. 10.

18. Zimmerman, "Daughters of Main Street," p. 158.

19. Daniel Katz and Floyd Henry Allport, *Students' Attitudes: A Report of the Syracuse University Reaction Study* (Syracuse: The Craftsman Press, 1931), pp. 146–47.

20. For example, see Hilding B. Carlson, "Attitudes of Undergraduate Students," *Journal of Social Psychology* 5 (1934): 211; and Paul J. Fay and Warren Middleton, "Certain Factors Related to Liberal and Conservative Attitudes of College Students: Sex, Classification, Fraternity Membership, Major Subject," *Journal of Educational Psychology* 30 (1939): 380.

21. A. J. Harris, H. H. Remmers, and C. E. Ellison, "The Relation between Liberal and Conservative Attitudes in College Students, and Other Factors," *Journal of Social Psychology* 3 (1932): 335.

22. Orden Smuckler, "The Campus Clique as an Agency of Socialization," *Journal of Educational Sociology* 21 (1947–48): 163–68; quote from p. 164.

23. Ben Willerman and Leonard Swanson, "Group Prestige in Voluntary Organizations: A Study of College Sororities," *Human Relations* 6 (1953): 55–77.

24. Paula S. Fass, *The Damned and the Beautiful: American Youth in the 1920s* (New York: Oxford University Press, 1977), pp. 262–70.

25. Willard Waller, "The Rating and Dating Complex," *American Sociological Review* 2 (1937): 727–34.

26. Lynn Montross and Lois Seyster Montross, "The Strangest Serenade," *Town and Gown* (New York: George H. Doran Company, 1923), pp. 221, 220.

27. Mary M. Crawford, *Student Folkways and Spending at Indiana University, 1940–1941: A Study in Consumption* (New York: Columbia University Press, 1943), p. 215.

28. J. E. Janney, "Fad and Fashion Leadership among Undergraduate Women," *Journal of Abnormal and Social Psychology* 36 (1941): 275–78.

29. Crawford, *Student Folkways and Spending at Indiana University*, p. 104.

30. Patricia Blake, "Why College Girls Dress That Way," *The New York Times Magazine*, April 7, 1946, p. 23.

31. Phyllis Blanchard and Carlyn Manasses, *New Girls for Old* (New York: The Macaulay Company, 1930), pp. 250–51; conversation with Daniel Katz, spring 1984.

32. Blanchard and Manasses, *New Girls for Old*, pp. 260–69.

33. Dorothy Dunbar Bromley and Florence Haxton Britten, *Youth and Sex: A Study of 1300 College Students* (New York: Harper & Brothers, 1938), pp. 287–89.

34. Ibid., pp. 47–86.

35. Ibid., pp. 87–116; quote from p. 88.

36. Laura Bergquist, "Kay Meyer Goes to College," *Ms.*, Oct. 1974, p. 53.

37. Evelyn Seeley, "Geography, Youth, and Idealism in the Colleges," *Literary Digest* 119 (April 13, 1935): 17.

38. Theodore M. Newcomb, *Personality and Social Change: Attitude Formation in a Student Community* (New York: Dryden Press, 1943).

39. Ibid., pp. 58–59.

40. Blake, "Why College Girls Dress That Way," p. 23.

41. The excellent study by Barbara Miller Solomon, *In the Company of Educated Women: A History of Women and Higher Education in America* (New Haven: Yale University Press, 1985), is useful here, pp. 189–91. It reminds me that in this chapter I am not attempting an overview of women's higher education, but rather an exploration of the subcultures of college women, particularly as revealed by studies of student attitudes before 1960.

42. Rose K. Goldsen et al., *What College Students Think* (Princeton: D. Van Nostrand Company, 1960), pp. 46–59; quote from p. 52.

43. Ernest Havemann and Patricia Salter West, *They Went to College: The College Graduate in America Today* (New York: Harcourt, Brace & Company, 1952), pp. 53–63; quote from p. 54.

44. Ibid., pp. 70–75; quote from p. 74.

45. Ibid., pp. 83–91; quotes from pp. 85, 90.

46. Ibid., p. 74.

CHAPTER TEN

1. As I draw here both on others' writings and on my own reflections as I lived through and came to terms with these years on campus, I am aware of the limited nature of this chapter. Protest in the 1960s called into question basic American assumptions and challenged its institutions. As a liberal, I never identified myself directly with the New Left movement, but I was deeply stirred by the questions radicals posed and the information they revealed. Both my belief in civil rights and my opposition to the Vietnam War meant my support of certain ends, if not of means. My concern here, however, is with the culture of college students, not with the nature of American politics or with elemental justice. What I want to understand is the dynamics of the 1960s within the specific context of student life, before and after. The danger is that I may trivialize what were profound statements about American society. The other side, however, is that this narrow approach may reveal aspects of college experience in the 1960s. Moreover, because I am looking at college students and the worlds that they create, not at the nature of American politics and society in the 1960s, much that was important to the decade gets truncated in these pages. The cultural revolution critically affected student attitudes about dress, sex, drugs, and the future. Protest against racial discrimination and American foreign policy occurred in many contexts. In both cases, I am concerned only with the way they came on campus.

2. Richard E. Peterson, "The National Campus Reaction to Cambodia and Kent State: Themes and Variations," in Richard E. Peterson and John A. Bilorsky, *May 1970: The Campus Aftermath of*

# Notes

*Cambodia and Kent State* (Berkeley: Carnegie Commission on Higher Education, 1971), pp. 15, 17.

3. Arthur Levine, *When Dreams and Heroes Died: A Portrait of Today's College Student* (San Francisco: Jossey-Bass, 1980), pp. 4–5. The number rose to roughly one-half in the spring of 1970 (Seymour Martin Lipset, *Rebellion in the University* [Chicago: University of Chicago Press, 1976], p. 90).

4. Richard Flacks, "Who Protests: The Social Bases of the Student Movement," in *Protest! Student Activism in America,* ed. Julian Foster and Durward Long (New York: William Morrow & Company, 1970), pp. 134–57; and Flacks, *Youth and Social Change* (Chicago: Markham Publishing Company, 1971). Flacks has influenced my thinking far more than this single note suggests; I am indebted to his discussions for reminding me of the importance of music and dress and for his sensitive discussion of the interplay between events and the process of radicalization.

5. Paul Goodman, *Growing Up Absurd: Problems of Youth in the Organized System* (New York: Random House, 1960), pp. 159–60, original in italics, and p. 161. Goodman's Appendix D, "The Freedom to Be Academic," contains an impassioned plea for academic freedom, the right of professors to be enthusiasts rather than strive for a false neutrality, and the value of John Dewey's reconstruction of education. It also expresses Goodman's hostility to the Big University (pp. 256–79).

6. C. Wright Mills, *The Power Elite* (New York: Oxford University Press, 1957), passim; quotes from p. 296.

7. C. Wright Mills, "Letter to the New Left," *New Left Review,* Sept.–Oct. 1960, pp. 18–23; quote from p. 22.

8. While André Schiffrin emphasizes the weakness of the radical student movement in the 1950s, he nonetheless testifies to its existence ("The Student Movement in the 1950's: A Reminiscence," *Radical America,* May–June 1968, pp. 26–41).

9. Flacks, "Who Protests," p. 152.

10. Flacks, *Youth and Social Change,* pp. 60–73.

11. Kirkpatrick Sale, *SDS* (New York: Random House, 1973), deals not only with the organization of its title but also with student radicalism and protest in the 1960s. Here I drew on pp. 35–36. As this account makes clear, radical alumni—not students—formed the leadership of SDS.

12. *The Port Huron Statement* (New York: Students for a Democratic Society, 1964); quotes from pp. 3, 4, 7, 9, 63.

13. Sale, *SDS,* is the indispensable source.

14. An excellent introduction to the vast literature on the 1960s is the balanced account in Allen J. Matusow, *The Unraveling of America: A History of Liberalism in the 1960s* (New York: Harper & Row, 1984), Chapter 11: "Rise and Fall of the New Left" (pp. 308–44). I have drawn extensively on these pages. I have also found useful the less sympathetic account offered by Diane Ravitch, *The Troubled Crusade: American Education, 1945–1980* (New York: Basic Books, 1983), pp. 182–227.

15. Seventeen percent of those surrounding the police car had taken part in at least seven demonstrations (Lipset, *Rebellion in the University,* p. 98).

16. Ibid., p. 317. A full account is Max Heirich, *The Beginning: Berkeley, 1964* (New York: Columbia University Press, 1970). Useful is Irwin Unger, *The Movement: A History of the American New Left, 1959–1972* (New York: Dodd, Mead & Company, 1974), pp. 62–79.

17. Mario Savio, "An End to History," in *The New Student Left: An Anthology,* ed. Mitchell Cohen and Dennis Hale (Boston: Beacon Press, 1966), pp. 253–57; quotes from p. 257. The essay was an edited version of Savio's taped speech during the Sproul Hall sit-in at Berkeley, 1964.

18. Arthur Levine, *Handbook on Undergraduate Curriculum* (San Francisco: Jossey-Bass, 1978), pp. 376–78.

19. Flacks, "Who Protests," p. 153; Sale sympathetically chronicles the calculated actions of SDS and other radical groups on campus.

20. Gallup poll, reported in Lipset, *Rebellion in the University,* p. 43. One survey of student opinion found that alongside the intense idealism of 1960s college youth was an even deeper commitment to privatism. The draft, administrative directives, and police response to building takeovers thus felt like personal violations (Jeffrey K. Hadden, "The Private Generation," *Psychology Today* 3 [Oct. 1969]: 32–35, 68–69).

21. Sale, *SDS,* pp. 202–52; Matusow, *Unraveling of America,* pp. 325–31.

22. Matusow, *Unraveling of America,* pp. 331–35. For a full narrative by the staff of the Columbia

*Daily Spectator,* see Jerry L. Avorn et al., *Up Against the Ivy Wall: A History of the Columbia Crisis,* ed. with intro. Robert Friedman (New York: Atheneum, 1969).

23. Sale, *SDS,* pp. 444, 632–33, 713.

24. By the final demonstrations, 1969–70, participants came as well from farther down the economic spectrum, but remained always proportionately wealthier than non-participants. Lipset summarizes studies of protest participants and left-wing students in *Rebellion in the University,* pp. 80–123.

25. Leonard R. Baird, "Who Protests: A Study of Student Activists," in *Protest!,* ed. Foster and Long, pp. 123–33.

26. My problem with so many of the studies of student protests is that they failed to consider the role of undergraduate culture. Protest did not simply occur if a campus contained a given number of students of certain socioeconomic characteristics. Those students entered an undergraduate world that profoundly reshaped them. Socioeconomic position did help determine how students located themselves in that world.

27. Leading spokesmen for the positive assessment of radicals were Richard Flacks and Kenneth Keniston, who published articles and books repeatedly during the period. *Youth and Dissent: The Rise of a New Opposition* (New York: Harcourt Brace Jovanovich, 1971) contains a collection of Keniston's articles. The opposition included Lewis S. Feuer, *The Conflict of Generations: The Character and Significance of Student Movements* (New York: Basic Books, 1969). A more recent study from the opposition, examining radical students in the early 1970s, focused on the differences between Jews and Christians. Jewish radicals emerged out of "a tradition of radicalism held by upper-middle-class ethnic Jews" in contrast to the Christian radicals, who were "in overt rebellion against the social and political conservatism of their middle- or working-class parents." Moreover, Jewish radicals reacted against domineering, intrusive mothers; Christian, against traditional, patriarchal fathers (Stanley Rothman and S. Robert Lichter, *The Roots of Radicalism: Jews, Christians and the New Left* [New York: Oxford University Press, 1982], quote from p. 223).

28. To focus on the triumph of the culture of collegiate rebellion is not meant to deflate the issues that college radicals raised about the nature of American society and the war in Vietnam or to deny that campus unrest may have hastened the withdrawal of American troops from Southeast Asia. The justice or injustice of a cause and its relative effectiveness do not spring from the abstinence of its adherents from the pollution of culture.

29. See Chapter 9; Theodore M. Newcomb, *Personality and Social Change: Attitude Formation in a Student Community* (New York: Dryden Press, 1943).

30. James Simon Kunen, *The Strawberry Statement—Notes of a College Revolutionary* (New York: Random House, 1969), pp. 19–20, 27.

31. Ibid., pp. 36, 71–72.

32. Ibid., p. 89.

33. Ibid., pp. 108, 109, 151.

34. Alexander W. Astin, Helen S. Astin, Alan E. Bayer, and Ann S. Bisconti, *The Power of Protest* (San Francisco: Jossey-Bass, 1975), pp. 50–53. This team did find protesters to be from less affluent families than counter-protesters, to see themselves as differing in beliefs more than others, and to be pessimistic about the future. The data base of the groups surveyed differed from other studies in that the students surveyed by the Astin team were freshmen, followed up a year later, and were composed of two distinct groups treated as one—blacks involved in demonstrations against discrimination and white anti-war protesters.

35. Avorn et al., *Up Against the Ivy Wall,* passim.

36. Steven Kelman, *Push Comes to Shove: The Escalation of Student Protest* (Boston: Houghton Mifflin Company, 1970).

37. Studies of the New Left or black protest do not generally consider the black movement on campus. A useful source for a specific campus is Lawrence E. Eichel et al., *The Harvard Strike* (Boston: Houghton Mifflin Company, 1970), pp. 261–88. Blacks who participated in demonstrations did not share the socioeconomic profile or aspirations of whites: blacks tended to be poorer, of parents who had not been to college, and clearer about future careers (Lipset, *Rebellion in the University,* p. 88).

38. J. Anthony Lukas, *Don't Shoot—We Are Your Children!* (New York: Random House, 1971), pp. 65–113.

39. Sara Evans, *Personal Politics: The Roots of Women's Liberation in the Civil Rights Movement and the New Left* (New York: Alfred A. Knopf, 1979).

40. Ibid.; quote from pp. 98–99.

CHAPTER ELEVEN

1. Arthur Levine, *When Dreams and Heroes Died: A Portrait of Today's College Student* (San Francisco: Jossey-Bass, 1980), p. 85.

2. Eleanor D. Macklin, "Cohabitation in College: Going Very Steady," *Psychology Today* (Nov. 1974): 53–59.

3. Daniel Yankelovich, *The New Morality: A Profile of American Youth in the 70's* (New York: McGraw-Hill Book Company, 1974), pp. 87, 91.

4. Joyce Maynard, "The Embarrassment of Virginity," *Mademoiselle* 75 (Aug. 1972): 259, 258.

5. Christopher Buckley, "A Keening of Weenies," in *My Harvard, My Yale,* ed. Diana Dubois (New York: Random House, 1982), pp. 263–64. According to the head of Yale's campus security, the rumor was nonsense.

6. Jerald G. Bachman and Lloyd D. Johnston, "The Freshmen, 1979," *Psychology Today* 13 (Sept. 1979): 79–87.

7. Levine, *When Dreams and Heroes Died,* p. 85.

8. "8 in 10 College Students Use Alcohol, Study Finds," *The Chronicle of Higher Education,* Oct. 29, 1979, p. 2.

9. Michiko Kakutani, "New Haven Blues," in *My Harvard, My Yale,* ed. Dubois, p. 282.

10. Levine, *When Dreams and Heroes Died,* pp. 5–6, 86.

11. Ibid., pp. 61–63.

12. Ibid., Chapter 6 subtitle, p. 103.

13. Alexander Astin, "The New Realists," *Psychology Today* 11 (Sept. 1977): 50, 53, 105–6.

14. Dean R. Hoge, Cynthia L. Luna, and David K. Miller, "Trends in College Students' Values between 1952 and 1979: A Return of the Fifties?" *Sociology of Education* 54 (1981): 263–74; quotes from pp. 266, 273.

15. Levine, *When Dreams and Heroes Died,* pp. 105, 111–12. Levine offers a fine summary and analysis of the survey data of Alexander W. Astin's annual study of entering freshmen.

16. Ibid., pp. 107, 109.

17. Ibid., p. 109.

18. Lansing Lamont, *Campus Shock: A Firsthand Report on College Life Today* (New York: E. P. Dutton & Co., 1979), p. 59. Lansing Lamont is the nephew of Corliss Lamont.

19. Buckley, "Keening of Weenies," pp. 266–67 (ellipses in the original).

20. Lamont, *Campus Shock,* p. 61.

21. Levine, *When Dreams and Heroes Died,* pp. 66, 70–73.

22. Ibid., pp. 66–67.

23. Lamont, *Campus Shock,* title of Chapter 2; statistics, p. 19.

24. Buckley, "Keening of Weenies," p. 267.

25. Lamont, *Campus Shock,* p. 1.

26. Kakutani, "New Haven Blues," p. 285.

27. Buckley, "Keening of Weenies," p. 261.

28. Levine, *When Dreams and Heroes Died,* pp. 78–83.

29. Buckley, "Keening of Weenies," p. 266.

30. Alan N. Schoonmaker, *A Students' Survival Manual: Or How to Get an Education Despite It All* (New York: Harper & Row, 1971); quotes from pp. 1, 14.

31. Kakutani, "New Haven Blues," p. 286.

32. Buckley, "Keening of Weenies," p. 272.

33. Levine, *When Dreams and Heroes Died,* p. 97.

34. Ibid., pp. 94–97.

CHAPTER TWELVE

1. Jonathan Lutz, "Are You Asking Questions?" *Stanford Daily,* Nov. 8, 1983.

2. "For Students, a Dramatic Shift in Goals," *The New York Times,* Feb. 28, 1983.

3. During the academic years 1983–84 and 1984–85, I conducted a number of student interviews, many of them taped, at colleges and universities on the East Coast, in the Midwest, and in the South. I also draw on informal talks with students, the children of friends, and family members. Most students with whom I talked preferred not to be identified in any way, even by college. To respect their privacy I have not documented the interviews.

4. "Class of '83: Working Its Way into Tight Job Market," *Daily Princetonian,* Nov. 28, 1983.

5. "40% of Seniors Choose Grad School," *Harvard Crimson,* Oct. 6, 1983.

6. "Age of Awareness—the Activist Years," *Duke Alumni Register,* May–June 1983, p. 12.

7. "Daily Student Survey," *Indiana Daily Student,* Nov. 29, 1983.

8. "Sophomores Stage Cheating Incident to Test Honor Code," *Daily Princetonian,* Nov. 16, 1983.

9. "An Old System in Need of Modernization," *Daily Princetonian,* Nov. 17, 1983.

10. Sharon Rosenthal, "Back Home Where You (Don't) Belong," New York *Sunday News Magazine,* June 5, 1983.

11. Alexander W. Astin's 1984 survey of entering freshmen revealed that 73 percent regarded as an essential or very important objective to "become an authority in my field"; 71.2 percent, to "be very well off financially" (Alexander W. Astin, *The American Freshman: National Norms for Fall 1984* [Los Angeles: Cooperative Institutional Research Program of the American Council on Education and the University of California at Los Angeles, 1984], p. 52).

12. "Study Finds Significant Drop in Financial Aid for Students," *The New York Times,* Jan. 16, 1984.

13. Gene I. Maeroff, "The Class of '84 Is Another Disappointment for Blacks," *The New York Times,* June 10, 1984.

14. "Asian-Americans Question the Admissions Policies at Ivy League Colleges," *The New York Times,* May 30, 1985.

15. "University Recognizes Sorority," *Stanford Daily,* Oct. 28, 1983; "Sigma Alpha Mu Fraternity Gets University Recognition," *Stanford Daily,* Nov. 3, 1983.

16. "Students Get Richer: Survey," *Daily Northwestern,* Nov. 10, 1983.

17. "College Council Submits Report to Trustees," *The Amherst Student,* Dec. 5, 1983.

18. Scott Cobb, "End Segregation in Greek System," *Daily Texan,* Nov. 16, 1984.

19. "Porcellian Club Chooses Its First Black Member," *Harvard Crimson,* Nov. 22, 1983.

20. "Poster Depicts Fraternity as Racist, Stirs Controversy," *Daily Tar Heel,* March 29, 1985.

21. "Momma's a Daddy at UNC," *Daily Nebraskan,* Nov. 9, 1983.

22. "Pi Eta Club to Reopen; Inquiry Continues," *Harvard Crimson,* Nov. 22, 1983.

23. "College Council Submits Report to Trustees."

24. "When Tradition Turns Tragic," *The Diamondback* (University of Maryland), Nov. 16, 1983; "Fight Against Hazing Rituals Rages on Campuses and in State Legislatures," *The Chronicle of Higher Education,* March 12, 1986, pp. 34–35.

25. "Trees and Trolls Tumble at Tiger," *Daily Princetonian,* Nov. 21, 1983.

26. "Cornell Student Files Complaint against Fraternity," *Daily Collegian* (Pennsylvania State University), Dec. 8, 1983.

27. "Alpha Tau Omega Suspended; Ruling Called Disappointing," *Pennsylvania Gazette,* March 1984, pp. 9–12; quote from p. 10.

28. Fred M. Hechinger, "Fraternities, After Years of Disfavor, Show Signs of New Strength in U.S.," *The New York Times,* May 21, 1985; Elizabeth Greene, "Campus Gang Rapes Are Found Most Likely to Occur at Fraternity Parties," *The Chronicle of Higher Education,* Oct. 16, 1985, p. 35; Julie K. Ehrhart and Bernice R. Sandler, "Campus Gang Rape: Party Games?" Project on the Status and Education of Women, Association of American Colleges, Nov. 1985, quotes from pp. 6, 2.

29. Astin, *National Norms for Fall 1984,* p. 2.

30. "Michigan U. Daily, Muckraker of 1960's, Strives for Relevance," *The New York Times,* March 20, 1985.

31. Articles in *The Missing Link* seem mainly to be written by graduate students, however.

32. "Libraries Open Football Saturdays," *Daily Nebraskan,* Oct. 7, 1983; "But We Study Weekends," *Stanford Daily,* Oct. 12, 1983; "Students Call for Extended Hours," *Pitt News,* Nov. 4, 1983.

33. "English Tests for Foreign TAs Sought," *The Diamondback* (University of Maryland), Sept. 7, 1983.

34. Scott Heller, "Watchdog Group Says Students at 110 Colleges Now Monitoring Classrooms for 'Liberal Bias,'" *The Chronicle of Higher Education,* Oct. 16, 1985, p. 27.

35. "YCT Still to Monitor Classes," *Daily Texan,* Jan. 16, 1986, p. 1.

36. Larry Rohter, "Protests Indicate Activism Is Stirring on Campuses," *The New York Times,* April 25, 1985.

37. "Police Seize 46 Anti-Apartheid Protesters at Yale; Dozens Arrested at Other Campus Demonstrations," *The Chronicle of Higher Education,* May 7, 1986, p. 36.

38. "Students Protest 'Racist' Fraternity Party," *Daily Texan,* March 17, 1986, p. 7.

39. "Graduates Facing Good Job Outlook," *The New York Times,* Dec. 16, 1984.

40. Rand Cooper, "Confessions of a Pre-med Dropout," *Amherst,* June 1980, pp. 28–32; quotes from pp. 28, 31.

41. Ibid., p. 32.

# Index

*Index*